SAINTS OF THE IMPOSSIBLE

SAINTS OF THE IMPOSSIBLE

Bataille, Weil,
and the
Politics *of the* Sacred

Alexander Irwin

University of Minnesota Press
Minneapolis
London

Copyright 2002 by the Regents of the University of Minnesota

Published by the University of Minnesota Press
111 Third Avenue South, Suite 290
Minneapolis, MN 55401-2520
http://www.upress.umn.edu

Printed in the United States of America on acid-free paper

The University of Minnesota is an equal-opportunity educator and employer.

Library of Congress Cataloging-in-Publication Data

Irwin, Alexander
    Saints of the impossible : Bataille, Weil, and the politics of the sacred / Alexander Irwin.
        p. cm.
    Includes bibliographical references and index.
    ISBN 0-8166-3902-7 (alk. paper) – ISBN 0-8166-3903-5 (pbk. : alk. paper)
    1. Bataille, Georges, 1897-1962. 2. Weil, Simone, 1909-1943. I. Title.
B2430.B33954 I79 2002
194 – dc21

                                                                        2001007761

12 11 10 09 08 07 06 05 04 03 02   10 9 8 7 6 5 4 3 2 1

CONTENTS

Acknowledgments   vii

Abbreviations   ix

Introduction
THE SACRED, TRANSGRESSION, AND THE POLITICS OF DESPAIR   xi

1. BATAILLE'S SACRIFICE
   Mutilation, Revolution, and the Death of God   1

2. TRANSFORMING THE WARRIOR'S SOUL
   Simone Weil's Poetics of Force   41

3. IF REVOLUTION IS A SICKNESS
   Politics and Necrophilia in Le Bleu du ciel   82

4. EXERCISES IN INUTILITY
   War, Mysticism, and Bataille's Writing   124

5. THE SPECTACLE OF SACRIFICE
   War and Performance in Simone Weil   169

Conclusion
COMMUNICATION, SAINTHOOD, RESISTANCE   213

Notes   227

Works Cited   245

Index   253

ACKNOWLEDGMENTS

A grant from the Amherst College Faculty Research Award Program facilitated work on the final stages of this project. I am grateful to the college administration and to my colleagues at Amherst, Robert Doran, Jamal Elias, Janet Gyatso, Susan Niditch, and David Wills, as well as Diane Beck, for creating a stimulating collegial atmosphere in which to teach and write.

I wish to thank the mentors, colleagues, and friends whose comments on *Saints of the Impossible* were indispensable. Thanks in particular to those who read through full or partial drafts, including (in rough chronological order) Margaret R. Miles, Martin Andic, Susan Rubin Suleiman, Richard R. Niebuhr, Amy Hollywood, the two anonymous reviewers of the University of Minnesota Press, and Janet Gyatso. Input from attentive readers at every stage helped to clarify and strengthen the arguments presented here. Whatever errors and infelicities remain are entirely my own responsibility.

For inspiration and moral support not immediately related to this project, yet without which it could not have been completed, I would like to thank Olivier Abel, Ximena Arnal, Laurent Gagnebin, Monica Gandhi, all Irwins, Joyce Millen, Tim Morehouse, Raphaël Picon, Shelley Salamensky, and all those connected with the Institute for Health and Social Justice and Partners in Health. Above all, my gratitude goes to Laurie Wen.

ABBREVIATIONS

The following abbreviations have been used for in-text citations of selected sources. Full references appear in the Works Cited. Where not otherwise indicated, translated citations from French originals are my own. Italics in all citations are those of the original authors, except where added emphasis is explicitly noted. Unbracketed ellipses within quotations are those of the original authors. Bracketed ellipses indicate that a portion of the original text has been omitted for clarity.

AD	*Attente de Dieu*, by Simone Weil
BOC	*Oeuvres complètes* (12 volumes), by Georges Bataille
C1, C2, C3	*Cahiers*, by Simone Weil
CdS	*Le Collège de sociologie*, edited by Denis Hollier
CO	*La Condition ouvrière*, by Simone Weil
CS	*La Connaissance surnaturelle*, by Simone Weil
CSW	*Cahiers Simone Weil*
E	*L'Enracinement*, by Simone Weil
EF	*Elementary Forms of the Religious Life*, by Émile Durkheim, translated by Joseph Ward Swain
EHP	*Écrits historiques et politiques*, by Simone Weil
EL	*Écrits de Londres*, by Simone Weil
ENL	"Essai sur la notion de lecture," by Simone Weil
FLN	*First and Last Notebooks*, by Simone Weil, translated by Richard Rees
FW	*Formative Writings*, by Simone Weil, translated by Dorothy Tuck McFarland and Wilhelmina Van Ness

GG	*Gravity and Grace,* by Simone Weil, translated by Arthur Wills
HDS	"Hegel, Death, and Sacrifice," by Georges Bataille, translated by Jonathan Strauss
IPF	"The Iliad, or the Poem of Force," by Simone Weil, translated by Mary McCarthy
LRC	"Letter to René Char on the Incompatibilities of the Writer," by Georges Bataille, translated by Christopher Carsten
ML	*Georges Bataille: La Mort à l'oeuvre,* by Michel Surya
NB	*Notebooks,* by Simone Weil, translated by Arthur Wills
NM	"Un Nouveau Mystique," by Jean-Paul Sartre
OL	*Oppression and Liberty,* by Simone Weil, translated by Arthur Wills and John Petrie
PG	*La Pesanteur et la grace,* by Simone Weil
PSO	*Pensées sans ordre concernant l'amour de Dieu,* by Simone Weil
RCL	*Réflexions sur les causes de la liberté et de l'oppression sociale,* by Simone Weil
SG	*La Source grecque,* by Simone Weil
SL	*Seventy Letters,* by Simone Weil, translated by Richard Rees
SNF	*Sacrifice: Its Nature and Function,* by Henri Hubert and Marcel Mauss, translated by W. D. Halls
SP	*La Vie de Simone Weil* (2 volumes), by Simone Pétrement
WG	*Waiting for God,* by Simone Weil, translated by Emma Craufurd
WOC	*Oeuvres complètes,* by Simone Weil

THE SACRED, TRANSGRESSION, AND THE POLITICS OF DESPAIR

The saint turns away in fright from the voluptuous man. She does not realize the unity of his unavowable passions and her own.
— Bataille, *L'Érotisme*

IN A PIVOTAL SCENE of Georges Bataille's 1935 novel *Le Bleu du ciel*, the narrator, Henri Troppmann, physically and mentally exhausted by orgies of alcohol, sex, and tearful self-pity, finds himself an unwilling participant in a discussion of the political responsibility of intellectuals. The conversation takes place in the Paris apartment of Louise Lazare, a young revolutionary activist to whom Troppmann feels mysteriously drawn despite her physical ugliness. Wandering in a state of despair and suffering from a massive hangover, Troppmann has called on Lazare on an impulse. He finds her in the company of her stepfather, Antoine Melou, a professor of philosophy. Oblivious to Troppmann's half-delirious condition, Melou begins to hold forth on the subject of politics and the crisis of workers' movements across Europe. He ruminates aloud on the "agonizing dilemma" before which intellectuals find themselves placed by the "collapse of socialist hopes." Gesticulating theatrically, the professor asks: "Should we bury ourselves in silence? Or should we give our support to the last resistance of the workers, committing ourselves to an implacable and sterile death?" (*BOC* III, 422).

Troppmann's response is to ask for directions to the toilet, where he "takes a long piss" and, hoping to relieve the pressure of nausea, tries unsuccessfully to make himself vomit by sticking his fingers down his throat. Emerging from the bathroom, Troppmann wants to make a rapid escape. But before he does so, he turns to Melou and Lazare and asks a question:

"All the same, there's one thing I'd like to know. If the workers are screwed, why are you still communists ... or socialists ... or whatever?"

They looked at me fixedly. Then they looked at one another. Finally Lazare answered, so softly that I could barely hear her: "Whatever happens, we must stand beside the oppressed."

I thought: She's a Christian. Obviously! [...] " 'We must'? In the name of what? What for?"

"One can always save one's soul," said Lazare. (*BOC* III, 424; unbracketed ellipses in original)

Written, the author tells us, in a "spasm of rage" in the spring of 1935, *Le Bleu du ciel* offers a snapshot (slightly retouched)[1] of an era of radical cultural and political disorientation. A novel of violent excess written amid a decade of violent excess, Bataille's book exhibits the anguish of an epoch that saw itself — not without reason — as in the grip of a "total crisis of civilization."[2]

The questions Troppmann throws at Lazare and Melou are the same ones Bataille himself had been raising in a series of articles published in 1933–34 in the independent leftist journal *La Critique sociale*. What could the notion of revolutionary commitment mean in a context in which the proletariat showed itself divided, cowed, and incapable of effective action, while "all vital forces have today taken the form of the fascist state" (*BOC* I, 332)? Where did the responsibility of progressive intellectuals lie, when the objective hopelessness of the workers' fight was matched only by the "jovial blindness" of the Communist party leadership: "human parrots" who continued to proclaim an inevitable triumph guaranteed by the logic of history itself (333)? For those who had ceased to accept the infallibility of Marxist doctrine, few choices seemed open beyond cynical withdrawal or a sacrificial commitment to the lost cause of proletarian struggle, promising only "implacable and sterile death."

The attitude of Bataille's characters was, then, less histrionic than realistic. Contemporary political events in Europe gave little ground for optimism. Exploiting factional divisions within the German left, Hitler had risen to power over the ruins of Europe's most advanced workers' movement. Meanwhile, the fascists consolidated their grip on Italy, while in the Soviet Union Stalin butchered workers and peasants in the name of communism. On February 6, 1934, riots by right-wing groups in Paris left dozens dead and nearly toppled France's own floundering parliamentary democracy. For leftist French intellectuals in 1935, the issues discussed by Troppmann, Lazare, and Melou were real, urgent, and paralyzingly complex. And the questions would only become more tortuous as the decade advanced: through German remilitarization, the Spanish Civil War, and the disintegration of the Popular Front, into the abyss of World War II. If an "apocalyptic" tone recurred among writers of the period (Bataille not least among them),[3] it was perhaps because daily life had indeed begun to resemble the end of the world.

Le Bleu du ciel formulates these issues as memorably as any literary work produced in the period. Yet Bataille's novel is intriguing not only for the political questions it raises, but for how — and through whom — it raises them. Troppmann is not Bataille, yet the close complicity between Bataille and his narrator is evident. The character of Lazare, meanwhile, with her combination of "hallucinatory" Christianity and analytic rigor (*BOC* III, 401), her masculine dress and her asceticism, has been recognized as a detailed literary portrait of Simone Weil.[4]

To meet a figure modeled on Weil in one of Bataille's erotic novels seems incongruous, to say the least. The contrast between Weil and Bataille amounted to a veritable antithesis of metaphysical beliefs, moral values, and personal styles. Bataille was an atheist, a devotee of Sade and Nietzsche, enchanted by the scatological. He was best known in the Paris of the mid-1930s as the author of eclectic articles that celebrated perverse sexuality and the poetic dimension of slaughterhouses or glorified the sacrificial excesses of the ancient Aztecs. Setting aside the pseudonymous publication of the pornographic novel *Story of the Eye*, the most impressive public achievement of Bataille's intellectual career to this point was having been denounced by André Breton, in the *Second Manifesto of Surrealism*, with the label *"philosophe-excrément."*[5]

Simone Weil, a dozen years younger than Bataille, had studied philosophy under Alain (Émile Chartier) at the Lycée Henri-IV, then moved on to the ultraprestigious École Normale Supérieure. Weil was known among her peers for a passionate commitment to social justice and an ascetic personal lifestyle. Weil had a reputation for relentless rational rigor (she had written her philosophy thesis on "science and perception in Descartes") and a principled pacifism that condemned all violence except that strictly necessary for the liberation of the workers and the poor. Beginning in 1935, a series of mystical experiences would lead Weil (born a Jew) to embrace Christianity, whose moral teachings she had long admired. Bataille's and Weil's only personal contact — through the circle of ex-communists and disaffected Surrealists around the journal *La Critique sociale* — had been marked by sharp ideological clashes and all the appearances of a deep personal antagonism.

What, then, was Weil doing in Bataille's novel?

The most natural assumption would be that she is there as a figure of ridicule, a minor *personnage à clef* who can serve as the target for a few jibes at religion, then vanish from the scene so Bataille's hero, Troppmann, can get on with the serious business of fornicating in cemeteries. Yet even a casual reading shows that matters are not so simple. Lazare is not a minor character, but a pivotal figure in Bataille's narrative, centrally involved in the novel's crucial action. More important, Troppmann's feelings toward Lazare are by no means limited to mockery and contempt. On the contrary, Troppmann emphasizes again and again the compelling, otherworldly power the black-clad revolutionary exerts. Lazare "casts a spell on people who listen to her," appearing to be "from another world" (*BOC* III, 442). She inspires devotion so fervent that the workers Lazare meets in Barcelona quickly yearn "to get killed for her" (442). "She spoke slowly," Troppmann notes, "with the serenity of a spirit foreign to everything. Sickness, fatigue, dispossession and death had no importance in her eyes. [...] She exerted a fascination, as much by her lucidity as by her hallucinatory thought. [...] Most of the time I thought she was positively insane" (401).

Lazare's name is already a clue to her mysterious liminal state, on the boundary between life and death, spiritual purity and sepulchral corruption. Troppmann presents Lazare as weaving a spell tinged with blood and madness, provoking simultaneous effects of attraction and repulsion. In other words, Bataille's narrative exhibits Lazare/Weil as a sacred figure according to the technical understanding of this concept Bataille had begun to develop in his articles for *La Critique sociale* and that would be central to his work with the College of Sociology at the end of the decade (see *CdS*, 188–231). Lazare evokes the prestige and horror of death, the ultimate horizon of the sacred for Bataille. She is a "bird of ill omen" [*oiseau de malheur*], "rather strange, even ridiculous." But for her followers, she is a "saint" (*BOC* III, 401, 442). Among the women in the novel, it is ultimately to Lazare that Bataille's narrator feels the closest connection: a link so intense that in the later stages of the book Troppmann is forced to ask himself if he is not in love with Lazare. "The idea that, maybe, I loved Lazare tore a cry from me that lost itself in the tumult. I could have bitten my own flesh" (445). Ultimately, Troppmann will be mesmerized to the point of volunteering to risk his own life in one of Lazare's "impossible" (458) revolutionary schemes.

Bataille's staging of Lazare/Weil as a sacred figure at the heart of his most "political" novel opens intriguing perspectives that scholars have as yet done little to pursue. These perspectives concern both the intellectual relationship between Bataille and Weil and wider questions about politics, literary practice, and sacrificial religion. Until now, the scholarly communities concerned respectively with Bataille's and Weil's work have remained isolated from one another, in keeping with the dominant perception that Bataille and Weil themselves belonged to different worlds.[6] The portrayal of Weil in *Le Bleu du ciel*, however, challenges this assumption of incommensurability. Troppmann's complex attitude toward the Christian revolutionary prompts a series of concatenated hypotheses. First, Bataille and Weil have more pertinent things to say to and about each other than have generally been recognized. Second, fresh light can be shed on the achievements of these two major intellectual figures by rereading them through the lens of Troppmann's and Lazare's perverse complicity. Third, exploring politics, writing, and sacrality in Weil and Bataille illuminates a wider set of issues concerning the performative deployment of the sacred in political space, issues important both for the historical period in which the authors wrote and for contemporary efforts to rethink the possibilities and impossibilities of the political. These hypotheses provide the point of departure for my study.

In this book, I will pursue these problems by examining aspects of Bataille's and Weil's life and writing in the period from 1930 until the end of World War II. (For Weil, the war ended early, with her death from tuberculosis in August 1943.) I want to show that the obvious differences between the two authors are less interesting than what Bataille and Weil turn out to share: namely, a political mobilization of the category of the sacred by means of self-sacrificial performance. Distinct (if not antithetical) as their worldviews were, Bataille and Weil concurred in stretching the boundaries of the political through a subversive channeling of sacrality into the political realm. This unexpected convergence and its implications constitute the focus of this book.

Frustrated with conventional political movements as the 1930s advanced, Bataille and Weil came (separately and by very different routes) to the conclusion that individual and collective regeneration had to begin, as Bernard Sichère has indicated for Bataille, "at the crossroads of the literary act, philosophy, and mystical experience."[7] Both writers believed a positive renewal of political forms, if such a renewal were practicable at all, depended on a transformation for which the language of religion provided the least inappropriate vocabulary. Of course, Bataille and Weil were by no means the only French intellectuals prospecting on this terrain in the 1930s and 1940s. Calls for a "spiritual revolution" and a "return to metaphysics" as the basis of political action went up from the young contributors to *Cahiers,* strongly influenced by the ultraconservatism of Action Française.[8] Arnaud Dandieu and Robert Aron of Ordre Nouveau echoed in 1931 that the revolution they believed imminent would have to be "above all spiritual"; otherwise it would "change nothing."[9] Writing in *Esprit* in 1934, Raymond de Becker proclaimed that the solution to political, social, and economic crisis lay in the cultivation of an "inner purity" that "Personalist revolutionaries" could not hope to achieve "without themselves being saints."[10] Yet in this context in which religious and political discourses formed confusing hybrids, Bataille's and Weil's enlistment of the sacred was, I will argue, distinctive: in its critical and self-critical complexity; in its refusal of political and religious orthodoxies; and above all in its dimension as literary performance.

I want to show that Bataille and Weil attempted not merely to destabilize or circumvent conventional political frameworks through the categories of the sacred, but to transform themselves into (stage themselves as) sacred beings in a violent performance fusing life and writing. Bataille and Weil responded to the crisis of political responsibility not only with intellectual analysis, but through practices of self-stylization, a construction or writing of the self as sacred. Bataille's and Weil's scripting of their selves and lives took divergent forms. Yet their disparate self-constructions sprang from a concern and an impulse common to both authors: the sense of intellectual, political, and moral crisis they shared with their generation and the intuition that one could respond to this challenge by turning the self into a work, a text, an embodied event of meaning, in Bataille's words a "place of communication" (*BOC* V, 21).

All that Bataille said, wrote, and lived, he "imagined it *communicated*," imagined it *as* communication. "Without that, I could not have lived it" (*BOC* VI, 31). Simone Weil signaled a similar shaping principle in her own life when she affirmed that spiritual perfection was the duty of all Christians and that "Each perfect existence is a parable written by God," that is, a text in which God communicates supernatural truth (*CS*, 121). Weil stressed her own distance from the spiritual ideal; yet she strove to give her life a poetic form, hoping the text of her existence could indeed be read as a parable, if not of attained perfection, then of indefatigable desire for the good. Weil published relatively little in her lifetime. But that she meant for her *self* to be read was made clear in many overt and subtle ways in her last years, not least in a letter to Gustave Thibon in 1942, which Thibon, appropriately, included in full in his introduction to *Gravity and Grace*, the first collection of Weil's writings to see print. In the letter, written by Weil from Oran on her way to America, Weil detailed to Thibon her intentions for the notebooks she had consigned to his care. But Weil was concerned not merely about her writings. She was also concerned about her self *as* writing. Weil observed that she hoped to be remembered by her friends in the way they remembered "a book [...] read in childhood":

> I also like to think that after the slight shock of separation you will not feel any sorrow about whatever may be in store for me, and that if you should sometimes happen to think of me you will do so as one thinks of a book one read in childhood. I do not want ever to occupy a different place from that in the hearts of those I love. (*GG*, 12)

Bataille claimed to have written books "with his life" (*BOC* VI, 17). Weil transformed and distilled her very self through verbal alchemy into a book seeking its place in readers' hearts. The best way to communicate a message, both authors seem to have reasoned, was to *be* the message: to put in the reader's hands a text consubstantial with the writer's own self, to live a life crafted as a vehicle of poetic, spiritual, and political meaning.

Saints of the Impossible will explore how for Weil and Bataille the practice of writing and the work (or *désoeuvrement*) of life flowed together, as both authors sought to transform themselves into sacred symbols. Bataille's vehicle for this transformation was his provocative textual performance of a mystical martyrdom on the margins of World War II. "Crucifying himself in his spare time" (*BOC* V, 70), Bataille both mocked the notion of redemptive sacrifice and ambiguously mimed the self-oblation of an abandoned God, voluntarily suffering torture and humiliation for the sins of the world. Bataille's metamorphosis into a perverse, provocative spiritual figure was crowned with success when Jean-Paul Sartre sarcastically proclaimed Bataille a "new mystic," the heir of Pascal, if not indeed of Christ himself (*NM*, 144, 175–76). Simone Weil, meanwhile, sought to shape her life and above all her death as an act of communication. By entering into a consented death in the service of the afflicted, Weil meant to become what she termed a "real metaphor" (*CS*, 163) for the courage, devotion to the supernatural good, and pure sacrificial love she believed were the qualities required not only of the Christian, but of the loyal citizen of a country in the throes of affliction. Weil and Bataille believed the moral and political attitudes their epoch demanded could be most effectively communicated not by conventional political discourse and argument, but through "dazzling realities" (*WOC* 2.3, 118) or a saintly "dramatization" (*BOC* V, 22–23).

But why? If the point was to communicate, why reject plain language in favor of mysterious pantomimes? To spurn the discursive procedures that make reasoned political and philosophical debate possible would seem an unpromising route to understanding and consensus. Why short-circuit rational argument by a turn to "religious" figures, especially in a context where the political stakes were as high as those evoked in the discussion between Troppmann, Melou, and Lazare?

Part of the answer lies in historical precedents. We have noted that many intellectuals struggling in the political morass of the 1930s believed affective forces shaped the course of political events, that political convulsions necessarily had "spiritual" roots. Converging with this willingness to envisage an aesthetic or religious dimension of politics was French intellectuals' long tradition of perceiving the writer as an exemplary, in some sense sacred, being. The national literary canon included prominent figures in whom literary genius coincided with a demanding personal spiritual quest, above all Pascal, to whom both Weil and Bataille have been compared (sometimes ironically, as in the case of Sartre's review of Bataille's *Inner Experience*). Pascal's work had enjoyed a renaissance in the 1920s, in part by way of Russian émigré Leon Chestov, an important early influence on Bataille.[11] Near at hand was also the example of Charles Péguy, the poet and nationalist mystic whose battlefield death in 1914 elevated him to martyr status. One should by no means underestimate the importance of the fact that, thanks in part to writers like Péguy, France's identity was still entwined with the image of its patron Jeanne d'Arc, historical archetype of saintly solutions to apparently intractable political and military crises.[12]

Meanwhile, since the Romantic era, the artistic avant-garde had been developing its own alternative pantheon of holy figures (often marginalized and "accursed"), along with various permutations on the doctrines of the artist's redemptive suffering and of the self as artwork. Dandyism's self-stylizing gestures and the progressive rehabilitation of the Marquis de Sade as a misunderstood victim and artistic martyr belonged to this process, as did the glorification of the rebellious poet-"seer" Rimbaud.[13] At first aligning Sade, Poe, Baudelaire, Rimbaud, and other admired predecessors in genealogies with a hagiographic tone,[14] the Surrealists in the late 1920s and 1930s went a step further. In books like *Le Paysan de Paris, Nadja,* and *L'Amour fou,* Louis Aragon and André Breton put themselves on display as representative figures, offering minutely detailed accounts of their own private lives as maps or models of the poetic existence they advocated.[15] These different facets of the tradition of viewing the writer as a "chosen," exemplary being helped form the background for Bataille's and Weil's elaboration of their communicative vocation. Bataille and Weil inherited from French intellectual history elements of the idea that the writer's message reaches beyond the words he or she puts on the page, that the writer's life may itself constitute the medium of a decisive revelation. But if Weil and Bataille found models of literary self-stylization ready to hand, they radicalized these preexisting patterns and turned them in bold (and troubling) directions.

While historical precedents are important, certain stakes of Bataille's and Weil's self-sacralizing practice can also be clarified not by looking to these authors' intellectual predecessors and contemporaries, but by considering philosophical proposals from our own era. In her recent study *Saints and Postmodernism,* Edith Wyschogrod has argued that the urgency of today's moral and political crises mandates a radically new ("new" because ancient) approach to transmitting values and teaching moral responsibility. Wyschogrod claims that contemporary moral theory finds itself at an impasse, characterized by a chaotic proliferation of mutually incompatible doctrines and the glaring failure of these theories to nurture real moral action in society. Wyschogrod's proposal is a turn away from the conventions of moral theory toward a focus on flesh-and-blood human exemplars — saints — as concrete embodiments of active virtue. "A postmodern ethic must look [...] to life narratives, specifically those of saints, defined in terms that both overlap and overturn traditional normative stipulations and that defy the normative structure of moral theory."[16] Narratives that record the lives of saintly figures, Wyschogrod argues, can offer direct and compelling "insight into what moral lives are and how one might go about living a moral life," while circumventing the procedural and linguistic disputes in which modern ethics has become entrapped.[17] Saints are beings who, instead of trying to crystallize the abstract essence of courage or justice in yet another theory, enact courage and justice in real-life situations and inspire others to do likewise. Saints offer not airy discourse but their own flesh, a "saintly corporeality," risked in the service of the other.[18] In a historical context marked by the collapse of cultural grand narratives and the chaos of legitimating structures, Wyschogrod urges that the appeal to "hagiographical narratives" offers an outlet from the stalemate provoked by the inextricable tangle of competing doctrines and systems.

I believe it was an intuition in some respects comparable to Wyschogrod's that motivated Weil's and Bataille's most characteristic literary, spiritual, and political strategies in the 1930s and 1940s. French society in the *entre-deux-guerres* was also marked by a collapse of consensus on fundamental political, social, and moral issues and a drastic breakdown of peaceful communication between opposed groups, due in part to the radical irreconcilability of the assumptions and background claims such groups brought with them. This disintegration of the foundations of dialogue shaped the "agonizing dilemma" before which Troppmann, Melou, and Lazare found themselves in *Le Bleu du ciel* (prompting Troppmann to seek a haven in the WC, Lazare to "save her soul" alongside the doomed workers). In the wake of events like the riots of February 1934, Bataille and Weil became convinced that the search for theoretical common ground among antagonistic parties, even if possible, would be too slow, given the racing course of political events within France and outside. Like certain postmodern thinkers more than half a century later, Bataille and Weil followed the conviction that what was required to guide responsible action was "not a theory, but a flesh and blood existent."[19] The virtues demanded by the historical moment did not need to be (perhaps could not be) formulated in a coherent theory. But they could be inscribed, presented, and enacted in a human figure and set forth in the story of a life. Anticipating moves made later by Wyschogrod and in a very different sense by Philippe Lacoue-Labarthe and Jean-Luc Nancy, Weil and Bataille sought a way to break free from the traditional schema of Western political and moral thought, ossified in an opposition between theory and practice that must be deconstructed to open a space for new possibilities.[20] Needless to say, the appeal to/performance of the sacred does not belong to the overflowings of conventional political categories Lacoue-Labarthe and Nancy endorse. Yet it might be argued that in the life of the literary saint, theory and practice relate to one another in a new way "consonant with the retreat" of traditional political meanings.[21]

At this point, a basic definitional question forces itself on us. The claim of this book is that Bataille's and Weil's politics pivoted on a staging of themselves as sacred figures. But how exactly did Weil and Bataille define sacredness, so as to be persuaded of its political relevance? Answering this question requires attention to the derivation and shape of the ideas of sacrality in circulation among French thinkers in the *entre-deux-guerres*. The views of the sacred available to Bataille and Weil stemmed largely from two sources: on the one hand, the Christian theological and hagiographical tradition and, on the other, the work of Émile Durkheim and the French school of sociology. Christianity's linking of holiness to voluntary sacrificial death, exemplified in the crucifixion, furnished an enduring template for Weil's and Bataille's thought. My study will be centrally concerned with the two writers' variations on the Christian motifs of divine self-sacrifice, expiation, and salvific agony. Fundamental to the Durkheimian view, meanwhile, was the axiom of an inherent mobility or "ambiguity" of the sacred (*EF*, 409). Indeed, for Durkheimians, the sacred is less a concept with a fixed content than a shifting marker of radical otherness, separation, opposition. For Durkheim and his followers, sacrality is not in the first instance a positive property; rather, the sacred is defined negatively, as sheer "heterogeneity" (39). In the words of Roger Caillois: "Basically, with regard to the sacred in general, the only thing that can be validly asserted is contained in the very definition of the term — that it is opposed to the profane."[22] The sacred is the very principle of opposition, contestation, and radical difference.[23]

Standing in absolute dichotomy over against the profane, the sacred is also internally divided. The alterity that is the sacred takes on, in the Durkheimian model, two forms, defining a powerful polarity: on the one hand, a pure, noble, elevated, life-giving form (the "right" sacred); on the other, an impure, vile, degraded, and dangerous form (the "left" sacred). "[E]ach in its own sphere extremely hostile to the other," the right and left sacred are "regarded as similar from a certain point of view by the profane world to which they are equally opposed."[24] Mutually inimical, the right and left, high and low forms of sacrality nonetheless also display, according to Durkheim, patterns of complicity. Not only is there "no break of continuity" between the propitious and destructive forms, but the same object "may pass from one to the other. [...] The pure is made of the impure, and reciprocally. It is in the possibility of these transmutations that the ambiguity of the sacred consists" (*EF,* 411). Thus, for example, the cadaver, object of sacred horror par excellence, becomes at a later stage a loved and venerated relic, bestowing blessings where it previously radiated pollution and chaos (410).

Bataille's debt to Durkheim is evident (see chapter 1). Weil read Durkheim with skepticism (e.g., *EL,* 103), yet her concept of the sacred exhibits striking structural parallels to the Durkheimian view, as regards both the radical opposition of sacred and profane and the ambiguous double character of the sacred. If anything, Weil is more insistent than the Durkheimians on the absolute heterogeneity of the sacred (as the transcendent good) with respect to the domain of ordinary human experience. Sacred powers enter human life, Weil asserts calmly, from "outside the world" (74–75). Moreover, Weil frequently insists that the holy or supernatural can only be characterized negatively: as that which has no place in the realm of matter, natural necessity, or social domination. Meanwhile, Weil's theory of affliction [*malheur*] shows that Weilian sacrality, too, exhibits a double or split structure involving high and low, life-giving and death-dealing aspects, between which a striking reversibility can operate (see chapters 2 and 5).

I believe it was the negative, transgressive, oppositional character of the sacred that drew Bataille and Weil to this concept and that made the term useful to them as an instrument of social analysis and as a device for positioning themselves in a cultural and political landscape. Both Bataille and Weil undertook an "othering" of the political for which ideas of heterogeneous sacrality served as enabling devices. Meanwhile, the mobility and internal doubleness built into the concept also enhanced its tactical value. The later chapters of this study will explore the particular ways Bataille and Weil capitalized on this ambiguity.

Yet tormented artists and mystical saints were not the only "heterogeneous" figures influencing the politics of the interwar epoch. There was also, for example, Hitler. Both Weil and Bataille were outspoken critics of fascism. Both had discerned in the blending of pseudoreligious impulses with political drives one of the characteristic traits of the fascist program. Why, given this fact, would Bataille and Weil have remained committed to the idea of mobilizing sacred forces and exhibiting themselves as sacred figures? Did Bataille and Weil, despite their protestations, fall prey, perhaps unconsciously, to fascist seduction? Or did they genuinely believe the elusive heterogeneity of the self-scripting saint could challenge Nazism's *"ersatz de religion"* (*EL,* 191)? If such was their conviction, was this belief a disastrous political and moral miscalculation? These questions will remain in play in the chapters ahead. Bataille's and Weil's mobilizations of the sacred as a poetic resource and a political positionality responded to a situation of "intellectual confusion and the muddling of political identities" in France in the interwar years.[25] I will try to show that their staging of the sacred, of themselves as sacred, allowed the two thinkers to find orientation in the chaos of the era's "irresistible expenditure of commitments and ideas."[26] Yet for some recent critics, the determination to blend religion, art, and politics in a "reenchantment of the [political] world" was the tragic *error* of the French intelligentsia in the interwar years and in no way a *solution* to the multiple crises with which thinkers, artists, and activists found themselves confronted.[27] Weil's and Bataille's proposals must be assessed carefully and critically in light of this challenge. It will be vital to show if and how sacred force as theorized and performed by Weil and Bataille differs from the "power" [*puissance*] at the heart of the Nazi "myth": a myth "which is nothing 'mythological,' " but rather presents itself as "the very power of the uniting of the fundamental directions and forces of an individual or a people, that is to say the power of a profound, concrete, and embodied identity."[28]

Though critical attention to the relationship between Weil and Bataille has been very limited, trends in the scholarly literature suggest that the moment is appropriate for a study to engage the politics of sainthood in these two authors. Important recent work on Weil has begun to explore how Weilian categories might illuminate both the politics of the 1930s and contemporary political and social challenges.[29] At the same time, critics have asserted the destructive impact of Weil's religiosity, urging that flaws in her understanding of the sacred may have crippled Weil as a political philosopher.[30] Did religion paralyze Weil's political thought or expand her vision, enabling a constructive recasting of political problems? Clarity on such questions is decisive for a balanced assessment of Weil's achievement. Recent years have seen a marked growth of interest in Bataille as a theorist of the sacred and in the relationship between mysticism, politics, and strategies of writing in Bataille's corpus.[31] Yet concurrently, as Carolyn Dean points out, some scholars are challenging with renewed insistence the ethical and political defensibility of Bataille's literary mysticism.[32] Was Bataille's atheistic "religion" a liberation from ossified political forms or a rejection of real responsibility in favor of self-indulgent textual transgression? My research aims to contribute to these conversations, bridging the separation between the scholarly communities at work on Bataille and Weil and helping to show the importance of both thinkers for the theorization of relations between literary practice, the sacred, performativity, and politics.

Thus, two interwoven lines of questioning will be in play in what follows. One considers specific issues in Bataille's and Weil's politics (e.g., Bataille's wartime political "withdrawal" and the apparent senselessness of Weil's obscure self-squandering in an English tuberculosis hospital). The other line of inquiry raises broader theoretical questions about politics, "religion," and resistance. I want to show that these two sets of questions illuminate each other. Perplexing aspects of Bataille's and Weil's political (or antipolitical) attitudes are clarified when our analysis takes account of the two authors' use of the sacred and related categories. Meanwhile, Bataille's and Weil's specific literary/political strategies open broader perspectives and initiate broader interrogations about connections and disjunctions between political reason and the performance of heterogeneity. *Saints of the Impossible* by no means aims to exhaust either the historical or the theoretical issues introduced here. However, I hope the book can provide a useful foundation for further work.

My study's five chapters represent discrete but thematically interconnected approaches. Chapters 1 and 4 are devoted to Bataille, chapters 2 and 5 to Weil, and in chapter 3 the work of both authors is considered. Thus, though the sequence of chapters obeys a broad chronological structure — moving from Bataille's treatment of sacrifice in the early 1930s (beginning of chapter 1) to the shared problematics of mysticism and commitment that mark both authors' World War II writings (chapters 4 and 5) — the movement is not linear. As one would expect with Weil and Bataille, there will be detours, leaps, retreats and retracings, and moments when a phenomenon or text previously discussed reappears from a different angle. Bataille's postwar writings are largely left out of consideration not because they are uninteresting (indeed, it is clear that works such as *The Accursed Share* contain some of Bataille's most important political ideas), but because it was in selected texts of the 1930s and in the *Atheological Summa* that Bataille cultivated most strikingly the image of himself as a sacred being. To focus primarily on Bataille's earlier writings also makes for a rough chronological symmetry with the authorship of Simone Weil, cut short by Weil's premature death.

Chapter 1 looks at the concept of sacrifice in Bataille's writings, in light of Jean-Luc Nancy's call for the closure of the "fantasm of sacrifice" that has obsessed (and possibly defined) the "West."[33] The avatars of sacrifice in Bataille's work in the 1930s are surveyed. In an early article on Van Gogh, Bataille saw the self-mutilation of the rebellious artist as the paradigmatic sacrificial act. Four years later, collaborating at *La Critique sociale,* Bataille used the language of sacrifice and ritual destruction (potlatch) to frame an original and provocative theory of political revolution. At the end of the decade, sacrifice internalized as spiritual violence became the basis of Bataille's model of mystical experience.

Chapter 2 explores Simone Weil's notion of force, a pervasive yet elusive concept. Force bridges the realms of natural science, psychology, politics, and spirituality, ambiguously mediating between spirit and matter, persons and things. I discuss force in relation to two other Weilian themes: hunger (force inhabiting the human body as natural need) and reading (in Weil's acceptation, the cognitive automatism by which we see/interpret objects and persons around us as intrinsically invested with meanings that demand actions: e.g., when we "read" a man as enemy, we kill). I show that in the period after her explicit turn to Christianity, Weil pursued two distinct but related strategies with respect to force: seeking, on the one hand, to theorize and practice resistance to oppressive force in the political realm and, on the other hand, to internalize and use force in the mystical transformation ("decreation") of the ego.

Chapter 3 proposes a reading of Bataille's political novel *Le Bleu du ciel*. I argue that important but relatively neglected aspects of the novel — and of Bataille's and Weil's intellectual relationship — can be illuminated by focusing on the character of Lazare/Weil. Understanding the link between Lazare and Bataille's narrator, Troppmann, involves situating *Le Bleu du ciel* against the background of Bataille's and Weil's disputes over the nature of revolution during their shared association with the journal *La Critique sociale*, immediately preceding the period in which Bataille's novel was written.

Chapter 4 explores the relationship between war and mysticism in Bataille's writings, principally the texts composed from 1939 onward that mark Bataille's mystical retreat and ostensible political "demobilization." Bataille's apparent withdrawal from political involvement at the beginning of World War II has been attributed by some commentators to intellectual cowardice or a tacit endorsement of Nazism. I argue that Bataille's mysticism should be seen not as a rejection of political responsibility, but rather as a provocative effort to model an alternative mode of resistance (through literary self-sacralization) in a context where notions of duty, virtue, and virile action seemed to Bataille to have been emptied of their content. Bataille never abjured his taste for transgressive violence. Yet, positioning himself as a spiritual teacher and ironic saint, Bataille sought to convert his readers to a better — that is to say, more evil — form of violence than war could offer.

In contrast to Bataille, for whom inner experience was "the opposite of action" (*BOC* V, 59), Weil theorized authentic mystical experience as the decisive source of empowerment for active political struggle. Chapter 5 explores Weil's efforts to participate in the Allied military action against Hitler, considering this effort in relation to the central doctrines of Weil's mysticism. I claim that Weil's view of all human action as communication and her concern with death as the determining moment of existence came together in her plan to expose herself to a sacrificial death on the battlefield. Through such a death Weil intended to transform her existence into what she termed a "real metaphor" expressive of religious and political truth.

Before approaching the multiple issues at stake in the authors' wartime treatments of mysticism and *engagement*, we must trace the trajectories of Bataille's and Weil's interrogation of politics, religious experience, and violence through the decade preceding the outbreak of the war. The place to begin this investigation is with Bataille's concept of sacrifice.

Chapter One

BATAILLE'S SACRIFICE

Mutilation, Revolution, and the Death of God

What is involved, therefore, is above all a *mimesis:* the ancient sacrifice is reproduced — up to a certain point — in its form or its scheme; but it is reproduced so as to reveal an entirely new content, a truth hitherto hidden or misunderstood, if not perverted.

— Jean-Luc Nancy, "The Unsacrificeable"

Doubtless, as we have seen, in every sacrifice the victim has something of the god in him.

— Henri Hubert and Marcel Mauss, *Sacrifice: Its Nature and Function*

TO INVESTIGATE THE POLITICS of sainthood in Georges Bataille and Simone Weil, one could choose no more appropriate starting point than the concept of sacrifice. In Bataille's writing, sacrifice is a ubiquitous motif, ambiguously bridging the domains of religion, art, eroticism, and politics. Yet precisely because of its centrality, the Bataillean theory of sacrifice has given rise to contradictory evaluations. Some commentators have praised the sophistication of Bataille's politics of sacrifice and the impossible.[1] Others have critiqued Bataille's sacrificial theories as harboring a nostalgia for primal unity linked to fascism.[2] Jean-Luc Nancy has argued that in Bataille's work, a millennial Western obsession with sacrifice culminates and reveals the urgent need for its own dissolution, while Giorgio Agamben has countered that the Nancian critique is far from exhausting the problematics of sacrifice and sacrality adumbrated by Bataille.[3] At stake in such discussions is the permeability of the political to disturbing forces that can be labeled as sacred or religious. The very vehemence of reactions to Bataille's effort to explore and exploit this permeability shows the need to clarify the fundamental textual, political, and performative mechanisms Bataille puts into play.

1

What was sacrifice to Bataille? (And what was Bataille to sacrifice?) How and why did Bataille use the sacrificial motif (while celebrating its uselessness)? This chapter aims to identify key facets of sacrifice in Bataille's thought, following major steps in the evolution of the concept from the early 1930s to the outbreak of World War II. Tracing variations on sacrifice through some of Bataille's principal writings of the 1930s helps to explain the gradual movement from public activism to inward-turning mysticism that characterized Bataille's work in this decade. The shift in Bataille's attitude reflects and exploits ambiguities within the concept of sacrifice itself, as Bataille adapted it from Durkheimian sociology: sacrifice's double function as both representation of social unity and concrete unleashing of violence, its simultaneous reference to external social processes and to intrapsychic events. Even as Bataillean sacrifice modulates increasingly into the realm of written performance, I will argue, it incorporates political problems and continues to function as a critical marker of the individual's relation to collectivity and history. But where Durkheim's sacrificial rites solidified social bonds, Bataille's sacrificial writing stages a rebellious psychological and social dismemberment.

Durkheim: The Reasonableness of Sacrifice

It has been argued that much of the most important twentieth-century French thought has taken shape in critical response — avowed or implicit — to Émile Durkheim's "carefully worked out synthesis of rationalism, anthropological humanism, and secular religion."[4] This claim applies in exemplary fashion to Bataille. Numerous references reflect the determining role of Durkheimian problematics in Bataille's intellectual program.[5] The Bataillean concept of sacrifice in particular bears the marks of a sustained engagement with theses advanced by Durkheim and his pupils. In *The Elementary Forms of the Religious Life* (1912), Durkheim formulated a theory of sacrifice that became an unavoidable reference point for later work on the topic. In order to grasp the force of the Bataillean reconceptualization of sacrifice, it is necessary both to examine briefly the interpretation of the sacrificial dynamic in *Elementary Forms* and to note the rather different emphases brought out in the analysis proposed by two of Durkheim's disciples, Henri Hubert and Marcel Mauss.

In *Elementary Forms,* Durkheim's project was to uncover, through an analysis of the beliefs and rituals of "primitive" religions (primarily those of Australian and North American aboriginal peoples), the fundamental conceptions and ritual attitudes that define "religion in general" (*EF,* 5). Not (ostensibly) in order to debunk religion and unravel its mystifications, but to reveal the nature of its enduring truth, no less vital for modern societies than for the nonliterate tribes on which Durkheim's study focused.

The eminently rational inner truth of religion for Durkheim is the power of society itself and the complex ties of interdependence binding the human individual to the social group. The real object of worship in aboriginal rites is the society in which these rites take place, the social body that the ceremonies simultaneously represent and constitute. "Religious force is nothing other than the collective and anonymous force of the clan" (*EF,* 221). Once the truth of this basic equation has been grasped, "religion ceases to be an inexplicable hallucination and takes a foothold in reality" (225). In fact, it becomes clear that "the believer is not deceived when he believes in the existence of a moral power on which he depends and from which he receives all that is best in himself: this power exists, it is society" (225). The "error" of the Australian tribesman (or of any other religious believer) lies merely in taking the "figures and metaphors" that represent the social force (e.g., the clan's totem symbol) for the "concrete and living reality" that lies behind these representations: society itself (225). Seen in this light, Durkheim claims,

> Religion acquires a meaning and a reasonableness that the most intransigent rationalist cannot misunderstand. Its primary object is not to give men a representation of the physical world. [. . .] Before all, it is a system of ideas with which the individuals represent to themselves the society of which they are members, and the obscure but intimate relations they have with it. This is its primary function; and though metaphorical and symbolic, this representation is not unfaithful. (225)

For Durkheim, religious rituals are structured to manage, by symbolic means, the relation of interdependence between individuals and the collectivity. Central among these ritual operations is sacrifice, in which "the give and take between person and community reaches its most developed phase."[6]

The concept of sacrifice epitomizes all that in religion appears most "inadmissible" to the modern mind (*EF*, 344). Yet in a key chapter of *Elementary Forms*, Durkheim sets out to demonstrate that the logic underlying sacrificial operations is fully rational and coherent. Durkheim acknowledges that sacrifice follows — as Robertson Smith had suggested in *The Religion of the Semites* — a circular pattern of reciprocal giving between human beings and their gods. Yet Durkheim sees in this circle not a "logical scandal" (344), but a profoundly rational exchange and mutual "revivification" between individuals and the collectivity (whose sacred force the "gods" represent). "There is an exchange of services, which are mutually demanded, between the divinity and its worshippers. The rule *do ut des* [I give that you may give], by which the principle of sacrifice has sometimes been defined, is not a late invention of utilitarian theorists: it only expresses in an explicit way the very mechanism of the sacrificial system." The circular pattern pointed out by Robertson Smith is real, "but it contains nothing humiliating for reason. It comes from the fact that the sacred beings, though superior to men, can live only in the human consciousness" (347). The members of the society must assemble periodically to regenerate within themselves the sense of the divinity (the society) on which they depend and to nourish the sacred beings with a sacrifice of symbolic gifts, in order in turn to be nourished and sustained by the collective life the divinity symbolizes. As the focus of these periodic assemblies, the sacrificial rite constitutes the decisive mediation between the individual and the community, the source of a "renovation" in which the individual soul is "dipped again in the source from which its life comes" (348–49).

Again following Robertson Smith, Durkheim nonetheless acknowledges an "ambiguity" in the concept of the sacred (*EF*, 409). "Religious forces are of two sorts. Some are beneficent, guardians of the physical and moral order, dispensers of life and health," while a second set of sacred forces are "evil and impure [...], productive of disorders, causes of death and sickness." Religious life gravitates around these "two contrary poles between which there is the same opposition as between the pure and the impure, the saint and the sacrilegious" (409–10). Durkheim offers an eminently rational explanation for this apparently illogical double character of the sacred. Both categories of religious energies arise from society itself, in the shared experience of ritual. According as such rituals mark either occasions of communal joy or moments of shared woe, the sacred forces with which the participants feel themselves in contact will be experienced as either beneficent or malign (412). That is, the sacred is double because the collective rites that produce it are of two types, celebratory or anguished/expiatory. The two categories of sacrality are joined by the common trait that for Durkheim remains essential: both emerge through collective practices typified by sacrifice. In triumph or in tragedy, human beings assemble to reconstitute the communal bonds equally indispensable in both situations.

Allan Stoekl identifies a less conspicuous but more insidious tension in the concept of sacrifice as Durkheim employs it. Sacrifice functions both as a "representation of social exchange" between person and community and as an "active device by means of which society can remain unified."[7] On the one hand, that is, sacrifice is understood as a means by which the members of the society symbolically project the group and their allegiance to it. It thus forms part of the "vast symbolism" that constitutes the basis of social life (*EF*, 231). It is this representational (rational-symbolic) aspect of sacrifice that Durkheim privileges in *Elementary Forms*. But, on the other hand, as Durkheim himself obliquely acknowledges, sacrifice not only represents but also *imposes* unity by unleashing forces of actual violence. To this basic ambiguity is linked another one: it is not entirely clear on Durkheim's treatment *where* sacrifice actually happens — whether the essential operation occurs in the observable violence of the external act or whether the "real" sacrifice takes place in the minds of the participants. Durkheim never formulates the question explicitly, yet his rationalistic emphasis on the thought behind sacrificial operations makes the latter interpretation appear to be the more accurate. At the very least, it is clear that from the modern point of view primary importance attaches to the symbolic inner meaning of sacrifice as the representation of interdependence between individual and collectivity, rather than to the rite's outer forms.[8] The violent external procedures of primitive rituals have no contemporary relevance for Durkheim, other than as objects of scientific curiosity. The rational meaning of the sacrifice (hidden to the participants themselves, grasped by the scholarly investigator) retains crucial importance. The concluding section of *Elementary Forms* is a meditation on the erosion of this meaning in the modern West, punctuated with speculations about how this decisive social content might be represented in new symbolic forms appropriate to the contemporary era. Durkheim's work thus offers a significant instance of the West's ongoing "interiorization," "spiritualization," and "dialecticization" of sacrifice.[9] In Durkheim, the "old," primitive sacrifice is mimetically reinscribed and reinterpreted in such a way as to reveal that the form of the primitive sacrifice is merely an "exterior figure — vain in itself" — of a deeper truth that the modern world discerns and purifies: "that truth in which the subject sacrifices itself, in spirit, to spirit."[10] Or in Durkheim's case, in the society, to the society.

A somewhat different analysis of the sacrificial mechanism had been furnished a decade earlier by two of Durkheim's disciples, Henri Hubert and Marcel Mauss, in *Sacrifice: Its Nature and Function* (1898). Hubert's and Mauss's general conclusions regarding the social utility of sacrifice are similar to Durkheim's (*SNF*, 101–3). However, Hubert and Mauss show a relatively greater interest in the violent and morally ambiguous nature of sacrificial rites. They link blood sacrifice explicitly to the notion of crime, describing the initial phases of the sacrificial procedure in terms of an anguished transgression demanding expiation: "That which now begins is a crime, a kind of sacrilege. So, while the victim was being led to the place of slaughter, some rituals prescribed libations and expiations. [. . .] Under the influence of these same ideas, the instigator of the slaughter might be punished by beating or exile" (33).

Hubert and Mauss also devote a lengthy chapter to a species of sacrifice that complicates the fundamental idea of usefulness and rationality, namely, the mythical representation of the "sacrifice of the god." The divine (self-)sacrifice defies the utilitarian principle that commands the circularity of ordinary sacrificial procedures. The god has, by definition, no utilitarian motivations;

his gift or sacrifice cannot be compensated by any meaningful return. Yet precisely for this reason, Hubert and Mauss regard the god's self-offering as the form in which sacrifice attains its "highest expression" (*SNF,* 77). All other types of sacrifice involve an "ambiguity" insofar as the *do ut des* principle inevitably tinges them with "self-interest." The sacrifier "gives in order to receive" (100). Only in the case of divine self-sacrifice is the sacrificial operation entirely pure, untainted by "selfish calculation." In this instance, the sacrificial circle is contracted to a single, explosive point: sacrifier, victim, and sometimes even sacrificer[11] are one in an act of divine self-destruction that seeks no reward and is oriented toward no utilitarian aim. "The god who sacrifices himself gives himself irrevocably": without reserve, without return (101).

The sacrifice of the god represented a nonutilitarian anomaly, a puzzling remainder with respect to the norm of the *do ut des* principle proposed by Durkheim as the key to the rationality of sacrifice. It was — typically — this useless remainder that would attract Bataille's attention.

Self-Mutilation as Promethean Sacrifice: Van Gogh's Ear

Bataille's important series of articles for the magazine of art history and ethnography *Documents* included several texts treating the theme of sacrifice. The article "Vanished America" (*BOC* I, 156–58) evoked in hallucinatory terms the sacrificial excesses of the ancient Aztecs. "Rotten Sun" (231–32) described Mithraic bull sacrifice. But Bataille's most important early treatment of sacrifice came in the article "Sacrificial Mutilation and the Severed Ear of Vincent Van Gogh," published in *Documents* in 1930 (258–70). In the essay, Bataille interpreted the famous incident of Van Gogh's ear, along with more contemporary cases of self-mutilation culled from medical and psychiatric annals, as expressions of the sacrificial impulse at the root of religious behavior throughout history. The gesture of the automutilator is "uncontestably linked to madness." Yet it can nevertheless be "designated as the adequate expression of a true social function," of the "generally human" institution of sacrifice (264). While the automutilation of mad men and women shocks and revolts, there is continuity between these pathological acts and religious practices both ancient and contemporary, which have also included "the most varied and maddest forms of automutilation" (264).

The details of both group religious practices and individual acts vary widely. However, Bataille claims that a shared underlying sacrificial principle can be discerned, whose goal is to "liberate heterogeneous elements and to rupture the homogeneity of the person" (*BOC* I, 269). The aim of the automutilator is "to throw oneself or to throw something of oneself *outside oneself*" (265), overflowing and shattering the constricted closure of individuality. The sun (with which both Van Gogh and another automutilator whose case Bataille cites were obsessed) serves as the emblem and model for this "throwing out" of the self. Automutilation as sacrifice expresses human beings' desire to "resemble perfectly," through "the laceration and tearing away of one's own parts," the ideal of the "solar god" who constantly sacrifices and spends himself, ceaselessly burning his own substance (263).

By linking sacrifice to madness, Bataille refuses Durkheim's harmonizing depiction of sacrificial operations as reasonable and useful. On the contrary, sacrificial automutilation is a paradigmatically irrational gesture of pure and purposeless destruction. To interpret the action theoretically, Bataille appeals not to Durkheim, but to the earlier study of sacrifice by Hubert and Mauss, specifically to the concept of the "sacrifice of the god" in which the utilitarian *do ut des* principle is suspended by the gesture of the god who gives without any hope of recompense. Bataille cites Hubert and Mauss: " 'The god who sacrifices himself gives himself without return. [...] The god who is the sacrifier is one with the victim and sometimes even with the sacrificer. All the diverse elements which enter into ordinary sacrifices interpenetrate and blend together here' " (*BOC* I, 268). Yet Bataille disagrees with the sociologists' conclusion that " 'such a blending is only possible for mythical, imaginary, ideal entities.' " Hubert and Mauss, he asserts, "neglect here the examples of 'sacrifice of the god' which they could have borrowed from automutilation and by which alone the sacrifice loses its character of pretense" (268).

Bataille concludes the essay by stressing the way in which the sacrificial gesture can also function not, as in Durkheim, as an enactment of social order and unity, but rather as an act of revolt against the established order and the values it upholds. Bataille describes the power of self-mutilation as a "marvelous liberty." Even the most violent religious fanatics, he claims, have never "abused" this liberty as gloriously as Van Gogh transporting his severed ear to the house of prostitution, "the place which is most repugnant to good society." Bataille declares "admirable" the way in which the painter thus "spat in the face" of the defenders of "elevated, official" bourgeois morality (*BOC* I, 270). Van Gogh's severed ear "abruptly breaks out of the magic circle inside which rites of liberation aborted stupidly," shockingly claiming a menacing freedom (270). Bataille associates Van Gogh with other automutilators who defied authority: Anaxarchus of Abdera, who bit off his own tongue and spat it "bleeding in the face of the tyrant Nicocreon," and Zeno of Elea, who similarly spat his tongue in the face of Demylos after having been subjected to "frightful tortures" (270).

It is no coincidence that Bataille focuses on rebellious artists, intellectuals, and other mad men and women whose automutilating gestures challenge the established authorities and their moral and medical codes. In contrast to Durkheim, for whom collective ritual serves to unite society, Bataille here treats sacrificial mutilation in the same way he will shortly deal with the subject of sexual perversion: as a form through which the individual's disunity and disenchantment with the collectivity finds subversive expression.[12] Yet in another sense, the automutilating madman may experience through his act an ecstatic connection comparable to that which Durkheim attributes to the participants in ritual sacrifice. For in the shattering of the integrity of their bodies, automutilators know a deeper, paradoxical unity accessible only through the violent rupture of apparent wholeness. If sacrifice both represents society and imposes unity in an act of violence, the automutilators' "personal economy will impossibly incorporate the same violence" the larger social economy simultaneously depends upon and struggles to repress. The automutilator "will come to embody and reflect the larger community, just as Durkheim's person does when [that person] engages in sacrificial ritual."[13] To submit him/herself to symbolic-sacrificial mutilation may be precisely the role of the artist (or writer), who incorporates and represents the conflicts lacerating the social body, as s/he rebels against society's norms.

The Notion of Expenditure: Revolution as Sacrifice

The revolt of the automutilator was a spectacular gesture on the part of an artist, intellectual, or other solitary figure. As the cases of Anaxarchus and Zeno showed, self-mutilating performance could confront oppressors with a potent symbolic act of defiance. Yet such acts were political only in an inchoate sense. Three years later, Bataille transferred the concept of sacrifice explicitly to the realm of revolutionary politics, using the idea to construct a theory of class conflict and revolution.

From 1931 to 1934, Bataille was a principal contributor to the dissident communist journal *La Critique sociale,* one of the most adventurous forums of leftist political debate in France in the period. The mission of the anti-Stalinist review was to revitalize the tradition of revolutionary social analysis threatened by repressive party dogmatism. Even the progressive editorial board of *La Critique sociale* was dismayed, however, when Bataille submitted to them his essay "The Notion of Expenditure." The text was eventually published (in January 1933) accompanied by a disclaimer in which the editors signaled their disagreement with the contents and their intention to give space to a critical analysis of the piece in a later issue (the promised critical response never appeared).

In the essay, Bataille develops his concept of expenditure in close connection with that of sacrifice, drawing on Mauss's sociology, in particular the exploration of potlatch in *The Gift* (1925). Bataille argues that classical economic theories that focus their attention on categories of utility and production have failed to grasp a deeper dynamic underlying all economic and social arrangements: namely, the "principle of loss," of "unproductive" or "unconditional expenditure" (*BOC* I, 305). Such pure expenditure is the ultimate end of all human activity (indeed, perhaps, of all activity in the universe). As exemplary social forms of unproductive expenditure Bataille cites "luxury, mourning, wars, cults, the construction of sumptuary monuments, games, spectacles, the arts, perverse sexual activity (that is to say, turned away from genital finality)" (305). The common characteristic of these diverse behaviors is that they are oriented toward no external purpose and "have their end in themselves" (305). Expenditure stands in opposition to the productive mode, in which each action or element is instrumentalized in the service of an end beyond itself, which alone endows it with meaning. Expenditure signals the triumph of exuberant, useless waste over the principles of order and utility.

Not only does expenditure exist as an alternative to the productive practices and patterns of accumulation reflected in conventional economic theory, but expenditure commands production and accumulation, as their real (though unacknowledged) reason for being. Classical economic theories (including those of Marxism) have obscured this fact, but the theoretical bases of the traditional conceptions have been "ruined" by recent scholarly advances, in particular Mauss's study of potlatch and the primitive economy (*BOC* I, 308–9). Mauss's research shows that economic production and the conservation of goods "are only means subordinate to expenditure" (308). The real end and defining moment of economic activity comes with the "spectacular destructions of riches" by which potlatch "rejoins religious sacrifice" (309).

For Bataille, the principle of uselessness is a defining quality of the sacred or "heterogeneous" realm. Thus, Mark C. Taylor's claim that Bataille's distinction between sacred and profane "is strictly parallel to Durkheim's"[14] requires qualification. Taylor is right to stress Bataille's debt to the father of French sociology. The description of the social field as structured by a dichotomy between sacred and profane (heterogeneous and homogeneous) elements is pivotal to Bataille's theory, and this framework is obviously Durkheimian. Yet Bataille resists Durkheim's reading of the sacred as simply equivalent to unifying social force, together with the accompanying analysis of sacrifice as an operation whose eminently useful aim is the symbolic representation/mediation of the mutually sustaining relationship between individual and collectivity. In his writings for *La Critique sociale*, Bataille is not interested in sacrifice as a representation or catalyst of social unity, but rather primarily in the immediate violence unleashed in the act of sacrificial killing (the aspect of sacrifice Durkheim acknowledged but sought to downplay) and in the opportunities for social *dis*-unity and *dis*-integration that the sacred might afford. Sacrifice for Bataille is the unleashing within the social framework of an "unknown and dangerous force" (*BOC* I, 346) that takes no account of rational goals. Not only does it not, as Durkheim claimed, primarily generate social utility; its role is to strip away from beings and actions the utility that under normal circumstances they possess, exposing them to (or as) absolute loss. Durkheim's thesis on the identity of the sacred and the social, Bataille asserts explicitly in "The Psychological Structure of Fascism," exemplifies the tendency of science to reduce the sacred to the level of the profane (the "homogeneous") "in order to escape from the sensible presence of heterogeneous elements" that would threaten the stability of the rational-utilitarian order and shake the foundations of science itself (345, note). Bataille's aim is not to integrate the sacred as a category into a scientific construct, but to exhibit and summon forth expenditure and heterogeneity as "lived states [*états vécus*]" (339).

Moreover, Bataille's language in "The Notion of Expenditure" indicates that the violence he envisions is not to be merely symbolic, but quite real. Denouncing the ravages of the "masters and exploiters," Bataille calls for a "*grand soir* where their pretty words will be covered by the death screams of riots." The vision of this social sacrifice is the "bloody hope which blends each day with the existence of the people" (*BOC* I, 318). Thus, the fact that "the forces released in sacrifice cannot always be controlled"[15] is for Bataille a decisive argument for, not against, the use of sacrificial categories to interpret (and transform) the political situation. Though Bataille's language does (in the 1930s and later) "ech[o] Durkheim,"[16] the political aspirations Bataille connects with sacrifice are crucially different.

In "The Notion of Expenditure," Bataille analyzes a number of areas in which the principle of loss is operative: religious worship (the "bloody wasting of men and animals of *sacrifice*" [*BOC* I, 306]); various forms of competition; but also art and literature. "The term poetry," which is applied to the "least degraded, least intellectualized forms of the expression of a state of loss," can be considered "as a synonym of expenditure." Poetry "signifies, in effect, in the most precise fashion, creation by means of loss. Its meaning is thus close to that of *sacrifice*" (307). But the centerpiece of Bataille's essay is the claim that the fundamental Marxist concepts of class struggle and revolution must be reread through the categories of sacrificial expenditure.

Bataille suggests that class divisions spring from a sacrificial impulse inherent in society itself. Useless expenditure is the true end of human life; yet access to expenditure's potent forms is a privilege jealously guarded by those with high social status. It is to maintain their monopoly on the pleasures of waste and destruction that the rich exclude the "miserable" classes from all access to social, political, and economic power. In earlier historical periods, moreover, not only were the poor denied the right to engage in the ecstatic prodigality of expenditure, but they themselves — as captives or slaves — were liable to become the *objects* of sacrificial expenditure for the pleasure of the rich. This same pattern, Bataille argues, remains operative in contemporary capitalist society, with the difference that slavery is now called wage labor and is "reserved for proletarians" (*BOC* I, 315). In modern society, just as in earlier times, "the rich man consumes the loss of the poor man." "*The end of the activity of the workers is to produce in order to live, but that of the activity of the bosses is to produce in order to condemn the laboring producers to a horrible downfall*" (315).

Understanding the annihilation of the workers as the concealed goal of the process of production, Bataille defines the struggle between the classes as a sacrificial operation, oriented toward pure destruction. The break with Marx is drastic. As Sylvère Lotringer indicates: "If the proletarians were simply exploited by the rich, a social revolution with utilitarian goals would be sufficient to free them from their servitude." Such, however, is not the case. "The rich, Bataille argues, do not just oppress the workers for their own benefit." Rather, both exploiters and victims "obey 'a decisive impulse *constraining* society [...] to realize as tragic and as free a mode of expenditure as is possible.' The rich do not want just to exploit the proletarians. *They want to sacrifice them.*"[17] Under the force of this "constraining" impulse, the oppressed have few options. Either the workers must continue to submit themselves as sacrificial victims, or they must become sacrificers in their turn. "The miserable have no means for entering the circle of power other than the revolutionary destruction of the classes which now occupy it." Bataille exhorts the oppressed to initiate precisely this "bloody and in no way limited social expenditure" (*BOC* I, 308).

Revolution is not — at the very least, not primarily — a means to a practical end (the overthrow of capitalism, the creation of a workers' state); it is an end in itself, a sacrifice in defiance of the principle of utility. The Bataillean revolution aims not at victory, but at pure loss. The political triumph of the proletariat, if it were in fact to come about as a result of such an effort, would have to be seen as a kind of accidental by-product. Yet Bataille is not entirely limpid on the questions of ends and means. Certain passages in "The Notion of Expenditure" (including the lines just cited on the desire of "the miserable" to enter "the circle of power") can be read as positing overarching political aims for the sacrificial revolution, thus calling into question the purity of "pure loss" in the political realm. While he challenged Durkheim's domestication of the sacred, the reduction of sacrifice to social utility, Bataille recognized that such utility did in fact attach to sacrificial operations (as Mauss had shown that it did to potlatch) and that not only sociologists but the practitioners of "primitive" sacrifice themselves might very well, if questioned, describe their ritual behaviors in terms of utilitarian aims. Bataille did not deny the utilitarian aspects of sacrifice and its equivalents, but he did maintain that these aspects were secondary and that in the concept of pure expenditure he had identified sacrifice's essential nature.

It is easy enough to denounce Bataille's apparent equivocation on the question of whether revolution as sacrifice could or should be justified in relation to specific political goals. Yet one can argue that Bataille's tolerance for a certain logical inconsistency on this issue sprang less from intellectual laziness than from a genuine commitment to the cause of the oppressed in a historical context where rigorous logic seemed to lead ineluctably to despair. The sincerity of Bataille's concern for the miserable and excluded, for the workers as victims of capitalist exploitation, should not be ignored when we consider the genesis of Bataille's theory and its possible flaws.[18] If Bataille groped for a theory of revolution that might somehow continue to justify political struggle in the face of what appeared as objectively hopeless conditions, it was to a considerable degree because of his genuine hunger to see the end of a political and economic order that crushed the masses for the profit of a small elite. Real moral anger is palpable in Bataille's protests against the destruction of "human nature" inflicted on the workers by the dominant classes (*BOC* I, 318). Within Bataille himself, utilitarian motivations and hopes for social transformation cohabited with the fascination of pure expenditure for its own sake.

This is not to say that Bataille's concern for the victims of oppression liquidates the troubling questions to which the concept of class conflict as useless expenditure gives rise. Indeed, it renders these questions more urgent. If from the start the rich play their exploitative role in obedience to an irresistible impulse "constraining" and shaping society at all levels and in all historical epochs (*BOC* I, 318), can the oppressors legitimately be held accountable for their actions?[19] If sacrificial expenditure suspends ordinary ethical concepts, where can the proletariat and its intellectual allies situate themselves to voice a moral condemnation of the rich? Must the idea of such a condemnation itself be sacrificed if one is to affirm the triumphant "insubordination" (318) of *dépense*? The revolutionary workers are exhorted to reproduce precisely the "crime" of which the rich stand accused — destining another group of human beings to bloody sacrificial loss. In what sense could the workers' sacrifice of the bourgeoisie be considered more legitimate than the capitalists' current immolation of the oppressed?[20]

The rather sketchy justifications Bataille offers in "The Notion of Expenditure" are predominantly of an aesthetic nature. Bataille attacks the mediocrity and *mesquinerie* of the modern bourgeois, for whom the hatred of the more glorious forms of expenditure has become a "raison d'être." Simply looking at these degenerate beings, "all human life seems degraded" (*BOC* I, 314). Bataille ridicules their weakness in comparison with the unapologetic cruelty of the "former masters" (314) of feudal and aristocratic societies. The "attenuation of the brutality of the masters" discernible among the bourgeois does not reflect an increase in humanitarian virtue, but rather simply "corresponds to the general atrophy of the ancient sumptuary processes which characterizes the modern epoch" (316).

Such critiques of course attack less the violence of capitalist oppression per se than the embarrassing inability of the decadent bourgeoisie to live up to the higher standard of brutality set by the more vigorous oppressors of old. It is not the fact of oppression that is challenged, but rather the aesthetic quality of the bourgeoisie's staging of its cruelties. Supplanting bourgeois insipidity, the revolutionary proletariat has the chance to offer a new and superior mise-en-scène of social sacrifice, raising class struggle again to its proper aesthetic-spectacular dimension, as "the most grandiose form of social expenditure" (*BOC* I, 316).

The dangers involved in this aestheticization of politics seem clear in retrospect.[21] To conceptualize revolutionary struggle in terms of the goal-less exaltation of pure violence was to risk playing directly into the hands of fascist irrationalism. Fascism asked for nothing better than the unleashing of violent passions steered only by the will to exterminate those groups whose unpleasing existence seemed to degrade "all human life." The picture was further complicated by Bataille's insistence that the fascist leaders and the miserable and excluded social categories were closely linked, insofar as both exhibited a "heterogeneous" character that opposed them to the profane order of productive, bourgeois society (*BOC* I, 348–49). A profound complicity existed between the "sovereign" and base forms of social heterogeneity, making it possible to understand that the revolutionary energies of one could easily be captured and absorbed by the other.[22]

Yet Bataille's recognition of the fascination Hitler was capable of exerting was no endorsement of Nazi politics. Bataille maintained, not unreasonably, that an understanding of the means by which fascism had gained its ascendancy was required in order to combat it. Along with others at *La Critique sociale,* Bataille saw that orthodox Marxism provided insufficient tools for an analysis of the fascist phenomenon. He was convinced that to understand fascism a new theoretical vocabulary had to be forged that would move beyond economic determinism to give their full weight to the quasi-religious elements that defined fascism's specific ethos. Their success in providing elements of such a vocabulary assures

Bataille's essays on expenditure and heterogeneity a place among the most perceptive critiques of the totalitarian mentality.[23] For Bataille, however, heterogeneity/sacrality and sacrifice were more than intellectual categories for analyzing fascist power. They were also devices for resisting it.

From Proletarian Revolt to "Sacred Conspiracy"

La Critique sociale ceased publication in 1934. Bataille's image of the political applications of sacrifice underwent a series of significant metamorphoses in the years that followed. Bataille's search for theoretical and practical resources in the struggle against authoritarian incursions led him through an eclectic series of political organizations, scholarly groups, and "religious" communities in the chaotic atmosphere of the late 1930s.

Bataille's participation in the Contre-Attaque group (1935–36) represented the apogee of his interwar political activism. In Contre-Attaque, Bataille's "fundamental pessimism" yielded momentarily to a surge of aggressive political passion carried by a "lyricism of the call, the shout, the crowd, the street."[24] The intellectual leadership of the militant organization was shared (uncomfortably) by Bataille and his Surrealist nemesis André Breton. In its broad outlines, their program was clear, trenchant, and consciously inflammatory. The menace of fascism abroad and the continued agitation of the Croix de Feu and other right-wing groups in France itself demanded a response drastically more resolute than the anemic "phraseology" and political maneuverings of the French communists or the compromises of the Front Populaire, which, though able to place itself at the head of the country by parliamentary means, was doomed (as the Contre-Attaque manifesto rightly predicted) to a rapid "bankruptcy" (*BOC* I, 379–80). Refusing reformism, Contre-Attaque's manifesto called for a violent seizure of power by the proletariat and the installation of a *"ruthless dictatorship of the people in arms"* (380). For a time, at least, Bataille sought to shape the group as a disciplined revolutionary organization committed to pragmatic thinking, resolute action, and concrete results.[25] Contre-Attaque declared itself "determined to succeed and not to talk" (379).

The orientation toward concrete (if perhaps not entirely "realistic" [*BOC* I, 379]) political goals coincides with a conspicuous downplaying, in the writings and speeches Bataille contributed to Contre-Attaque, of the vocabulary of sacrifice and unproductive expenditure. The sacrificial terms in which Bataille analyzed class struggle and revolution at *La Critique sociale* are almost completely effaced in the Contre-Attaque texts. Bataille may have reckoned, understandably, that these ideas possessed a rather limited propaganda appeal for a political movement seeking to catalyze popular rebellion in the streets. The tone of Contre-Attaque was set not by calls for useless social potlatch or reflections on the dynamic value of despair, but by plans for the nationalization of major industries and the effective redistribution of wealth to workers and peasants, after a revolution that would see the extermination of slave-driving capitalists (380–82). Such hard-nosed talk notwithstanding, disputes between the Surrealist contingent and Bataille's faction precipitated Contre-Attaque's dissolution in May 1936. The disappearance of the group marked a crucial turning point for Bataille.

Contre-Attaque's failed experiment in no-nonsense activism left Bataille convinced of the futility of party politics and mass organizing efforts. Bataille's attention now turned in a different direction, toward the formation of a " 'secret society' " that would eschew politics and "envisage only a *religious* goal" (*BOC* VI, 485). The entity that emerged was Acéphale, a double organization comprising a journal and a mysterious closed community enacting rituals designed to expose the participants directly to the virulent force of the sacred. If sacrificial terminology had gone underground in Bataille's Contre-Attaque writings, the language (and the promised reality) of sacrifice reemerged with a vengeance in Acéphale. Here, in what Maurice Blanchot believes was "the only group that really counted for Bataille," the "sliding [*glissement*]" between sacrifice as an object of "historical and religious interpretation" and sacrifice as an "infinite exigency" putting Bataille himself in play reached its most "obsessive" intensity.[26]

Acéphale's manifesto, entitled "The Sacred Conspiracy" (*BOC* I, 442), declared, "WE ARE FIERCELY RELIGIOUS" (443), signaling Bataille's will to disentangle himself from conventional political discourse and patterns of behavior. "If nothing could be found beyond political activity, human avidity would meet only the void" (443). The void was to be filled by a return to and of the sacred, which Bataille presented as a total transformation of being, repairing the damage and humiliation wrought by a degenerate civilization. "It is time to abandon the world of civilized men and its light. [...] [I]t is necessary to become totally other, or to cease to be" (442–43). The rejection of an ossified rationality and the cultivation of violent ecstasy were symbolized by the headless being who served as Acéphale's graphic emblem (drawn to Bataille's specifications by André Masson). The acephalic figure holds a sword in his left hand, "flames similar to the Sacred Heart" in his right. He represents the man who by mutilating himself of a servile rationality has "escaped from his head like a condemned inmate from prison" (445).

The setting in which the sacred was to be cultivated and made effective was no longer — as in "The Notion of Expenditure" — a mass proletarian movement bent on unleashing an uncontrolled social potlatch. The structure in which Bataille now placed his hopes was that of the elective community, to which he also referred as a secret society or an "order" in the religious or initiatory sense (*BOC* I, 469; cf. *CdS*, 217–44). The community was the setting for the examination of "truths which lacerate, which absorb those to whom they appear, while the mass of humanity does not look for them and is even animated by a movement which distances from them." The "disintegrating movement" which held the masses in its grip could only, Bataille argued, "be compensated with a stealthy slowness by that which will gravitate anew around figures of death" (489). Centered on the contemplation of such figures and charged with their sacred energies, the community would be united by a bond able to withstand the entropy corroding the wider society.

The sacred community must stand apart from the political order and its instrumental logic, incapable of forging intense bonds. In the draft of a program for Acéphale, Bataille outlined his hopes for the group: "To form a community which will create values, values which will create cohesion. [...] To take upon oneself perversion and crime not as exclusive values, but as needing to be integrated into the human totality. [...] To participate in the destruction of the world that is, eyes open toward the world that will be" (*BOC* II, 273). The issue of crime was not only a theoretical problem, but an immediately practical one. Notoriously, Bataille's plans for Acéphale included the performance of an actual human sacrifice. Bataille had succeeded in locating a person ready to serve as voluntary victim of the rite. (Prudently, he thought to ask the prospective victim to prepare in advance a document absolving the sacrificer and the group of legal responsibility.) The planned sacrifice did not take place: allegedly because, despite the availability of a consenting victim, no one could be found to assume the role of sacrificer-executioner.[27]

Acéphale was to have no explicit political agenda, no positive goals beyond its own existence: "EXISTENCE, THAT IS TO SAY TRAGEDY" (*BOC* I, 482). Bataille envisioned the group as sacred — purely unproductive — in character. Yet Bataille was once again unwilling to renounce entirely the notion of political impact. He hinted that the "unproductive" presence of the group might ultimately prove more politically potent than the verbiage and agitation of conventional political organizations. Modeling a contestatory, convulsive existence both for the individual and the collectivity, the acephalic community would embody a contagious liberation from the tyranny of all structures of hierarchical domination, a shattering of the "principle of the head" (469).

Bataille denounced the domination of the "head" both as a moral and psychological rule (subordination of all vital structures and desiring energies to reason) and as a template of political organization (concentration of power in a unified, elevated, commanding authority). Bataille now perceived that his earlier model of proletarian revolution as social sacrifice was inadequate, not because revolutionary destruction was wrong, but because such destruction did not go far enough. Revolt was "regularly followed by the reconstitution of the social structure and of its head" (*BOC* I, 469). Revolutions historically simply tended to replace one form of tyranny (one "head") with another. For this reason, Bataille now affirmed, "The formation of a new structure, of an 'order' developing and seething through the entire earth, is the only real liberatory act — and the only one possible" (469). The model of political sacrifice evoked in "The Notion of Expenditure," where the proletarian masses rise up in unison to overthrow their masters in a single grand gesture, yields to the picture of sacred energies filtering subversively, stealthily through the social system from the multiple, disseminated nodes of a secret network.

Bataille was of course not alone in his frustration with the inertia of bourgeois democracy, nor in his flirtation with conspiratorial alternatives. Antiparliamentarian sentiments and a generalized dissatisfaction with what Emmanuel Mounier termed the "established disorder" were widespread in French intellectual circles in the 1930s. Bataille's program had much in common with the vision of some of those working in Mounier's orbit at the journal *Esprit.* At *Esprit,* too, there was talk of circumventing traditional political formations through the creation of an "order" modeled on medieval monastic groups. In the February 1935 issue of Mounier's review, Raymond de Becker called for a "new Order" working with revolutionary fervor toward the resacralization "of art, of culture, of political, social, and economic life." The organization would be founded on ideals of "friendship and poverty, [...] with an intense community and liturgical life, with a profound ascetic and contemplative formation."[28] But where *Esprit* imagined its new order as the vanguard of a "Christian revolution,"[29] Acéphale's program was predicated on the death, more precisely the ongoing sacrificial expulsion, of God. Bataille saw in monotheistic Christianity the historical template of centralized, hierarchical domination, thus in a sense the very root of authoritarian politics. The worship of the Christian God established a pattern that culminated in the servile adoration of the Führer. Thus, to combat fascism required killing God: not merely as a theological postulate, but on the deeper level of ingrained psychological and social reflexes. The Acéphale figure — graphic symbol of liberating headlessness — negated the principle of unified, centralized power that undergirded both monotheism and fascism. The Acéphale incarnated "sovereignty destined to destruction, the death of God" (*BOC* I, 470). He attacked God by sacrificing that part of himself (the head) that had wished to exercise a unilateral, quasi-divine authority.

Bataille-Dionysos

While Acéphale sought communal bonds, the accents of a defiant individualism also reemerged in Bataille's writings in this period. One expression of this ambiguous coexistence of group identification and individual authority was the "shamanistic" position occupied within the secret society by Bataille himself. Roger Caillois notes that for Bataille, the "theoretical interest" of shamanism was vivid "only to the extent that he could aspire to become a shaman himself."[30] At the same time that he preached the ideal of the headless community "without a chief" (*BOC* I, 489), there can be no doubt that, in the group Acéphale as actually constituted, Bataille himself claimed the clear and unequivocal leadership role, amounting to a sacerdotal authority. "The cards were in his hands alone; he dealt them out in his own way following a hierarchy of participants of which he remained the only master" (*ML*, 252). If the community was to be the matrix of a rekindling of sacred forces, Bataille in his own person was the primary channel and vector of those forces. Pierre Klossowski, who participated in some of the group's rituals, affirms that the acephalic figure that symbolized the aspirations of the community was in fact a portrait of Bataille himself. The Acéphale is "purely Bataille emblematized by Masson. The figure of the god with his attributes" — the sword, the flame, the labyrinth represented by the visible entrails — "formed a sort of *mandala* in which Bataille contemplated, and invited us to contemplate, his own experience."[31] Bataille thus cast himself in a double role incorporating the two dimensions of Durkheimian sacrifice. As the Acéphale, Bataille became both a symbolic figure representing the community to itself and a shaman or sacrificial priest palpably unleashing sacred forces through rituals intended to fuse the members in intense solidarity. The Acéphale is a forbidding and isolated figure, but his solitary self-mutilation liberates the energies that make possible the cohesion of the group.

Nietzsche had also been a lonely thinker haunted by the notion of community. Placing Acéphale under Nietzsche's intellectual sign, Bataille underscored the significance for the community of the emblematic or heroic individual. Thus, Bataille's mythologizing of "Nietzsche-Dionysos" in the pages of the journal *Acéphale* constitutes not only a homage to a philosophical predecessor, but an account of the role Bataille envisaged for himself. Following Karl Jaspers's suggestions in *Nietzsche: Einführung in das Verständnis seines Philosophierens* (1936), Bataille believed an "imitation of Nietzsche" (atheistic rewriting of the *imitatio Christi*) was possible and necessary, for those willing to abandon the confines of a "small politics" for the open-ended exploration of the "total possibilities of humanity."[32] Shaping oneself to the Nietzschean ideal opened the road to a community freed from all forms of servility.

In the *Acéphale* texts devoted to defending Nietzschean thought against fascist co-optation, Bataille stressed both Nietzsche's representative character (which enables Nietzsche to point to, in some sense to *become,* the binding force of a new form of human community) and the terrible solitude that was Nietzsche's lot. "Because he could not confuse emasculation and knowledge, and because his thought opened on a lucid explosion which could not cease before having exhausted his forces [. . .], Nietzsche collapsed in a humiliating solitude." But Nietzsche became by his very isolation a symbol and rallying point, the "hero" of all who refused conformity and servitude (*BOC* I, 480). "In the image of the one [Dionysos] he was avid to be even to his madness, Nietzsche is born of the Earth torn by the fire of the Sky, is born lightning-struck and in that way charged with this fire of domination becoming FIRE OF THE EARTH" (484). Nietzsche, fused with Dionysos, rises to messianic stature: "THE SACRED — NIETZSCHEAN — FIGURE OF TRAGIC DIONYSOS DELIVERS LIFE FROM SERVITUDE" (484). Bataille salutes in Nietzsche the "incarnation" of humanity's maddest and most exalting possibilities, life and thought transformed into a "festival," the assertion of a freedom so vast that "no language would suffice to reproduce its movement" (547).

As a sacred figure, Nietzsche forms a pendant to the "heterogeneous" fascist leader, radiating a "*force* that shatters the regular course of things" and inspires ecstatic communal devotion (*BOC* I, 349). Yet the community summoned by Nietzsche is rooted not in imperative violence but in a "tragic experience of self and world," an "experience of the negative [. . .] or of the *impossible,*" consisting precisely in the "affirmed certainty that it is not possible to place oneself outside the reach of tragedy."[33]

This is what Bataille means by "religion": a community without domination, united at once by the demand for a mad freedom and by the awareness of shared vulnerability to tragedy. From the conjunction of freedom and tragic consciousness springs a paradoxical, nonhierarchical, permanently wounded sovereignty. Such sovereignty separates people from each other irrevocably in the very moment that it exposes them to each other in the nakedness of tragic compassion. (The Acéphale stands naked and isolated, with his heart in his hand and a death's head lodged in his groin.) Decisive for Bataille's subsequent thought is the understanding that humans commune in the limit experience of the tragic sacred and that sacrality must be crystallized or channeled ("incarnated") by a sacred-symbolic individual. This figure animates community while at the same time remaining separated from community in an infinite solitude that is both sovereignty and "humiliation."

The College of Sociology: Power and Deicide

Bataille's interrogations of sacrality, violence, and communal bonds continued at the College of Sociology (March 1937 to July 1939). The college's lectures and debates brought together an array of talented and ideologically disparate thinkers with the goal of exploring social phenomena in which "the active presence of the sacred is revealed" (*CdS*, 27). Acknowledging their debt to Durkheim even as they judged the results of conventional sociology "timid and incomplete," the college's leaders (principally Bataille, Michel Leiris, and Roger Caillois) theorized the sacred as the affective force grounding authentic community and hoped to mobilize this "virulent" force not simply as an intellectual postulate, but as experienced reality. Via the sacred, the college aimed to connect "the fundamental obsessive tendencies of individual psychology" with the "guiding structures that preside over the social organization and command its revolutions" (26–27).

The college did not entirely eschew conventional politics (the group issued, for example, a "Declaration on the International Crisis" following the Munich accords of 1938 [*CdS*, 355–63]). Yet Bataille was increasingly haunted by the Kojèvian notion of the "end of history" and the idea that while political involvement was still in some way a moral imperative, in a deeper sense individual agency was meaningless. In the face of the impersonal mechanics of history, represented abstractly by the Hegelian system Bataille had studied under Kojève and concretely by Europe's irresistible slide toward war, what was to become of the anguished individual who knew himself as *"négativité sans emploi"*?[34] In what sense might it still be possible for the "unemployed" individual to act? What would appropriate action look like in a situation that seemed in advance to strip people's gestures of meaning and efficacy? Such questions set the background for Bataille's lecture on power, delivered at the college's session on February 19, 1938. The talk gave Bataille the opportunity to clarify a new stage in his thinking on subjectivity, sacrifice, and the political.

Bataille's approach to the concept of power is unusual in a number of respects. Most obviously, his analysis focuses on power not as a structural or institutional phenomenon, but as an attribute of individual human beings. Bataille is concerned with a dimension of power that "in the large majority of cases appears individualized, that is to say incarnated in a single person. The name of king is commonly given to this person" (*CdS*, 183–84). The prestige of fascist chiefs is the riddle Bataille hopes ultimately to solve, by applying social-scientific insights concerning the figure and functions of the king. The primary reference here is J. G. Frazer, whose *Golden Bough* analyzed "the prerogatives of primitive kings and the taboos which strike them" (185). The key figure in Frazer's monumental work was the priest of the sacred grove of Nemi, outside Rome. This priest, known under the name of Dianus, was a runaway slave or criminal who had managed to reach the grove and kill its defender, thereby earning the right to take his place and claim the title "King of the Wood" (Rex Nemorensis). The victorious combatant lived on as king/priest of the grove until killed in his turn by a new challenger.[35] In his talk on power, Bataille evokes Dianus as exemplar of the paradoxical intertwining of crime, royalty, and sacrality (185).

The example of Dianus reveals that power stands in a direct relation to the sacred.[36] Power as Bataille defines the concept can in fact be understood as a denatured outgrowth of the sacred, which turns back violently against its own religious sources.

Power in Bataille's specific sense emerges when religious prestige and military force converge and the resulting authority is
enlisted for the profit of a dominant individual or group. The
process that gives rise to power is thus a parasitic co-optation
of sacred force, welding the sacred to coercive armed strength.
"Power would be the institutional joining of sacred force and military might in a single person using them for his individual profit"
(CdS, 189). While such a notion might appear anachronistic in
modern civilization, the emergence of fascism had shown that the
hybridization of religion and military force was by no means restricted to "primitive" societies. As Bataille addressed his audience
in 1938, such archaisms were unleashing political effects no one
could ignore.

Violence per se is not the problem, Bataille thinks. His attitude
"does not imply any hostility with regard to the energy [*puissance*]
that is generated by the human play of force" (CdS, 190–91). What
inspires Bataille's "profound aversion" is the use made of volatile
puissance by those who seek to "capture" the energy for their
own "conservation" (191), who direct force unilaterally against
others, failing to realize that the first target of a sacred war should
be oneself. Those who capture and channel outward the energies of
violence block the process of expenditure by refusing to put themselves into play. Seeking victory and acquisition, they freeze the
exuberance of pure loss and deny the identification between sacrificer and victim that is the basis of the true sacrificial economy.[37] "In
other words, power is what escapes from the tragedy demanded
by the 'movement of the ensemble' animating the human community." Power consists in the channeling for private advantage
of the forces of the tragic economy (190). On this basis, without
denying the link between the sacred and violence, Bataille could
attempt to show that those who affirm the sacred will critique and
resist oppressive power.

The pivotal figure in Bataille's argument is Jesus, seemingly a cu-
rious choice, given Bataille's Nietzschean allegiances. But Bataille
sees in the torture and death of Christ and the subsequent tri-
umphalist reinterpretation of this event the paradigmatic passage
between the sacred's two branches: "left" (terrifying and repellent)
and "right" (high, glorious, noble). The shift from the left to the

right sacred prepares the way for the ossification of the authentic sacred into a rigid apparatus of power. "At first," Bataille writes,

> Christianity valorized the poor, the pariahs, the unclean [*les immondes*]. It put a king into play in the person of Jesus, but this king aligned himself with the miserable. Much more, Jesus let himself be treated as a criminal and reduced to the state of a tortured body, identifying himself in this way with the left and immediately repulsive form of the sacred. (*CdS*, 192)

The original Christian myth "emphasized the defaming character of the death on the cross, adding that [Jesus] had taken upon himself the sins of the world, that is to say the whole of human ignominy" (192).

Yet at the same time that he was a "tortured body" associated with the repellent left forms of the sacred, Jesus was also, theologically speaking, a king. And it was this royal, triumphal aspect of the figure that the developing church would soon come to emphasize, in effect initiating a profound transformation of the original sinister sacrality of the death of Jesus at Golgotha into a "right," noble force capable of entering into a successful alliance with the political might of the Roman Empire under Constantine (*CdS*, 193). In this way Christianity metamorphosed its founder from a vector of the sacred into the very archetype of unilateral power.

Three points in Bataille's discussion stand out. First, Jesus' sacrificial death underscores the idea that potent irruptions of the sacred will exhibit the character of crime.[38] In the story of the crucifixion, the redemption of humanity is procured by a horrifying crime (the murder of God). In the absence of this supreme transgression, the salvation brought by Christ would have remained inoperative. The crucified Christ united in his person "the pure and redoubtable king and the king put to death." He "took upon himself the very crime" of his own murder, then perpetuated the crime and its guilt through the institution of the Eucharist. The Christian sacramental meal is a "rite of the killing of the king, endlessly renewed by priests who identified themselves with the victim, living themselves like kings put to death, taking on themselves in turn the crime of the whole world" (*CdS*, 192).

The communion in tragedy and guilt associated with Christ's self-sacrifice opens the possibility of a new conception of authority, though this is a possibility Bataille believes institutional Christianity ultimately rejected. Christ as a "tortured body" and emblem of the left sacred incarnates a form of authority and community utterly different from those associated with dominating power. Where imperative power denies tragedy while exploiting its violence, the cross indicates a submission to the tragic and a critique of power from the position of the sacrificial victim. Denis Hollier observes that Bataille establishes a sharp opposition between "the power that kills and the power that dies, the lictor's ax which makes unity reign by its cutting gesture and the cross which propagates a tragic communion." Where the "military structure of power exports the works of death," authentic religious authority "takes them on itself" and suffers violence rather than inflicting it (*CdS*, 169). The opposition between the "Caesarian" and Dionysian-tragic figures developed in *Acéphale* is reinscribed, but with the Crucified now — pace Nietzsche — occupying the place of Dionysos.

The third crucial thrust of Bataille's lecture is the suggestion that powerlessness, or rather a certain performative renunciation of power, possesses paradoxical political efficacy. Christ's death symbolically crystallizes this process. The paradox of the crucifixion lies in the notion of an omnipotent being who has stripped himself of power, submitted willingly to torture and death, and brought redemption by an act of irrational self-expenditure. At the moment when the crucified Christ appears utterly powerless and humiliated, he has saved the world. Not through the mobilization of coercive political or military might, but by engaging in a supreme form of automutilation. By inaction (hanging helpless on the cross) that is at the same time senseless action (divine *dépense*), he has accomplished what rational, purposive action could never have achieved.

The closing sections of the lecture focus primarily on the paradox (long dear to Bataille) that a viable communal order is inseparable from crime. The rituals of regicide in primitive societies indicate that "the renewal of crime is necessary to the intense movement produced in the center of human groups." This situation is a tragic one, in the sense that what is necessary is also (and equally) intolerable. The king must be killed for the good of the group; yet to participate in the killing is an unpardonable transgression. This "strange situation," Bataille notes, gives rise to a question "charged with all the anguish of humanity": the problem of which figure in this primal drama one ought to emulate. Two responses to the problem have been offered: "Tragedy proposes to man to identify himself with the criminal who kills the king; Christianity proposes to him to identify himself with the victim, with the king put to death" (*CdS*, 195–96).

To be the king, the innocent sufferer who humbly bears the sins of the world, or to play the role of the guilty regicide: in his lecture on power, Bataille left his hearers with this alternative in the form of a binary choice. Shortly, however, Bataille would seek to reconcile the two positions in a final, ironic refiguration of sacrifice.

New Ways to Be Crucified

The activities of the College of Sociology had been scheduled to resume in the fall of 1939. Events decided otherwise. On September 2, 1939, Hitler's troops invaded Poland. On September 3, England and France declared war on Germany. Two days later, Bataille started the text that would become *Guilty* (*Le Coupable*): "The date on which I begin to write (September 5, 1939) is not a coincidence. I am beginning because of the events, but not to talk about them. [...] I will not talk about war, but about mystical experience" (*BOC* V, 245–46).

Faced with a world plunging headlong into an orgy of death, Bataille withdrew to the quiet suburb of Saint-Germain-en-Laye to celebrate a different form of violence: through meditative practice and the writing of a fractured confessional text. While Europe and then the world struggled in the throes of war, Bataille devoted himself to the transcription of a personal quest for mystical ecstasy in the books of his *Atheological Summa*.

The coincidence of Bataille's mystical turn with the outbreak of the war has generated an obsessive problem for Bataille's interpreters. Bataille's mystical writings have been perceived by some as marking an abrupt break with the political concerns that absorbed him during the 1930s. Some of Bataille's contemporaries, as well as more recent commentators, have denounced this apparent change of attitude as a cowardly flight from political responsibility, possibly signaling an endorsement of fascism. Other critics have come to Bataille's defense, arguing for a positive political interpretation of Bataille's mystical writings and fueling an ongoing, sometimes acrimonious debate.[39] In chapter 4, I will discuss in detail what I take to be the political use-value of Bataille's mysticism. For now, my aim is to expose some of the fundamental connections that make it possible to construe Bataille's mystical writing as political *at all*. The concept of sacrifice is pivotal in this regard. Focusing on the place of sacrifice in Bataille's mysticism uncovers continuities linking Bataille's mystical antiproject to the political efforts of the preceding decade. Viewed through the lens of Bataille's shifting interpretations of sacrifice, mystical writing reveals itself not as a break with politics, but as a gesture that carries forward a certain form of political contestation entwined with the subversive force of the sacred.

The pseudonym under which Bataille wrote and published the opening section of *Guilty* (first printed in the journal *Mesures* in 1940) provides an initial clue to the connections to be explored. The name is that of the "King of the Wood," the priest-king-criminal of Frazer's *Golden Bough*: Dianus. "One called Dianus wrote these notes and died. He designated himself (ironically?) by the name of the guilty one" (*BOC* V, 239). The inner violence enacted and written by Dianus constitutes an inscription of sacrifice that crowns Bataille's obsessive interrogation and reinterpretation of the sacrificial process over a decade. Dianus's self-lacerating mystical text completes a mimetic "metamorphosis or a transfiguration" of "ancient" forms of sacrifice, including Bataille's own previous theories, bringing sacrifice to (absurd) perfection as the parody of a messianic *kenosis*, or self-emptying.[40]

By taking on the persona of Dianus, Bataille ironically resolves the stark alternative sketched in his College of Sociology lecture on power, where a radical choice was offered between the Christian model of identification with the innocent sacrificial victim (Christ) and the tragic model of identification with the criminals who slay the victim and bear the guilt of this unpardonable act. Dianus collapses the opposition and unites its antithetical terms. Dianus, the priest of Nemi, the "King of the Wood," is in Frazer's account at once sacrificial priest and sacrificial victim. He is criminal and king, a fallen god condemned to expiate the most terrible of crimes.[41] Thus Bataille, writing as Dianus, fuses in his own person the Christian identification with the helpless divine victim and the tragic link with the guilty murderer. Writing his inner experience, Bataille is both sovereign and assassin, renegade deicide and self-annihilating savior. As in the "sacrifice of the god" analyzed by Hubert and Mauss, Bataille (again citing the sociologists' study of sacrifice explicitly [*BOC* V, 305]) conflates the roles of sacrifier, sacrificer, and victim, compressing the sacrificial event to maximum poetic density. Sacrifice remains a crime, but a crime in which there is no external victim, nor any outwardly directed brutality. There is no "cowardly" last-moment substitution of an arbitrary scapegoat (cf. *BOC* I, 268). The sacrificial priest absorbs the full violence of his own gesture, yet this acceptance of suffering does not lessen his culpability, his "sin" (*BOC* V, 305). The priest-victim dies and lives in the text that endlessly communicates his anguished, guilty passion.

In writing the *Atheological Summa,* Bataille declares, his aim is "to invent a new way to crucify myself," staging a paradoxical self-immolation at once tragic and risible, cruelly lucid yet on no account "less intoxicating than alcohol" (*BOC* V, 257). As the world marches toward glory and death, Bataille parodically assumes the position of a mutilated god, suffering for those who know not what they do. He ordains himself as priest and consecrates himself as victim of a senseless expiatory rite. Bataille incarnates sacrifice itself: a mad gesture that abolishes utility and dissolves identity in a spasm of inner violence. "Seated on the edge of a bed, facing the window and the night, I worked, toiled to transform myself into a *combat.* The fury to sacrifice, the fury of sacrifice [*la fureur de sacrifier, la fureur du sacrifice*] opposed each other in me like the teeth of two gears, if they snag at the moment when the drive shaft begins to move" (250). Bataille's mystical self-annihilation mimes the great founding sacrifices of Western ontotheology (those performed by Socrates and

Jesus) and reveals their hidden truth: that of a "divine impotence" that "intoxicates" and simultaneously "lacerates to the point of tears" (299).

Sacrifice has undergone a final, crucial metamorphosis in Bataille's writing. Whatever importance may be assigned to Acéphale's reported plans for ritual bloodshed, by the era of *Guilty* Bataille had understood that "sacrifice cannot be for us what it was at the beginning of 'time' " (*BOC* V, 289). Modern men and women have lost their access to sacrifice's elementary forms. Most reasonable people would assume this loss to be a victory. Yet as a self-proclaimed *fou* (217–18, note)[42] whose madness bore traces of Durkheimian method, Bataille was not willing to dismiss the violent/ecstatic unleashing of sacred forces as irrelevant to contemporary life (or politics). Like Durkheim, Bataille searched for sacrifice's modern equivalents, for what the sociologist had wistfully termed the "feasts and ceremonies of the future" (*EF*, 427). Unlike Durkheim, Bataille believed he had found these new ceremonies and that he was called not merely to describe but to enact them.

The new avatars of sacrifice include all behaviors that unleash the affective power of "communication," dissolving rigid boundaries and catalyzing a "compenetration" of subject and object, self and other (*BOC* V, 391). Bataille's lists of such comportments include laughter, tears, drunkenness, sexual love. Yet the most crucial modes of contemporary sacrifice, inextricably interwoven, are inner experience (meditation) and writing. Today the "effusion of sacrifice" designates "not only the rite," but also the whole range of "representations or stories in which the destruction (or the threat of destruction) of a hero or more generally of any being plays an essential role" (218, note). Through his poetic/mystical writing, Bataille/Dianus enacts the "destruction of a hero" (himself) and so unleashes the communicative forces of the sacred. Bataille puts himself in play as self-mutilating poet/saint, doomed or divinely chosen to "indefinitely write the tragicomic story" of his self-loss through a textualized sacrifice that is now irremediably "nothing but its own simulacrum."[43] Bataille brings to its summit his theory and practice of sacrifice by sublimating bodily violence into the perverse expenditure of mystical experience and the "hecatomb" of poetry (220). The false, simulated aspect of the sacrifice strips it of all dignity; yet precisely this destitution enables the mystic's communication.

If sacrifice indeed, as Durkheim claimed, represents the relationship between the individual and the collective, then Bataille's risible self-immolation at the margin of the apocalypse faithfully and cruelly represents the anguish of the situation in which this relationship degenerates into madness: in which individuals bear blood-guilt for actions over which they could exert no control; in which death unleashed mingles horror with a scandalous absurdity that demands laughter as well as lacerating sobs: "To laugh at the universe liberated my life. I escape from gravity by laughing. I refuse the intellectual translation of this laugh" (*BOC* V, 251). Bataille/Dianus represents society to itself, the universe to itself, in an absurd burlesque. But the gratuity and absurdity of the performance are central to its content. Under the name of the forgotten priest of an antique and vanished cult, Bataille's final sacrifice assumes its own inanity. In this ritual, society could contemplate (if it chose to ... as perhaps someday, "when I am dead" [251], it might) not its effervescent unity but the bankruptcy of its founding myths and the collapse of its moral order. Bataille's fragmented text and the shattered subjectivity the writing stages mirror this breakdown.

Yet the sacrifice does not merely represent or replicate. It also enacts, imposes. Bataille's sacrificial text unleashes the active force of a refusal of dignity, utility, coherence, and power, in a world that the worship of these values has propelled into death (but a false death, ornamented with the kitsch of patriotic glory [see *BOC* I, 471]). Bataille/Dianus — the two-headed writer taking the name of the two-faced God (Dianus, according to Frazer, was originally interchangeable with Janus)[44] — scorns the useful, officially sanctioned sacrifice of war. Through mystical self-mutilation, useless internalized violence, Bataille parodies the solemn, serviceable sacrifice on behalf of the military order and enacts a scandalous, "religious" alternative. As Dianus, Bataille is like the Christ of his lecture: mutilated and helpless, a mute and powerless critique of power. Or to be exact, he is like Christ, only better: better because more absurd, comic at the same time as tragic, not innocent but "lubricious, cruel, and mocking" (*BOC* V, 278). To the triumphant "right" sacred of the generals, ministers, and fascist chiefs, Bataille juxtaposes the "left and immediately repellent sacred" learned from extravagant automutilators who perished defying Caesarian powers. Like the sacrifice on Golgotha before its recuperation by an imperial church, Bataille's "new way of crucifying himself" catalyzes urgent emotional energies, actively modeling and inculcating an attitude of defiance. Challenging power through a scandalous performance turning sacrificial, "criminal" energies against the self (and exploding, in the process, the subject's fictive unity and homogeneity), Bataille returns to the position of the rebel philosophers who, as recounted in his early essay on Van Gogh, after "frightful tortures" spat their own severed tongues in the faces of the representatives of power. Bataille's mystical self-sacrifice replays this gesture of defiance: spitting at the ruling powers (governors, generals, and gods) a mutilated organ of communication (a fragmented text).

Thus, in its supreme form as mystical self-oblation through writing, Bataille's sacrifice conserved traces of its Durkheimian roots, even as it contested Durkheim's values. Where Durkheim had deployed prodigious erudition to prove sacrifice's reasonableness and social utility, Bataille's sacrifice trumpeted its own irrationality and purposelessness. Durkheim had dreamed sacrifice as the expression and catalyst of group unity, the *do ut des* mechanism by which individuals give their energies to society in order to receive back from the collectivity those creative forces multiplied and enhanced. Durkheim's rite forged the bonds of social integration. Bataille, too, was attracted by the idea that sacrificial participation could nourish communal bonds, "create cohesion" (*BOC* II, 273). Yet Bataille's sacrifice was as much concerned with marking alterity and separation as with imposing unity. Enacting his scandalous literary self-crucifixion as Dianus/Jesus, Bataille again seized sacrifice as an instrument of revolt. Like the automutilators of his Van Gogh article, Bataille used sacrifice not to model seamless integration, the submission of the individual to the group, but provocatively to perform his insubordination and refusal of collective norms. Durkheim's sacrifice conjured images of harmonizing incorporation. Bataille's mad people, untamed artists, and debauched mystics lived self-sacrifice as the opposite process: revolt against/amputation from the social whole.

Through the "throwing out of their own parts" (*BOC* I, 265), Bataillean mystics explode the myth of social organicity, perform their refusal to function as docile members of the social body. They announce themselves as useless, alarming waste matter, destined to disturb the functioning of the social metabolism. Their sacrifice is an expulsive rupture for which Bataille had offered a crude but apposite metaphor in the article on Van Gogh's severed ear: vomiting. Liberating the "heterogeneous elements" within self and society, sacrifice opposes itself "to its opposite, the common ingestion of foodstuffs, in the same way as vomiting. Sacrifice considered in its essential phase would be nothing but a rejection" of what had previously been "appropriated to an individual or to a group" (269). "The victim sunk down in a pool of blood, the finger, eye, or ear torn away do not differ significantly from vomited food" (269). Seen and practiced in this way, sacrifice as self-inflicted violence marks disintegration and incurable otherness even as it reaches toward a wounded communication. It confirms the mutual repulsion between the collectivity and the unassimilable being who rejects the role of proper subject. Where Durkheim's sacrifice catalyzed effervescent communal fellowship, Bataille's dynamically expresses "hatred and disgust," contestatory emotions in whose absence sacrifice itself would be, Bataille asserts, merely another form of "servitude" (270). Durkheim's primitives had sacrificed in and to society. Bataille's self-divinizing automutilators sacrifice *against* the social body (the mythologized *corps mystique*) and its imperious organization. Asserting his irreducible alterity, the automutilating mystic shows himself "free to throw himself abruptly *outside himself*" (270), to hurl himself perpetually toward an "outside" that would performatively mark (create as it designates) a space for the contestation of imposed identities.

This pattern clarifies pertinent distinctions between Bataille's understanding of sacrifice and the deployment of sacrificial language in fascism. The issue is crucial, for fascists, too, trumpeted the virtues of sacrifice as the war brewed, exploded, and then, for France under Pétain, abruptly ended. In the June 1940 address in which he announced the armistice with Germany, Pétain blamed the military debacle on the creeping subversion of France's "spirit of sacrifice" by the insidious "spirit of pleasure."[45] The national renewal to which Pétain summoned the citizenry in the wake of defeat was explicitly predicated on rekindling the will to sacrifice, obedience, and hard work, themes constantly interwoven in Vichy propaganda. Previously, Hitler himself, in *Mein Kampf,* had made of self-sacrifice the crowning Aryan virtue, hammering home the notion that "the Aryan is essentially the one who sacrifices himself to the community, to the race."[46]

That Bataille and fascist leaders both asserted self-sacrifice as a key value cannot simply be dismissed as insignificant. Yet the sacrifice enacted by Bataille differs drastically in its methods and effects from the self-offering evoked by Pétain and Hitler. Fascist thinkers associated sacrifice with disciplined obedience, the individual's service to and absorption within the community. Bataillean mystical self-annihilation was the defiant gesture of beings who refused to serve. Where fascist sacrifice promised freedom from guilt, a clear conscience in the knowledge of duty fulfilled, Bataille's useless mysticism pledged to deepen guilt and anguish *à l'infini.* Fascist sacrifice elevated its protagonists. Bataille's self-expenditure cast down, abjected its derisory "saints" (*BOC* V, 278), mediating a sovereignty inseparable from defilement. Insofar as fascist logics suppose a myth of purity and upward-oriented, ennobling self-transcendence, an "attempt to purify or cleanse the nation,"[47] Bataille, parading his own defilement, defies these logics with his sacrificial performance. If the fascist leader energetically "weeds out dissent, subversion, and 'filth,'"[48] Bataille brazenly declares himself to be such filth: repulsive, unclassifiable, unassimilable waste matter.

Bataille held firmly to his acephalic precept that "It is time to abandon the civilized world and its light" (*BOC* I, 443): not to return to an atavistic origin, an archaic communal bond, but to move forward toward a new, insubordinate freedom. Bataille had announced in *Acéphale* that sacrifice as he envisioned it sought to tear human destiny loose both "from the rational enslavement to production" and "from the irrational enslavement to the past." Since in the historical moment when Bataille wrote, "enslavement tend[ed] to encompass the whole of human existence," it was nothing less than "the destiny of that free existence which [was] in question," in the problem of releasing the sacred, of releasing/ rewriting the human *as* sacred (465).

Bataille's sacrifice, while it reached toward "communication," asserted itself *against* the fusional immanence of a community or communion that would confiscate the autonomy of its "members," abolish their sacredness (their guilt and inutility), and harness them as instruments for its own ends. Bataille's last lecture at the College of Sociology provides what may be his most pointed formulation of this idea. Here, "sacrifice" stands clearly for an antiauthoritarian attitude defying the appropriative claims of "communitarian narrowness":

> In the same way, men more religious than the others cease to care narrowly for the community for which sacrifices are made. They no longer live for the community. They live only for the sacrifice. Thus they are possessed little by little by the desire to extend by contagion their sacrificial frenzy. Just as eroticism slips without difficulty into orgy, sacrifice becoming an end in itself aspires beyond communitarian narrowness to universal value. (*CdS*, 811)

The heterogeneous character of the sacred being leads not to "heteronomy" in the Kantian sense of moral abdication, but instead becomes the necessary condition of moral and political autonomy, fueling resistance to the communitarian constriction of an ideology of blood and soil. Humans marked (consecrated) by sacrificial passion embody and seek to propagate the "contagion" of a mad freedom that transcends the limited interests of any "narrow" group, unleashing a "frenzy" whose value — like that of Kant's moral maxims — is measured by its "universalizability." It is precisely because these "men more religious than others" detach themselves from the comfort of parochial allegiances that their isolated sacrificial gestures can paradoxically claim "universal" significance.

Closing Sacrifice

Though the movement is by no means linear, a gradual internalization, sublimation, and textualization of sacrifice can be observed in

Bataille's work through the 1930s. Attracted early in the decade by the prolific hecatombs and collective delirium he imagined among the ancient Aztecs (and hoped for among modern proletarian revolutionaries), by 1939 Bataille had reduced sacrifice to writing and narrowed the circle of violence until it contained only himself. The potlatch-revolution failed to arrive; Acéphale's plans for human sacrifice aborted; Bataille's writings on sacrifice (writing as sacrifice) proliferated. What Durkheim would have called the "metaphorical and symbolic" and Nancy the "mimetic" aspects of sacrifice came increasingly to the fore.

For Nancy, Bataille's successive approaches to sacrifice through the 1930s offer a compact and ironic recapitulation of the sublimating appropriation of sacrifice that can be traced through (and is perhaps constitutive of) Western ontotheological discourse from Socrates to Hegel. According to Nancy, Bataille's conclusion that "true" sacrifice is a literary/mystical self-annihilation of the subject (an impossible transgression-sublation that for Nancy reinscribes and re-hypostasizes the "subject" in the very act of claiming to shatter it) must be understood as equivalent to the acknowledgment that "there is no 'true' sacrifice." The ostensible elevation of "old" forms of sacrifice into art and poetry is mere "manipulation."[49] Distilling sacrifice into writing does not eliminate the cruelty that lurked in the age-old fascination with sacred violence. Indeed, the transformation of sacrifice into art may lend this cruelty a new and dangerous power of seduction.[50] The moment has come, Nancy argues, to break the hold of the figure of sacrifice over the Western philosophical imagination (and over the political practices philosophy analyzes and legitimates). It is, Nancy claims, Bataille's own work (his tireless interrogation of sacrifice) that brings us to the point where a certain mode of "thinking according to sacrifice" that Bataille exemplifies must be left behind. "Isn't it time, finally, to take action: both the end of real sacrifice and the closure of its fantasm?"[51]

The importance of Nancy's question can hardly be overestimated. Here, the investigation of specific traits of Bataille's thought opens on the wider, normative problem of the haunting of politics by motifs of radical heterogeneity and figures of sacred violence. The analytic project of understanding Bataille's politics of sacrifice in relation to other aspects of his thought and to the historical tensions of the period in which Bataille wrote shifts, as it finally must, to an evaluative deliberation concerned with the political demands of our own day. Thus considered, in what light does Bataille's legacy appear? Are the conclusions to be drawn from his sacrificial teaching above all negative? Would it be our task to purge the political of "the tendency towards sacrifice" Bataille strove to incarnate, a tendency perhaps inseparable from a bloody "fascination with an ecstasy turned towards an Other or towards an absolute Outside"? Must the responsible sharing of a political space begin with the recognition that "there is no 'outside,' " that is, with the abandonment of sacrificial posturing and of dualisms whose root and archetype remains the opposition between sacred and profane?[52]

At the end of this study, after interrogating multiple facets of Bataille's and Simone Weil's sacred politics, we will be in a better position to respond to Nancy's questions, at the very least to discern their true stakes. For the moment, we may note with Giorgio Agamben that recent "demystifications of sacrificial ideology," important as they are, are far from having laid to rest the problems Bataille struggled to bring into focus through the lens of sacred violence.[53]

This chapter's exploration has already clarified significant points regarding Bataille's attitude vis-à-vis a possible "closure" of sacrifice. Even as he resisted the Durkheimian view of sacrifice's utility and reasonableness, Bataille remained Durkheimian enough to see sacrificial dynamics as the enduring paradigm for relations between individual and collectivity. Bataille never fully banished from his writing the Durkheimian schema of a sacrificial convulsion productive of shared meaning and communal cohesion (even if, for Bataille, what is shared is the calling into question of all meaning, at the "extreme limit of the possible"). Thus, the specter of a (constantly suppressed, constantly resurfacing) "utility of the useless"[54] haunts Bataille's writing on/of sacrifice. On the border (along the *déchirure*) where sacrificial violence passes into language, perhaps matters could not be otherwise.

Nancy's demand for a politics that renounces dark "outsides" retains its force. Yet if the price of dissipating the specter of sacred violence is subscription to the bald claim that "There is no 'obscure God.' There is no obscurity which would be God," then we can see that the closure of the sacrificial vision must be undertaken not only "after Bataille [...] and beyond him,"[55] but directly against him. For if it is undeniable that "fascination is already proof that something has been accorded to obscurity and its bloody heart,"[56] it is no less true that Bataille as the Acéphale held his own bloody heart in his hand and vowed to "live only from what fascinates" (*BOC* I, 445).

Through the avatars of sacrifice, Bataille interrogated the permutations of what he saw as the fundamental violence of the human being. He sought to understand, on the one hand, how violence connects humans to an acephalic universe and, on the other, how violence functions in the political realm. Violence (sometimes overt, sometimes veiled) is the key instrument of political tyranny, of "Caesarian" domination and the exploitation of the poor by the rich. How could such domination and exploitation be opposed? Since Bataille considered violence an irreducible aspect of human nature, it could not for him be a question of "nonviolent resistance," but of searching for a different *kind* of violence that could resist dominating force. Bataille's investigation of sacrifice was an ongoing quest for liberative potentials in the conjunction of violence and an atheistic "religious spirit."[57]

As Bataille pursued his obsessive investigation of sacrificial violence in its psychological, political, and poetic dimensions, another French thinker was exploring related issues. Simone Weil saw in the concept of "force" a principle connecting war, social exploitation, cosmic order, and mystical truth. For Weil, force was encountered as the instrumentality of dehumanizing oppression. Yet to eliminate force from human life was impossible, since in a real sense our existence is *made* of force: composed of that which destroys it. Chapter 2 will trace Weil's efforts to come to terms with the challenges posed by this contradiction.

Chapter Two

TRANSFORMING
THE WARRIOR'S SOUL

Simone Weil's Poetics of Force

In the same way, peace — social as well as international — consists of two equal wars in opposite directions.
And in the soul?

— Weil, *Cahiers*

IF GEORGES BATAILLE'S WRITING and life in the 1930s were shaped by figures of sacred violence, Simone Weil's work was informed by the idea of force. The concept of force traverses Weil's authorship, from the political writings of her early career to the mystical journals of her last years in New York and London. In a real sense, in Weil's view, force defines the human condition. Yet force itself is far from easy to define, and Weil's use of the term in disparate settings can lead to perplexity. A careful analysis of the notion of force is vital in order to grasp the boldness and originality of Weil's interlaced treatment of politics, poetic creation, and mystical truth. Weil's writings on force mark the crossroads of her political thought, her mystical teachings, and her lived experience of the ambiguity of embodiment.

According to Weil, it was Galileo who first "brought mankind [...] the notion of force" (*OL*, 141). The original home of the concept is the domain of natural science, in which force is closely connected with ideas of gravity, energy, law, and limit. In *Reflections on the Causes of Liberty and Social Oppression* (1934), Weil argued that all force has its source in nature, but that human beings encounter force primarily as social: the enabling instrument of oppression, which marks collective life at all levels and reaches its culmination in war. In "The *Iliad*, or the Poem of Force" (1940),

41

Weil defined force as that which has the specific power to abolish humanness, transforming persons into soulless things. Weil linked such transformations to her concept of perception as "reading" [*lecture*]. She investigated how the play of force in oppression and war leads people to read others (and themselves) as mere objects, and she strove to find strategies by which such destructive readings could be resisted or reversed.

In this chapter I will show that for Weil force marks the limit or breaking point of humanity. Yet this limiting element is also *constitutive* of the human situation and in an important sense of humanness as such. Force operates upon human beings not only from without, in the form of natural constraint, social oppression, and military violence, but also from within, in the form of bodily needs. Weil experienced and theorized subjection to physical needs, especially hunger, as a defilement and diminution of the human. However, if physical craving threatens humanness, hunger and force more generally also offer a decisive opportunity to grasp the deepest truth of existence. Some critics have claimed that Weil's political thought is weakened by her tendency to conflate natural and social force, collapsing boundaries between nature, politics, and the spiritual.[1] This objection locates real difficulties in Weil's thought. Yet I will argue that it would be unwise to dismiss Weil's political theories, and the provocative claims implicit in her political practice, simply because her notion of force may appear unwieldy and because she failed to respect the classificatory boundaries dominant philosophical and political traditions have found useful. Weil transgressed these boundaries with a purpose. This chapter will show how in her late writings Weil interwove distinct but related strategies with respect to force. On the one hand, she theorized and enacted resistance to the "empire of force" in the political realm. On the other hand, in her mystical practice, Weil harnessed the dehumanizing impact of force to catalyze spiritual transformation, mobilizing force as a crucial "technology of the self" (more precisely, in Weil's case, a technique of liberation from reductive constructions of selfhood).

In contrast to the fury of Bataillean sacrifice, Weilian force is not sacred. Nor is force simply equal to profane violence. Rather, force provides opportunities where, by means of a right *use* of violence, sacred (mystical) truth can erupt within and transform human life. Politics, mysticism, poetry, and a visionary "science" of material forces interweave in Weil's thought in a way that ultimately leads not to incoherence, but to a provocative remapping of the human psyche and a reconfiguration of the space of political action.

Early Years: "Avec la faim au ventre..."

Weil's mutifaceted theory of force attained its full development only in the late stages of her intellectual career. Yet during her student days at the Lycée Henri-IV and the École Normale Supérieure (1925–31), Weil had already begun to interrogate many of the themes she would later associate with the concept of force: notably war, work, the dynamics of social oppression, and hunger.

The point where these themes intersected was the human body, for Weil a site of deep and enduring conflicts. From the beginning, Weil's relationship to physicality was problematic. A dogged worker convinced that physical toil purified the mind and heart, Weil reproached herself bitterly with her own "laziness" and drove herself forward by relentless efforts of will. Her reverence for manual labor was accompanied by severe myopia, chronically poor health, and a native physical awkwardness. She was forced to struggle on many levels for mastery of her own body. In an article published in *Libres Propos* (the journal of Alain's philosophical disciples) in 1929, Weil exhorted: "Let us wake up again to the world, that is to work and to perception, not lacking courage to observe this rule [...]: to reduce our own body to the level of a tool, our emotions to the level of signs" (quoted in *SP* I, 147). Weil's need to question the body took on added urgency when in 1930 she began to suffer from violent migraine headaches that would plague her for the rest of her life. The urge to instrumentalize the body interwove with the desire to explore and honor its creative capacities and with the drive tirelessly to interrogate the body's relationship to mental and spiritual life. These contradictory impulses formed a pattern that determined much of Weil's later thought.[2]

The task of coming to terms with extreme physical pain and with bodily needs and processes experienced as crippling and dehumanizing constituted a crucial strand of Weil's intellectual project from its early stages. Her concerns crystallized around the phenomenon of hunger. Physical hunger became a paradigm of force for Weil: the symbol of servitude, of the powers in opposition to which human freedom must create and re-create itself in a constant struggle. Even more potently than war, hunger expressed the insurgence of force at the very core of human existence.

A poem Weil wrote during her student years intertwines the interrogation of the multiple meanings of hunger with Weil's ardent concern for social justice. The poem, entitled "To a Rich Girl" ("A une jeune fille riche"), explores hunger in the terms Weil will later use to theorize force more generally: as a power whose effect is to transform the human into the subhuman, living flesh into dead "stone." To submit to force means to lose one's full share in humanity. Yet suffering social violence oneself is still morally preferable to wielding it against others. Weil's poem challenges the beneficiaries of an unjust social and economic order to step outside the comfortable illusions of their privilege and confront the real effects of the oppression exercised quietly but pervasively in their name:

> Clymène, avec le temps je veux voir dans tes charmes
> Sourdre de jour en jour, poindre le don des larmes.
> Ta beauté n'est encor qu'une armure d'orgeuil;
> Les jours après les jours en feront de la cendre;
>
> Un jour peut te blêmir la face, un jour peut tordre
> Tes flancs sous une faim poignante; un frisson mordre
> Ta chair frêle, naguère au creux de la tiédeur;
> Un jour, et tu serais un spectre dans la ronde
> Lasse qui sans arrêt par la prison du monde
> Court, court avec la faim au ventre pour moteur.
>
> L'usine ouvre. Iras-tu peiner devant la chaîne?
> Renonce au geste lent de ta grâce de reine,
> Vite, plus vite. Allons! Vite, plus vite. Au soir
> Va-t'en, regards éteints, genoux brisés, soumise,
> Sans un mot; sur ta lèvre humble et pâle qu'on lise
> L'ordre dur obéi dans l'effort sans espoir.

T'en iras-tu, les soirs, aux rumeurs de la ville,
Pour quelques sous laisser souiller ta chair servile,
Ta chair morte, changée en pierre par la faim?[3]

[Clymène, with time, I want to see in your charms
The gift of tears dawn and well up from day to day.
Your beauty is still merely the armor of pride;
The passing days will turn it to ashes;

A single day can pale your face, a day can twist
Your sides with gripping hunger; a shiver bite
Your frail flesh, once sheltered in the hollow of warmth;
One day, and you would be a specter in the weary dance
That ceaselessly runs, runs through the prison of the world,
With hunger in the stomach as its motor.

The factory opens. Are you going to toil on the line?
Give up the slow gesture of your queenly grace,
Fast, faster. Go on! Fast, faster. In the evening
Go, gaze extinguished, knees broken, tamed,
Without a word; on your pale and humble lip let there be
    read
The hard order obeyed in effort without hope.
Will you go, in the evenings, through the noise of the city,
To let your servile flesh be soiled for a few coins,
Your dead flesh, turned to stone by hunger?]

Weil's poem represents two drastically opposed realities, two worlds between which hunger forms the dividing line. The rich eat their fill and enjoy life. The poor suffer a "gripping hunger" that turns their flesh to stone, reducing them to the status of inanimate objects. Yet precisely because of the vulnerability oppression imposes on them, the poor possess in Weil's eyes moral and epistemological superiority. Genuine moral insight belongs to those who labor and suffer under the tyranny of force, not to those who bask in the lazy voluptuousness of a "queenly grace." Under such circumstances, the chance to shed tears — to confront genuine suffering — becomes a "gift." Weil challenges the rich girl (A school acquaintance? Weil herself? Both?) to abandon the protections of her privilege and enter the world inhabited by the poor, which — though a "prison" — is also the world of truth. The poor at least recognize the prison they live in for what it is. The apparent freedom the rich enjoy is both corrupt and illusory: corrupt because their liberty is bought at the price of others' enslavement; illusory because contingent events can at any time reduce their merely external freedom, like their merely external beauty, to "ashes."

For Weil, an epistemological privilege attaches to the experience of hunger. The knowledge of the world available from the standpoint of poverty, suffering, and privation is painful, but for that very reason more accurate than the view with which the materially advantaged are content. To ignore hunger's and poverty's power to disfigure human lives is to cut oneself off from contact with reality. Only those who hunger — who have experienced the transformation of their own flesh through unsatisfied need — are in a position to recognize reality (the true character of an economic system, the truth of the human situation more generally). Protected by their "armor of pride," the rich have no access to the truth. Ginette Raimbault and Caroline Eliacheff emphasize the *"connaissance de la faim"* (knowledge of/through hunger) that for Weil is the necessary precondition of the "search for the meaning of existence."[4] The formula echoes a phrase from Aeschylus that will in later years become a touchstone of Weil's thought, copied and recopied tirelessly in her journals: *"Par la douleur la connaissance"* (Knowledge through suffering). True knowledge is knowledge of force and its consequences. And to know force, Weil asserts, one must feel its bite in one's own flesh.

Hunger in "To a Rich Girl" appears simultaneously as private distress, as social oppression, and as an aspect of cosmic truth. Lack of food provokes personal suffering. Yet hunger is also, the poem suggests, the "motor" powering the machinery of social exploitation (the factory and the assembly line, where workers toil in despair, spurred by the terror of bodily need). Weil perceives how hunger functions as a tool of social control, by means of which the powerful in society crush impulses of revolt, keeping the workers "tamed." Yet hunger's influence reaches still farther, propelling the entire world in its "weary dance." Weil raises hunger to the dimensions of a cosmic principle, adumbrating between force and the underlying structures of the universe a link that will become increasingly central to her thinking.

Oppression, Freedom, and Force

During the early 1930s, Weil had involved herself passionately in the revolutionary trade union movement, writing articles for left-wing workers' journals, participating actively in union organizing, and — to the horror of the local school authorities — leading demonstrations of unemployed workers in the small city of Le Puy, where she received her first teaching post. Yet Weil became increasingly frustrated with the bureaucratic inertia and short-sighted sectarianism of the unions. In *Reflections on the Causes of Liberty and Social Oppression* (completed in the fall of 1934), Weil drew together the strands of her early political and economic thought in a document that marked the end of her belief in the labor movement as a political force (though her reverence for manual labor itself was undiminished, and she never lost her conviction of the unions' ethical importance).[5] It was in *Reflections* that Weil first formulated a systematic conception of the role of force in human society. Weil's theory involved a stern critique both of industrial capitalism and of the alternative proposed by Marxist orthodoxy.

The notion of force, Weil writes in *Reflections,* "is the first that needs to be elucidated" in order to "pose social problems" in the correct perspective (*RCL,* 52). Marxists' failure to grasp the true nature of social force is the root of their naive economic messianism.[6] Marx and his followers mistakenly attributed to certain stages of economic evolution (especially capitalism) the responsibility for an oppressive dynamic that is in fact inseparable from any form of even minimally advanced socioeconomic order. No human society, Weil argues, can do without force because no society can survive without oppression.

Force and oppression are not identical (*RCL,* 52), but the two concepts are closely intertwined in Weil's analysis. Social oppression always relies on force (which can, but need not necessarily, take the form of overt physical violence). Oppression in Weilian terms can be broadly defined as the "negation of Kant's principle" that occurs when some human beings are treated as mere instruments in the hands of others, means instead of ends.[7] In all cases, "oppression is exercised by force" (52). Force itself is multifaceted. At its most blatant, it involves violence inflicted directly on vulnerable human bodies (e.g., by an army or a police). But force as Weil wishes to understand the term also includes social and economic *structures* (e.g., class relationships) that constrain human freedom and instrumentalize persons without deploying military violence. Weil argues that, the stubborn optimism of dogmatic Marxists notwithstanding, "The force the bourgeoisie possesses to exploit and oppress workers resides in the very foundation of our social life and cannot be abolished by any political or juridical transformation." This "force," the decisive instrument of social domination, is nothing other than "the regime of modern production itself: that is, large industry" with its accompanying division of labor (15).

Marx had believed the elimination of private property and the transfer of factories to collective worker ownership would end oppression, ensuring that workers would no longer be degraded to the status of "means." Yet the compulsion to reify and use the other is independent of questions of ownership, Weil maintains. This compulsion is built into the very structure of socially organized production. Modern production cannot occur without a division of tasks and thus a hierarchy. Yet in any hierarchy of command, those who give orders have no choice but to regard, to a greater or lesser degree, the people who execute these orders as means. The source of social oppression thus lies not in the specific attributes of feudalism or capitalism, but rather in the hierarchical relationships that inevitably appear when social and economic arrangements advance beyond the most rudimentary level. Even feeble degrees of economic specialization require coordination and a centralization of authority. They demand the division of society into "two categories of men: those who command and those who obey" (*RCL*, 83). Where it is not offered willingly (and genuinely consented submission is highly exceptional), obedience must be compelled by the application of force (overt or hidden). From this moment on, force becomes the glue required to hold the social order together. Short of a return to the anarchic patterns characteristic of the earliest threshold of civilization, the hierarchical division of the population into those who give orders and those who carry them out cannot be abandoned.

The impact of social force is further intensified by the "race for power" that social differentiation renders inevitable (*RCL*, 54–55). Perpetually afraid of losing their advantages, the privileged members of a society must do battle on two fronts, maintaining their power "simultaneously against their rivals and against their inferiors," who for their part "cannot do otherwise than seek to rid themselves of dangerous masters" (55). Moreover, "[T]he two struggles that each powerful man must conduct — one against those over whom he reigns and the other against his rivals — blend inextricably, and each ceaselessly rekindles the other" (55–56). To defeat his rivals he must have the obedience of his slaves; to assure himself of his slaves' support, he must oppress them relentlessly. Thus, as Richard Bell observes, "the human condition is caught in the grip of power," but oppression is "less a result of [specific abuses] by industrial barons or faulty bureaucracies than it is due to more general struggles for power," to patterns of rivalry and exploitation intrinsic to the social order.[8] Viewed from this perspective, social existence as such emerges as a constant, multilayered exercise of force (51–52).

Two implications of Weil's analysis of force in *Reflections* merit particular attention. First, even in its social manifestations, "all force has its source in nature" (*RCL*, 51–52). The fundamental forms of violence on which social oppression relies derive from humans' irreducible vulnerability to natural forces and material needs. The implications of this claim are far-reaching. Social oppression is not a poisoning of previously innocent, unspoiled, "natural" relationships. Rather, force saturates the social *and* the natural worlds. Consequently we must give up any hope of escaping from force by withdrawing from corrupt collectivities to a way of life more "in touch with nature." Banding together in society to resist environmental threats, human beings merely traded one form of servitude for another. Yet to grasp this is to understand that nature cannot free us from the constraints of social force.[9]

A second, related point is equally decisive for Weil. Social force always relies, when traced back to its root, on the threat of physical violence and ultimately of death. The impact of force is often discreet in the upper echelons of a modern society. Yet social force's effectiveness depends on the ever-present possibility of forms of privation and coercion that have nothing subtle about them. Weil argues that "those who obey and suffer" in society bend themselves to servitude, whatever may be the form of that servitude, because they are "perpetually under the pressure of a more or less disguised threat of death" (*RCL*, 83–84). For comfortable mid-level managers and members of the liberal professions, this threat may not impinge on consciousness. Yet the threat is never absent, and the farther down the social scale one goes, the more clearly the menace is felt. All hierarchies of social dominance and control repose ultimately on this principle, even though in modern industrial societies, the death threat wielded by bosses against their workers is unspoken and abstract, and harmonizing social discourses may be mobilized to mask the agonal character of class relationships. Though it is possible to conceive of forms of violence that do not involve oppression, oppression cannot exist without violence, without the possibility of taking away people's means of survival or of inflicting physical hurt on them. Social force depends on the at least implicit threat of a "crushing pressure" that is not only "moral" but also "physical" (*OL*, 56). In the case of force as in that of Weil's concept of affliction [*malheur*], the bodily dimension is decisive. It is the grim privilege of the poor and vulnerable in society not to be able to ignore the threat of physical violence that lurks behind all forms of social constraint.

The most effective antidote to force for the Weil of *Reflections* is thought. Force is the mechanism of constraint; as force's opposite, rational thought is the basis of human freedom. Freedom is realized exactly in the measure that human action is guided by reason. A truly free human being, Weil theorized, would be one whose every act was the fruit of her/his own unconstrained deliberation concerning the ends s/he wished to achieve and the most effective means for attaining those ends (*RCL*, 88). In Weil's "Theoretical Tableau of a Free Society" (the third major section of *Reflections*), she used this concept of freedom to sketch a utopian society in which force and oppression, though never eliminable, would be reduced to a theoretical minimum through decentralization of the political and productive apparatus and a strong emphasis on individual autonomy, reflection, and responsibility.

Needless to say, the industrial societies of Europe and North America, both capitalist and communist, were far from such an ideal, and Weil believed these societies were likely to increase rather than lessen their reliance on force, as they struggled with emerging crises. The political conclusions in the later pages of *Reflections* were pessimistic. Nevertheless, some hope persisted. For within the hearts and minds of the oppressed masses, a thirst for freedom would always linger, Weil claimed. As long as human beings retained their ability to think, the triumph of oppression and force would not be total. "[N]othing in the world can prevent man from feeling himself born for liberty. Whatever may happen, he can never accept servitude; because he thinks" (*RCL*, 85).

This hopeful affirmation would not survive Weil's own experience of the conditions of life and labor among the workers in modern industry.

The Factory: The Mark of Slavery

Weil completed *Reflections on the Causes of Liberty and Social Oppression* in the autumn of 1934. In December of the same year, she took up the challenge she had thrown to the "rich girl" of her student poem: she went to "toil on the line" of a factory and to experience in her own flesh the effects of the privation and degradation imposed by social force. Weil obtained a job as an unskilled factory worker in the Alsthom electrical equipment plant on the southwest fringes of Paris. Over the course of the next eight months (through August 1935), she worked in a variety of low-level positions at Alsthom and two other factories in the area of the capital. The direct experience of the existence of the industrial proletariat marked a decisive turning point in her life and thought.

In the factory Weil learned firsthand that the brutal routine of forced labor under the pressure of a thinly veiled threat of starvation was entirely capable of stripping people of their sense of being "born for liberty." Even a relatively brief period of work under such conditions — joining physical exhaustion to constant anxiety and social humiliation — was sufficient to make people willing and even anxious to give up the capacity for thought on which Weil had based her definition of freedom and human dignity. At first shocked by the lack of political consciousness and revolutionary anger among the workers, Weil soon came to understand their attitude and to share it. She noted in her factory journal how the effect of physical exhaustion "makes almost invincible for me the strongest temptation this life includes: the temptation not to think." To abandon thought became "the only way not to suffer":

> Revolt is impossible, except in flashes (I mean even as a feeling). First of all, against what? One is alone with one's work, one could only revolt against it — and to work with irritation would be to work badly, and so to starve to death. [...] One even loses awareness of this situation. One submits to it, that's all. Any reawakening of thought then is painful. (WOC 2.2, 192–93)

Here Weil learned directly what it means for a human being to be "at the disposal" of another, to be reduced to the status of a lifeless and instantly replaceable cog in the vast machinery of the factory. She sought and obtained a *"connaissance de la faim"* at the social level, learning in her own flesh how hunger is transformed into a constant threat ("to work badly" means "to starve to death") that coerces submission. Along with her fellow workers, Weil lived the condition she would later theorize as affliction, a simultaneous mutilation of the body, the social ego, and the soul. Later, summing up the bitter lessons of the factory, Weil stated: "I received there forever the mark of slavery" (AD, 36).[10]

Weil left the factory in August 1935. In 1936, she was deeply shaken by the outbreak of the Spanish Civil War. Though still a convinced pacifist, Weil felt it impossible not to engage herself bodily in a struggle to which she had deep intellectual and moral commitments. Unwilling to remain in safety while others risked their lives for ideals she also believed in, Weil joined the International Brigades.[11]

Her initial contacts with the communist and anarchist forces were positive, giving her briefly the sense that she was participating in one of those "historic periods" in which "those who have always obeyed assume responsibility."[12] Yet once Weil reached the zone of combat in Aragon and joined an anarchist column engaged there, the initial giddiness dissipated. She saw acts of gratuitous violence perpetrated not only by the fascists but by her anarchist comrades. The anarchists' sincere commitment to justice and the "spirit of brotherhood" did not hold them back from cruelty, as soon as cruel acts could be committed with impunity.[13] Weil observed with dismay how the unleashed violence of war canceled the high ideals with which many fighters entered the conflict. Imposing its own logic, war's violence became an end in itself, abrogating all rules of morality and rendering noble convictions irrelevant.

An accidental injury forced Weil to return to France after only two months, but her time on the front had provided a concrete taste of the realities of war that would inform Weil's thinking about power and violence in a lasting manner.

The *Iliad:* War as Transformation of the Soul

Weil's most developed treatment of the notion of force came in the essay "The *Iliad*, or the Poem of Force." The text was written during the summer of 1940, following France's military collapse before Hitler's forces. As the German army occupied Paris, Weil and her parents fled to the Free French zone in the south, settling temporarily in Marseilles while awaiting a passage to America. It was against a backdrop of military defeat and exile, in which she and her family had become refugees, that Weil composed her compelling study of the effects of force in war.

The essay argues that the "true hero, the true subject," of the *Iliad* is force itself (*IPF,* 3). For Weil, the Homeric epic's greatness lies in the manner in which it is able to display — with the noble and unsentimental "bitterness" (29) that is the mark of truth — the capacity of force to unmake human being at its most profound levels. *Reflections* had linked force to the notion of an implicit or explicit threat of death and posited in that threat the basic structure underlying all forms of social coercion and rivalry. In "The Poem of Force," Weil clarified this intuition by offering a lapidary definition of force as "that x which turns anybody who is subjected to it into a *thing*" (3). Exercised to its fullest extent, force turns human beings into things in the most literal sense, by killing them. Yet beyond this "grossest and most summary form" of force as the force that kills, another aspect of force emerges: "the force that does *not* kill, i.e., does not kill just yet," but instead uses the *threat* of violence to "tur[n] a man into a stone," robbing the victim of his humanity while he is still alive. "He is alive; he has a soul; and yet — he is a thing" (4–5).

For Weil, the paradigmatic image of this transformation — one that recurs at decisive moments in the epic — is that of the slave or captive kneeling unarmed and helpless before the triumphant warrior. The victim, placed entirely at the conqueror's mercy, perfectly illustrates subjection to force. Present simply as a looming menace, force undoes and abolishes humanity even before an actual blow has been struck. "Disarmed and naked," the victim "becomes a corpse before anybody or anything touches him." Under the threat of force, though still breathing, the captive is already "simply matter" (*IPF,* 5).

The kneeling victim's attitude of wordless abjection is equivalent to complete dehumanization. Those who have found themselves in this state, even if they are not killed instantly, are expelled from the human realm. If execution is delayed, the suffering of the victim is simply prolonged. It becomes "death strung out over a whole lifetime" (*IPF,* 8). This is the fate of the slave (or of the modern industrial worker), reduced for the duration of his/her existence to the mute, mindless, almost insensible condition of the condemned captive in the last moments before execution, the ultimate instants in which the victim is beyond even feelings of anger (10).[14]

The "Poem of Force" bears witness to the bitterest lesson of Weil's factory experience and her time on the front in the Spanish Civil War: the realization that all levels of human existence, including the most elevated and spiritual, are vulnerable to force. In 1934, when she wrote *Reflections,* Weil had not fully measured the capacity of force to abolish rational thought, dignity, compassion, and the aspiration to freedom: literally to obliterate the human spirit. Six years later, Weil declared in the first paragraph of her essay on the *Iliad:* "In this work, at all times, the human spirit is shown as modified by its relations with force, as swept away, blinded, by the very force it imagined it could handle, as deformed by the weight of the force it submits to" (*IPF,* 3). Force,

Weil now saw clearly, "can erase the whole inner life" (10), and it is precisely this power of destruction embracing both the physical and the spiritual that places force at "the very center of human history" (3).

The all-encompassing reach of force means that to consider its effects only on the victims of war and oppression is to see merely a part of the picture. The insouciant and brutal master and the (momentarily) victorious warrior are denatured and enslaved by force, just as are their powerless victims. "Force is as pitiless to the man who possesses it, or thinks he does, as it is to its victims; the second it crushes, the first it intoxicates" (*IPF*, 11).[15] This signifies, on a first level, that those who at any given moment play the role of triumphant conquerors will shortly find themselves beaten and humiliated in their turn (11–18). Yet for Weil the decisive point is not merely that those who have vanquished one day will themselves be defeated the next. Already in the very moment of his victory, the conqueror is no less a dehumanized object than the captive who kneels before him. The mighty warrior is himself in a deeper sense merely the passive instrument of force, a tool temporarily appropriated and destined to be rapidly cast aside. Thus, violence "obliterates" both its employer and its victim (19). Force's "power of converting a man into a thing is a double one. [...] To the same degree, though in different fashions, those who use it and those who endure it are turned to stone" (25).

Force takes possession of humans by metamorphosing them: turning what were communicative, thinking beings into objects over which "words are as powerless as over matter itself" (*IPF*, 25). Battles are won and lost, Weil writes, "by men who have undergone a transformation." Warriors in combat descend "either to the level of inert matter, which is pure passivity, or to the level of blind force, which is pure momentum." This transforming property of force is mirrored in the poetic language of the *Iliad*, whose similes liken warriors, on the one hand, to tempestuous elemental forces like "fire, flood, wind" and, on the other, "to frightened animals, trees, water," and other forms of passive matter (26). To provoke such "transmutations" of the human spirit into pure violence or pure inertia is the essence of force. The conscious practice of this alchemy is the "art of war" (26). War's "equipment, its processes, even the casualties it inflicts" are only means to its real aim: to produce a "transformation" of "the warrior's soul" (26).

In her "Essay on the Notion of Reading," Weil describes this transformation of the soul, toward which the apparatus of warfare is directed, in terms of a changed "reading" [*lecture*] of the world. Weil theorizes all perception as a process of reading through which "at each instant of our lives we are seized as though from outside by meanings that we ourselves read in appearances" (*ENL*, 14). "What we call the world is meanings that we read" (14). Vital to Weil's theory is the idea that we do not consciously *choose* our readings of phenomena. The "meanings" of the world "take possession of [one's] soul" imperiously (16). Yet our readings of complex constellations of phenomena are subject to abrupt shifts in which one reading replaces another not by gradual modification, but by a sudden and complete reconfiguration which can be compared to Wittgenstein's notion of "seeing an aspect."[16] In general, Weil suggests, "all action upon other people consists essentially in changing what men read." And this principle applies not only to "politics, eloquence, art, [and] teaching," but also — in a signal fashion — to war (17).

In her essay on reading, Weil again interrogates the situation in which an unarmed captive kneels before an armed man. The aim of war is realized when the armed fighter "reads" in the very physical being of the helpless victim the necessity to kill that being, as clearly and effortlessly as he "reads" the colors of the other's hair and skin. "If in civil disturbances or wars unarmed men are sometimes killed, it is because that which in these beings is vile and demands to be annihilated penetrates through the eyes and into the souls of the armed men" at the same time as the visual details of the victims' clothing and facial features (*ENL*, 16). The successful military leader is one who has trained his men to read in this manner, so that, looking at a defenseless enemy, "as in one color they read hair and in another flesh, they also read in these colors and with the same obviousness the necessity to kill" (17). The triumph of force is achieved when this transformation of the soul has taken place on all sides of the struggle, canceling each participant's ability to see his opponents otherwise than as objects to be destroyed.

Confronting the Empire of Force

The philosophical and political implications of Weil's analyses of force — from her youthful poetry through *Reflections* to her *Iliad* essay — appear deeply pessimistic. Deadly force saturates war, but also social, economic, and political life in peacetime. Force dominates the realm of nature, too, ruling out in advance the romantic notion that we could solve our social conflicts through a "return to the earth." Weil's perspective seems to admit no possibility of escape from the domain of force.

Some commentators have argued that such a pervasive, undifferentiated notion of force must lead to a paralyzing cynicism, if not to a kind of paranoia. Athanasios Moulakis sees Weil's political theory as hampered by her unwillingness to think the differences between physical, natural force and power as exercised in the social and political realms. Collapsing such distinctions, Weil and her mentor Alain remained "trapped in their physicalism"[17] and as a result unable to conceive of a constructive, creative exercise of political power. For Weil as for Alain, power and force are the same thing, and they are *always* bad. Whatever their official values and ideological commitments, governments will seek to oppress their subjects. And thus, in a perspective in which "every government is seen as tyrannical, mendacious, and usurpatory," political nonconformity "turns into a fundamental civic virtue, independent of the actual content of the dominant orthodoxy." The result is a tendency toward "anarchy, which Alain correctly pointed to as related to his liberalism." Yet, Moulakis argues, this "anarchic spirit" is no longer interested in "storming the Bastille," but manifests itself above all negatively, in a stance of undifferentiated "refusal."[18] Such an attitude, for Moulakis not untypical of the *esprit contre* of the disintegrating Third Republic, seems destined to lead to political paralysis.

Moulakis's interpretation is valuable and cogent in many respects. He argues convincingly that Weil's political theory is flawed by the one-sided depiction of force as necessarily destructive and oppressive. Yet this interpretation also underplays certain distinctive aspects of Weil's thinking about force and may overstate the continuity between Weil and Alain (even as it usefully exhibits the many ideas they share). During the 1930s, Weil, like her mentor, had indeed renounced the idea of "storming the Bastille." Despite her tireless vituperation against the social "great beast," however, Weil did not give up political action. As war broke over Europe, she was prepared to carry that action to extremes of risk and sacrifice. In the following pages I want to explore the hypothesis that in 1941–43 Weil's theory of force was precisely one of the crucial factors that led her toward distinctive modes of political practice, on the one hand, and toward a provocative reformulation of spirituality, on the other. It was just Weil's refusal to make radical distinctions between physical, political, and spiritual force that enabled her to advance original and provocative theses about the possible liberative *uses* of force.

There is indeed no way—no human way—out of the domain of force for Simone Weil. No person in the world is spared force's touch (*IPF*, 33). Yet to acknowledge this fact is not to abandon political responsibility. Nor is it to abandon hope for a healing transformation of human existence. In the last years of her life, following the completion of the "Poem of Force," Weil pursued both political action and mystical illumination. Far from isolating these undertakings from each other, force constituted the link between the two.

On the one hand, Weil sought to conceptualize and put into effect means by which the savage force unleashed in war could be effectively *opposed* through the identification and active propagation in society of values and "readings" counter to those demanded by force. On the other hand, she explored the possibility that force as that which destroys the human could be internalized and *used* in mystical practice as the motor of spiritual transformation. These two contrasting yet related approaches to the fundamental challenge posed by force are examined in the following sections. Practical opposition to force puts into play Weil's concept of attention and suggests how Weil believes the *Iliad* itself as a literary performance models an attitude of effective resistance to force and thus embodies a liberative political stance. Weil's mystical spirituality, meanwhile, seeks to enact in the inner realm a transformation of the soul that in some respects corresponds to the dehumanizing metamorphosis effected on the battlefield, yet is oriented in the opposite direction: toward an "upward" rather than a downward exit from the human condition.

The Politics of Attention

In a notebook entry, Weil suggested: "There are two ways of changing for other people the way in which they read sensations," a modification that is equivalent to changing their "relationship to the universe." The first of these methods is "force (that kind of which the extreme form is war)." The second means is "education" (NB, 24 [WOC 6.1, 296]).[19] If force unleashed in war transforms the warrior's reading of the universe (and thus simultaneously transforms his soul) by turning his humanity to stone, a different (symmetrical but opposed) transformation can also be imagined, effected not by violence but by a gentler in-forming of the intellect and the mind's higher capacities, through a systematic mobilization of what Richard Bell calls "benevolent practices," aimed at enhancing the "capacity for freedom."[20] Education opposes the petrifying effects of force in the social and political realm. It does so by bringing into play the faculty Weil calls attention.

The concept of attention becomes central in Weil's writing in the period following "The Poem of Force." Weil's elaboration of the notion constitutes in part a practical response to the challenge posed by the essay: the question of how "the empire of force" could be subverted. For Weil, this struggle involves an apprenticeship (ENL, 18) in attitudes of resistance to the dispositions of body and mind force seeks to impose, and which make possible force's unlimited propagation in war. The notion of attention is the cornerstone of the strategy of resistance Weil formulates.

Attention does not promise an escape from the domain of force. Such an escape is in Weil's view impossible for human beings whose very bodies are sustained by operations of force (e.g., hunger) that cannot cease as long as bodily existence itself continues. What an attitude of attention can do, however, Weil believes, is open up — within the matrix of natural and social force — interstitial spaces for the emergence of those qualities and energies that, while crystallizing within force's domain, contest and subvert its domination. These are the qualities Weil comes to designate as "supernatural": true courage, compassion toward the afflicted, justice, love (e.g., *EHP,* 79–81). Attention designates for Weil the attitude that allows these qualities to emerge and act upon reality.

Attention is a quiet, nongrasping openness to the world and other beings, a waiting [*attente*] Weil describes in terms of active receptivity, in which "the 'I' disappears" (*PG,* 134–35). Such an attitude might appear to offer few political possibilities. Yet Weil insists that not only is attention not politically negligible, but it is the only factor that can ground an effective subversion of the logic of violence in the social sphere. Attention enables us to see what is really in front of us, including the humanity of the other being, where before we perceived only the projected images of our own terrors or the phantoms conjured by propaganda and indoctrination. Attention is a transformation of the warrior's soul symmetrical but directly contrary to that provoked by the unchecked storm of force on the battlefield. Mary Dietz identifies in Weilian attention the opposite of and only effective "antidote" to force. Much of Weil's writing in the later stages of her career can in fact be "understood as a pedagogical attempt to bring attention to light in an increasingly bleak world dominated by force."[21] Richard Bell, developing insights from Peter Winch, argues that the " 'geometry' of human relations" revealed by attention embodies justice within the human community. This "*quality of attention to another human being is the fundamental building block for [Weil's] moral and political thought.*"[22]

Though the word "attention" is not used in the essay, the theme is signaled in the text of "The Poem of Force" in the passage in which Weil asserts that the destructive cycle of force can only be broken by interposing the "tiny interval that is reflection" between "the impulse and the act": that is, between the triumphant warrior's realization that another is at his mercy and the gesture that annihilates that other (*IPF,* 13). "Reflection" is here identical to attention, implying the notion of a changed reading. Weil sought to show that by developing the capacity for genuine reflection/attention, humans could cultivate a reading of the world that could begin to "challenge [. . .] the pervasive empire of force."[23]

Weil characterizes attention as an attitude of detached and patient receptivity. Attention does not involve the active search for "solutions" or right answers, but instead an alert contemplation through which the subject opens to the reality before her or him: "Attention consists of suspending our thought, leaving it detached, empty, and ready to be penetrated by the object." Thought hovers, "waiting, not seeking anything." The world is seen as a person sees it from a mountain: with a gaze that embraces a wide horizon, but maintains distance (*WG*, 111–12). It is through this attitude of detached availability that we enter into contact with the real, in particular with those aspects of reality that our cravings, fears, and hatreds otherwise tend to distort and conceal from our awareness: for example, for the victorious warrior, the tragic subjection to force uniting him to the helpless captive who kneels at his feet. Attention mitigates the impulses of force within the self (the violent movements of will and craving) and thereby enables a new degree of freedom, the precondition of moral choice. Without such a change of readings, there is no opportunity for "justice or prudence" (*IPF*, 14).

In *Reflections*, Weil had emphasized dispassionate, methodical thought as the key to limiting the effects of the struggle for power and moving toward the construction of a free and just society. In "The Poem of Force" and her other wartime writings, as Bell and Dietz show, her emphasis has shifted from methodical analysis to the evocation of a "compassion-based" moral and political order.[24] Here, Weil's concern is less with a critique of specific forms of conventional political and social analysis (e.g., Marxism) than with expanding the political vocabulary to embrace "moral judgment and the recognition of others."[25] Weil theorizes as the basis of liberation from violence the reflective capacity to recognize the humanity of the other through attention, to discern in the other's suffering and helplessness not an invitation to destroy him or her, but the tragic qualities that mark our shared humanity. In Peter Winch's words, attention changes the "soul of the reader" by revealing to me that both the victim of affliction and I myself are "equal members of a natural order which can at any time bring about such a violation of whoever it may be.... That is, I cannot understand the other's affliction from the point of view of my own privileged position; I have rather to understand *myself* from the standpoint of *the other's* affliction, to understand that my privileged position is not part of my essential nature but an accident of fate."[26] The recognition — effective reading — of a common vulnerability constitutive of the human condition is a first vital step toward suspending the ceaseless exchanges of violence that scar human history. To systematize and universalize this change of reading would be to place "an understanding of human suffering [...] at the center of moral and political theory."[27] War would be countered by an education for and through compassion.

Weil connects attention explicitly to "looking" (e.g., *GG*, 109), which in her conceptual system constitutes a value directly opposite to that of "eating." Attentive looking contrasts with the inherently violent action of eating, the symbol and seal of our subjection to force. Where eating serves as the central image of "destructive satisfaction," looking "becomes Weil's sensory image of renunciatory salvation":[28]

The great sorrow of human life is that looking and eating are two different operations. Only beyond the sky, in the land inhabited by God, are they a single operation. Children, when they look for a long time at a cake and take it to eat it almost with regret, yet without being able to stop themselves, already feel this sorrow. Perhaps vices, depravity, and crimes are almost always or even always in essence attempts to eat beauty, to eat what we must only look at. (*AD*, 124)

For Weil, war is basically a form of cannibalism. The soldier's rage on the battlefield is a desire to consume the other. To interrupt this process by means of a "looking" that would discern inviolable beauty where before one perceived only an object to be devoured: this cessation of action would be a "saving" act (*AD*, 124). To look, to experience the desire to eat (the urge to incorporate the contemplated object by violence), and yet to hold oneself back from eating: for Weil this pattern of renunciation grounds all effective resistance to dehumanizing force on the battlefield and in society. At the same time, it furnishes the basic template for spiritual life. The "temptation" to violent action must not be resisted by yet another violent action, but instead by adopting an attitude of "attentive immobility."[29]

Yet it is crucial to observe that for Weil the right kind of "looking," the right kind of "immobility," leads straight to action. For in a stance of looking and waiting not only can temptation be vanquished, it can be used as a source of energy. When one contemplates a "possible good" in an "immobile and attentive" attitude, "a transubstantiation of energy" is produced, "thanks to which one executes the good" (C2, 210–11). Only on the basis of this inner transubstantiation does genuinely just action become possible. But when rooted in attention, a *possible* good action also becomes *automatic*. The attentive person acts to realize justice with the same spontaneity and naturalness she shows in fulfilling her own most basic physical needs. Spiritual discipline and political commitment fuse, yielding what Moulakis aptly terms "contemplation *in actu*."[30] In chapter 5 we will look in greater detail at Weil's own efforts to theorize and to produce political action as contemplative "*action non-agissante*," "non-acting action," determined not by personal cravings or ideological allegiances, but by adherence to mystical truth.

Force, Politics, and Poetry

Weil is not naive about the chances that attention as she conceives of it could be practiced spontaneously by soldiers caught up in the storm of combat. Her own experiences on the Aragon front had taught her all too clearly how rapidly the machinery of war grinds down noble ideals and humanitarian impulses.[31] Moreover, as Weil notes, the *Iliad* itself serves as a grimly sober check on any such ingenuous idealism. Moments of genuine humanity emerge within the epic, but they are few, ephemeral, and ultimately without effect on the conflict. Words of reason are sometimes spoken, but immediately "drop into the void," drowned by the clamor of rage, greed, and thirst for vengeance (*IPF*, 20). The fury of battle is precisely the setting to which reflection is most alien, and where compassionate attention becomes most unimaginable.

Moreover, the virtual impossibility of applying force moderately — or a fortiori of renouncing force altogether — is not limited to the context of war. The power of Weil's analysis of the confrontation of Achilles and Priam (conquering warrior and helpless captive) derives in part from her suggestion that the social roles and positions of these two figures place them in a situation in which their interaction is overwhelmingly determined from without, by a configuration of social forces beyond their control.[32] Neither conqueror nor captive can in any sense freely choose their reactions to (readings of) the other. A person who holds overwhelming power over another by virtue of their respective positions within political and economic structures — whether in the situation of war or in the context of "peaceful" relations among classes and social groups — cannot simply *decide* to see and treat that other as an equal, a full human being. The two people are situated in a matrix of political and socioeconomic power relationships that make the idea of free individual choice inherently misleading. One of the major contributions of Weil's analysis of force is precisely that it calls into question the individualistic Kantian model of moral decision making that cannot grasp the structural reasons why "when Achilles meets Priam as suppliant he is not facing a person":[33] not because the triumphant warrior has made a considered choice to regard the captive as an object rather than a human being, but because that choice has already been made for him by the force relations operating in the situation, which determine the "readings" to which he has access.

Yet Weil's view of this situation (and of relations of force in general) is not fully deterministic. If force (culminating in war) is one means for shaping human beings' reading of phenomena (our "relationship to the universe" and to one another), the notion of education (training in and through attention) holds out another possibility. The idea of a spontaneous individual "choice" to reinvest the other being with a humanity of which he or she has been stripped describes the situation inadequately. But Weil does believe that a process of what she terms education or "apprenticeship" can prepare the ground for a transformed reading in which the humanity of the humiliated other can be discerned, though such discernment remains in a sense an act of "supernatural virtue." For Weil, the supernatural is available in the framework of the material world and of ordinary human life, through beauty. Thus, in the notebook passage in which she initially lists force and education as the two principal means of changing people's reading of experience, Weil goes on to add: "There is a third way: the beautiful" (*WOC* 6.1, 296).

If force as unleashed in war projects human beings downward into the subhuman, beauty exerts an in-forming and trans-forming effect in the opposite direction, lifting people upward, training minds and souls in the attentive receptivity that is at once the precondition and the substance of "supernatural virtue." Beauty offers access to the mode of awareness characteristic of true attention. Thus it is not incorrect to suggest that beauty "saves" us, spiritually and perhaps also politically.[34]

The experience of beauty is for Weil the supreme transformer and enhancer of human energy, because aesthetic experience trains us in a joy that incorporates detachment and renounces violent appropriation. "Beauty as such is the source of an energy that is at the level of spiritual life. This results from the fact that the contemplation of beauty implies detachment." We cannot assimilate beauty in a grasping manner, for to seize the beautiful object is to destroy it. The attraction of beauty "in itself implies a refusal" to seek to possess the object contemplated. Beauty's attraction "is an attraction that holds at a distance. Thus the beautiful is a machine for transmuting low energy into elevated energy" (*SG*, 120).[35] Beauty teaches us to look and wait, to content ourselves with a joy that does not require exclusive possession. To cultivate the love of beauty, then, is to train souls in progressive detachment from violence, in progressive liberation from the bonds of force. Thus the creation of beauty is for Weil a political act, and as a work of supreme beauty the *Iliad* itself is a powerful political intervention.[36]

Weil did not suggest that the citizens of a nation at war could simply substitute poetry for concrete military effort. Weil's own determination to participate actively in the French Resistance makes this point clear. Yet Weil held to her belief that the education of attention, in which the experience of beauty plays an indispensable role, constitutes the only means by which the dehumanizing power of force can be resisted in the long term. The "miraculous" beauty of the *Iliad* — laying bare with a stern tenderness the inner mechanisms of war — was charged with political importance precisely in the context in which Weil wrote.

The epic's political meaning consists above all, Weil claims, in the "extraordinary sense of equity" the poem embodies (*IPF,* 32). While the *Iliad* has habitually been read as a celebration of might and military feats, Weil argues that the text envelopes the warriors' actions in a "bitterness" (29) that does not glorify but instead critiques force. This bitterness emerges from a "tenderness" that "spreads over the whole human race, impartial as sunlight" (29–30). Neither side in the conflict is treated by the poet with hatred or contempt. Yet at the same time, no warrior, whether Trojan or Greek, is allowed to bask in an untainted glory. Rather, the poet stresses the corruption of *all* by the blinding power of force. "Everyone's unhappiness is laid bare without dissimulation or disdain; no man is set above or below the condition common to all men; whatever is destroyed is regretted. Victors and vanquished are brought equally near to us." Both those who triumph and those who perish are "seen as counterparts of the poet, and the listener as well" (30).

It is as a concrete model of this impartial seeing — this reading of the world that bathes both good and evil actions in the light of justice — that the *Iliad* makes a timeless contribution. The poet has been able to "read" (and therefore to write) his countrymen and their foes as equal, to read both victors and vanquished as deserving of compassion and respect, while declining to disguise the evil they commit or to sink into the false pathos of a puerile "lamentation" over their downfall (*IPF,* 30).[37]

"Only he who has measured the dominion of force, and knows how not to respect it, is capable of love and justice," Weil writes (*IPF,* 34). The *Iliad* embodies love and justice not through sentimental rhetoric, but by measuring force's empire with cold lucidity. Homer's sense of justice, lifting up the tragedy of all his characters, is the source both of the *Iliad*'s beauty and of its political meaning. Its beauty — inseparable from "equity" — *is* its political meaning. As Dietz in particular has shown, the poem inculcates in the reader the very attitudes of unsentimental compassion, impartiality, love for life, and sorrowful awareness of life's fragility that constitute the basis of effective resistance to force.[38]

The political lessons of the epic were especially vital, Weil believed, for a newly defeated nation like France, torn between numb despair, fantasies of vengeance, and the temptation to collaborate with the victorious invaders. Weil's commitment to the resistance effort and the defeat of Hitler was total; yet she was convinced that the fight against fascist domination risked simply reproducing that same type of domination under a different name, unless those involved in the struggle carefully examined their own motives and clarified their own relationship to force. Weil's experience in Spain had shown her how generous ideals could disintegrate under the pressures of war, reducing antithetical ideologies (e.g., anarchist and fascist) to a common denominator of pure violence. From the *Iliad,* Weil argued, one could "learn that there is no refuge from fate," yet that this fact does not cancel responsibility. One could "learn not to admire force," but at the same time "not to hate the enemy" (*IPF,* 37). Above all, one could be taught to strip oneself of "the armor of the lie" (36) that consists in the illusion that one's cause, nation, or leader is "superior to ordinary human misery" and that one's allegiance to the cause suspends moral accountability to and for the vulnerable human beings on *both* sides of the conflict (36). Fusing beauty and moral lucidity, recognizing force itself as the enemy, the great poem "offers us an example of what it means to be fully human and humane; it is, itself, an act of justice."[39]

Weil's own drive to invest political action with the communicative power of poetry would shortly take dramatic forms, in her effort to join the French Resistance. As the struggle against Hitler continued, Weil was not content merely to bring to light, in her writing, the political wisdom of ancient poems. She aimed to risk her life in real battlefield actions consciously invested with poetic-performative power. Weil's war activities, in particular her "Project for a Formation of Frontline Nurses" (*EL,* 187–95), will be analyzed in chapter 5. Weil's politics of attention and reading sought not only to extract a political and moral lesson from Homer's poem, but to reinscribe that lesson in the language of concrete — and dangerous — action.

Force, the "Training of the Animal," and Mystical Transformation

Weil's search for means to resist force in the political realm was only one facet of her approach to the enigma of force. In the years following the composition of her essay on the *Iliad,* even as she strove to clarify concrete strategies for minimizing the destructive effects of force in public life (politics and war), Weil also sought, in mystical practice, ways to use force for spiritual transformation.

Weil's mystical explorations interwove with the violent events of history. After a brief and frustrating interlude as a political refugee in New York (July to November 1942), Weil reached England, determined to join the resistance efforts of the Free French organization. However, her repeated bids to obtain an active mission on French soil were rejected. Instead, Weil was assigned amorphous editorial and informational tasks in the Gaullists' London office. Her frustration deepened. Meanwhile, her physical health declined rapidly after her diagnosis with tuberculosis in early 1943. Yet despite the anguish of exile, persistent physical suffering, and psychological torment leading to despair, the final years of Weil's life (1941–43) constituted a period of startling intellectual creativity and profound spiritual experience.

In Weil's later notebooks and in the texts published posthumously as *The Need for Roots,* the notion of force is brought into relation with other concepts decisive for the last stages of Weil's career, in particular energy and desire. During this period, Weil read mystical and religious texts (including the Bhagavad Gita and the Christian Gospels), but she was also plunged in the study of advanced mathematics and physics. Weil's use of the term "force" in different but related senses in her notebooks and late essays reflects this multiplicity of intellectual horizons and interlocutors. In general, force retains the specific connotations Weil had assigned the word in her study of the *Iliad:* force is "that x" that constrains human liberty and ultimately reduces human beings to inert matter. In some passages, force becomes simply a synonym for violence. In other texts, however, Weil uses the word in a broader and more neutral sense, closer to its meaning in the natural sciences, especially physics.

The themes of force, energy, and desire intersected crucially in the body for Weil in her last years. Large portions of Weil's late notebooks were devoted to exploring how the energies constitutive of human being — including somatic strength, desire, and will — feed into or inhibit one another. Weil's physical ill-health and food austerities meant that the question of how different kinds of energy could be produced, maintained, and "transmuted" was an issue of practical urgency as well as theoretical interest. Tortured by debilitating headaches and undernourished, while demanding from herself extraordinary levels of intellectual and physical effort, Weil had to confront the management of bodily and psychic energy as a matter of daily survival.

Weil's notes on economies of psychic and physical energy use the term "force" in a manner initially less indebted to military metaphors than to natural science. "Here below in the sensible universe there are only two forces: gravity on the one hand, and on the other all the energies that permit us to counterbalance gravity, and which all [. . .] proceed from the sun, that is to say from the same source as light" (*C3*, 187). However, scientific ideas of force concern Weil above all because they enable an understanding of spiritual realities. It is "literally true" that "solar energy descends into plants and thus into animals, in such a way that we can eat it after having killed it" (198–99). Yet this literal truth encloses a deeper and more important insight. It concretely symbolizes divine grace, God's endless self-giving. "We cannot capture solar energy. It is the energy that spontaneously transforms itself and takes a form in which we can seize it. This is an act of grace" (199).[40] Weil's analysis provides an intriguing counterpoint to Georges Bataille's glorification of solar self-squandering. In his article on Van Gogh and automutilation (as in numerous other texts), Bataille had presented the sun's endless outpouring of energy as the archetype of sacred (useless, irrational, self-expending) behavior. Weil, too, sees in the sun's activity a sacrificial gesture readable simultaneously as physical fact and moral-religious allegory. Yet Weil downplays the gratuitous quality of the sun's self-giving that so fascinated Bataille. Instead, Weil emphasizes the practical benefits that accrue to earthly creatures through the sun's pouring forth of warmth and light. For Weil, the sun's radiance becomes not a metaphor for irrational, violent excess, but a sacramental symbol expressive of God's love.

In an effort to describe more precisely the economy of energy operating in human existence, Weil divides the energies available to the human being into two categories: "vegetative" and "supplementary." Vegetative energy is body energy. It is the power that carries out basic somatic processes. Vegetative energy drives "the chemico-biological mechanisms indispensable to life" (*CS,* 178) in the purely corporeal sense. Supplementary energy, in contrast, belongs to the level of personality. It funds the ostensibly "higher" parts of human identity: desire, will, and the imagination (e.g., *C2,* 123–24; *CS,* 178). The processes of spiritual transformation as Weil theorized and attempted to enact them involved modifying the usual relationship between vegetative and supplementary energies by means of intense prayer, meditation, and bodily and psychic austerities.

Simone Weil is often criticized as a dualistic thinker hostile to human physicality (and merciless toward her own body). While there are elements of truth in this account, it is also in important respects misleading. The physical body as such is not the target of Weil's suspicion. For Weil, sin and distortion are located not in the flesh, but in what she terms the "carnal part of the soul" (e.g., *PSO,* 112): that is, the personality, the ego. Thus, the effort of genuine mystics is not to destroy their bodies, but to eliminate *from their souls* the ego component, the "part that says 'I' " (*EL,* 17). To obtain this transformation of the soul, however, the body — above all the suffering body — must be used as a tool.

External force, achieving its fullest expression in war, is characterized by its capacity to abolish human identity, to transform flesh into stone, a human subject into mere matter. A precisely analogous transformation in the inner realm becomes the key to Weil's mystical anthropology. Deadly force must be unleashed within the human being her/himself, in order to kill the isolated personality and open the way to spiritual liberation. Weil sketches the mechanics of this process in a passage from her last notebook of 1941. A striking comparison between the "supplementary energy" of will and desire and deadly "armed force" indicates the basis of Weil's strategy.

The essay on the *Iliad* had shown that force in combat produces a transformation of the warrior's soul, making of the fighter at least temporarily a being other than human (below the level of human existence, impervious to the power of language, akin to the blind and inarticulate forces of nature). But in 1941, Weil argues that we all carry within us a similar destructive principle: a force comparable to military power, and just as capable of unmaking humanity. "Supplementary energy corresponds to armed force" (C2, 175). That is to say, the components of our personal being — will, desire, goal-oriented rationality — that belong to the domain of the supplementary energy and that we ordinarily understand as constituting our unique self are at the same time the potential vehicles of a power that abolishes selfhood. Human personality carries its own built-in self-destruction mechanism. For the mystic, this apparent threat is also a promise.

Whereas force outside seethes without direction, the "armed force" inside us can be oriented. Society's warlike energies are aimless and therefore purely destructive. But "the soul's armed force can turn itself upward [*vers le haut*]" (C2, 175–76), toward God. This principle underlies Weil's model of spiritual transformation as a "training of the animal in oneself" (e.g., C3, 19). Such "training" involves ascetic renunciation that seeks not to eliminate desire, but to intensify and at the same time frustrate desires to such a degree that they literally disintegrate the individual's psychic substance. Hostile forces within the personality are pitted against one another, creating the equivalent of a war inside the self:

> Since one has within oneself a principle of violence, the will, one must also — in a limited measure, but to the full extent of that measure — use this violent principle violently; constrain oneself by violence to act as if one did not have such and such a desire, such and such an aversion; without trying to persuade the sensibility, but constraining it to obey. [...] Each time one does oneself violence in this spirit, one advances, a little or a lot. (19)

Violence inflicted by one part of subjectivity against other parts shatters the illusory integrity of the ego. Progressively, as material desires are dominated and greater energy focused "upward," one approaches the ideal of detachment that Weil conceives of as the "emission of the totality of [one's] energy toward God" (92). Ultimately, mystical transformation is the work of God's grace. Yet force — exercised as violence against the self — creates the conditions for grace's reception by overturning the ego's defensive structures and breaking open its monadic unity. This transformation is not merely an intellectual process. The role of the body and its energies is pivotal. Indeed, for Weil, spiritual revolution is not possible without a full engagement of the body. Bodily pain and bodily craving constitute opportunities for decisive progress in the "training of the animal."

‚ Weil's migraine headaches provided her with the model of a situation in which overwhelming physical suffering, submitted to in an attitude of spiritual "consent," leads to a palpable experience of liberation from selfhood and openness to the divine. Physical pain alters the relation between the supplementary energies of the conscious personality and the bodily, "vegetative" energies. Under circumstances of bodily suffering and privation, Weil claims, the elements of "force" within the personality can literally tear the somatic energies away from their investment in the maintenance of the body and orient those physical energies upward to God. Weil theorizes the supreme moment of mystical transformation not as the destruction of the body, but as the catalyzing — in the midst of pain that literally shatters the personality — of immediate contact between the body and God. "Supplementary energy, when it is entirely turned upward, serves as a lever to turn in this direction the vital energy itself, that of vegetative life" (C2, 175). This "tearing loose [*arrachement*] and orientation upward of the vegetative energy" possesses the quality of "redemptive suffering." It "redeems creation" — our creation as isolated human personalities — by "undoing" that creation: undoing our humanity in the mystical equivalent of death. In the moment of spiritual "decreation," one loses one's life quite literally. The life-energy is torn outside the self; or more precisely it is the self that is ejected, evacuated, leaving behind a still-living body emptied of its ego (175).[41] With the personality obliterated, the divine and material creation (the body) commune in renewed intimacy. Yet only a controlled "brutality" can bring this intimacy about.[42] Decreation demands that the subject "live while ceasing to exist so that in a self that is no longer itself God and his creation find themselves face to face" (C3, 80).

Among the bodily experiences to which Weil refers most frequently in analyzing mystical decreation is hunger. Hunger both figures and unleashes the anguished, unquenchable desire Weil believes must fuel the process of mystical change. The cry of the helpless, hungry child paradoxically illustrates the fullest deployment of spiritual force. For at its height, inner force expends and abolishes itself in impossible desire for what we "cannot reach":

> How could we look for God, since he is above, in the dimension we cannot reach? We can only walk horizontally. If we walk in this way, looking for our good, and the search succeeds, that success is illusory. What we will have found will not be God. A small child who in the street suddenly no longer sees his mother beside him runs in all directions crying, but he is wrong; if he has enough reason and strength of soul [*force d'âme*] to stop and wait, she will find him faster. One must only wait and call. Not call someone, as long as one doesn't know if there is someone. Cry that one is hungry, and that one wants bread. One will cry for a more or less long time, but finally one will be fed. [...] The essential thing is to know that one is hungry. (*PSO*, 44–45)

One must first know, recognize, one's hunger, in order then to know in and through one's hunger that there is no object, no earthly food, by which hunger can be assuaged. Our hunger is for the good, and the good is "outside the world" (*EL*, 74).

Hunger can be purified — and can in turn purge the soul — if hunger refuses to be satisfied by less than the good, which exists only "above." The force that in Weil's early poem was the "motor" driving the world's weary dance can itself become the power that moves us beyond the world. But the motor must learn to run not on the fuel of objects, but *à vide*. The paradoxical movement beyond the world occurs when one stands absolutely still. It is not an action, but a renunciation of action through which dehumanizing force is transmuted into the power to transcend the human. The figures Weil characteristically uses to symbolize this spiritual attitude are similar to the ones she has chosen to represent the helpless victims of force: the crying child, the future bride, the kneeling slave.[43]

The World as Poem of Force

Weil's analyses of force seemed to yield two possible (and sharply divergent) approaches for those determined not simply to accept force itself as the supreme value: on the one hand, a political program of "public action" (*E*, 240); on the other, an inner quest for mystical truth. The political path hinged for Weil on the notions of disinterested *"action non-agissante"* and of "education"; the aim was to counter force in the public sphere through the cultivation of compassionate attention and attention-guided action. In mystical practice, contrastingly, the transforming effects of force are sublimated and internalized for solitary spiritual purification. The first approach uses the resources of poetry and religious-philosophical wisdom along with conventional political analysis to inculcate attentive reading as the path to just action. The second, mystical approach appears to entail a blunt rejection of social action as the domain of the Platonic "great beast." The two efforts initially seem contradictory, or at the very least unrelated. Yet Simone Weil in the last years of her life practiced both simultaneously and affirmed their solidarity. In some of her last writings, notably the concluding section of *The Need for Roots*, she presented a view in which the mystical "decreation" of the self and the effort to shape a politics of beauty based on transformed "readings" fused in a vision that grasped the world as a "poem of force," and force itself as a transcription of divine wisdom. These pages unite the spiritual and the political dimensions of force in a cosmic vision that has proven both inspiring and disconcerting to readers.

Weil begins from the principle that the material world is shaped by a play of impersonal forces whose interactions are determined by laws of strict mathematical rigor. Gravity, light, the transformations and permutations of matter and energy: the operations of these principles are pitiless and mathematically exact. And not only insensible matter, but also human behavior and even human thought, to the extent it has its origins in the personality, are irremediably subjected to the operations of force. Under normal circumstances — insofar as she or he has not undergone spiritual transformation — the whole human being, including the "most

intimate of [her or his] thoughts," is "entirely subjected [...]
to the constraint of needs and to the mechanical play of force"
(*E, 366*).

Weil's use of the term "force" now condenses the series of meanings Weil had assigned to the term over more than a decade of
reflection. Force in the last pages of *The Need for Roots* encompasses the imperious drives that inhabit individual bodies; mental
functions, insofar as they originate in the personality; the social
structures of oppression and the dynamics of history; the shattering violence of the battlefield; and the immense, overarching
powers of the material universe. Yet force, Weil now affirms, has
limits, both within the human being and in the cosmos. Force is
"by nature blind and indeterminate"; whereas if we turn a pure
attention to the complex harmony and regularity of the natural
world, we discover the work of an ordering principle. Limits are
fixed to force's operations; determinations are imposed on it by
an authority outside force itself, which Weil terms "necessity." In
this sense, "The brute force of matter, which to us appears as sovereignty, is in reality nothing other than perfect obedience." Force
obeys necessity. And necessity is nothing other than the network
of determinations imposed on the universe by "eternal Wisdom"
(*E, 358–59*).

The laws regulating the universe are God's thoughts. This
means, "[F]orce which is sovereign here below is dominated in
a sovereign manner by thought." Thus, as "thinking creature[s],"
we humans are, at least potentially, "on the side of that which
commands force" (*E, 365–66*). To the extent that human beings
can bring our own thoughts into harmony with the pure, divine
thoughts that constitute the laws of the material universe, humans will no longer be mere blind instruments and objects of
force, but lucidly obedient participants in the unfolding of processes determined by the divine will. This fact, obscured by the
modern scientific worldview, was, Weil asserts, the very foundation of the science of classical Greece and of the Stoic and
Pythagorean philosophies from which that science was inseparable (365). The rational thought Weil had emphasized so centrally
in her earlier work, but whose power she had questioned as a result of her experiences of factory work and war, returned now,

transfigured. These are no longer the personal thoughts of an iso-lated human individual, asserting her freedom by determining each action through rational deliberation. The thoughts that concern Weil now are the impersonal thoughts of the cosmic creator, the pure laws underlying all reality. Human beings gain access to these thoughts through impersonal contemplation, in which "the opera-tion of the intelligence" discovers "necessity sovereign over matter as a network of nonmaterial relations without force" (365).

This reading of the "book of nature"[44] requires specific spiritual dispositions on the observer's part. Such reading is for Weil true and complete in a way that the reductive interpretations of mate-rialist science cannot be; yet to perceive its truth, the human being must undergo spiritual purification, progressing toward "detach-ment" and learning to disregard "the readings from lower and less comprehensive perspectives."[45] At the height of awareness, one perceives and experiences the unity of natural law (necessity), divine wisdom, beauty, and love. This unity is the key to the "per-fectly beautiful order of the universe" posited by the Greek Stoics (*E*, 364). Viewed from such a perspective, the world and all the events that occur within it appear saturated with beauty. "Like the oscillations of the waves, all successions of events here below [. . .], births and destructions, increase and decrease, make sensible the invisible presence of a network of limits without substance and harder than any diamond. This is why the vicissitudes of things are beautiful, even though they let us glimpse a pitiless necessity" (362). Pitiless, the necessity that governs the world is also without partiality and without cruelty. It is not force, but the "sovereign mistress of all force," love (362). This perception is the basis of the Stoics' *amor fati*, "the love of the order of the world, which they placed at the center of all virtue" (363).

Guided by the perceived unity of necessity, beauty, and love, the contemplation of the world resembles the contemplation of a work of art. The cosmos as a whole becomes a "poem of force," in which movement and transformation, the patternings of force and matter, no longer exist merely for themselves. Like the words of a poem or the brushstrokes of a painting, the configurations of force and matter obey and reveal the impersonal "thoughts" of their creator. Read with the detachment appropriate for the contemplation of beauty, force itself is poetry, a "medium" through which we decipher God's love.[46]

Faced with the spectacle of divine poetic creation, humans' task is not simply to admire the completed work (i.e., the world) passively. We are called instead, Weil affirms, to take part in the ongoing process, the manifestly incomplete divine *poiesis*, through forms of action obedient not to private whim, but to the demands of the divine law, read as cosmic regulation, aesthetic principle, and moral necessity. Weil insists that to obey God's commands rather than our own cravings leads not to a weakening of political effectiveness, but on the contrary to a multiplication of creative energies and to a more effective political application of the energies available. To discern the network of necessary laws that are "sovereign over matter" is not to resign moral hopes, but to see clearly the outlines of one's duty against a cosmic background that relativizes all private hopes and fears. Weil tried to show both by words and actions that the result of a lucid grasp of force and force's relationship to divine love is not cynicism, but a "supernatural courage" (*EHP*, 79) no longer held back from action by a fear of personal consequences.

Force and Transforming Action

Force shapes the natural world, determines social reality, saturates the human body, and structures the movements and transformations of the soul. Force destroys the human, yet to the impersonal gaze of pure attention, force is poetry, its diamond-hard beauty identical with divine love. In her culminating vision, Simone Weil unites the disparate dimensions of reality in a cosmic synthesis bound together by force.

Weil's final mystically inflected picture of reality has been labeled deeply "antipolitical."[47] The reasons that support such an assessment are clear. One may grant that Weil's understanding of just political action as pure obedience to God does not automatically imply quietism. Yet it is evident that conventional political thinkers will have difficulty simply understanding, much less accepting, the premise that right political action should begin with — and might never move beyond — a meditative attention and quiet waiting [*attente*] for the truth. Likewise, the Weilian thesis that divine commands are the preferred guides for our political interventions will in the eyes of many secular analysts foreclose political debate altogether. (Whereas by bringing this idea forward in her writings and political activities with the Gaullists in 1943, Weil sought to open, not to end, a substantive discussion about the orientation of French political life.) For most readers today, to conflate political and spiritual force, recasting military struggles in terms of spiritual transformation and vice versa, will appear — as it did to the majority of Weil's Free French comrades in 1943 — anachronistic, if not simply aberrant. Even recent authors sympathetic to Weil, such as Moulakis and Elshtain, argue that the conflation of different types and categories of force handicapped Weil's political thinking, caging her social and political analyses in structures that robbed them of flexibility and pushed her frequently toward a rigid, strident dogmatism.

Certainly, a good deal of truth must be acknowledged in such critiques. A more supple and differentiated understanding of force and forces, one that did not aspire to unify all levels of human and cosmic existence in an englobing whole, might have enabled Weil to grasp more clearly the nuances of the various political options on the table in the 1930s. Replacing the habit of universal suspicion inherited from Alain, this more nuanced view would have shown Weil that, while all leaders and governments risk corruption, they are not all bad in the same way nor to the same degree. With clearer and less metaphysically freighted ideas of force and power, Weil might have seen earlier, as Moulakis sternly puts it, that there is a not inconsiderable difference "between a Hitler and a Poincaré."[48]

Yet these critics may have underestimated the creative potentials of Weil's doctrine of force and discounted too rapidly the ways in which, precisely because of its all-englobing nature, Weil's theory of force dynamized her political thought and practice, even as it pushed her onto problematic paths. Her belief in the pervasiveness of force prevented Weil herself from conceiving of mysticism as an escape from force, thus from treating religious life apolitically. On the contrary, to contest standard forms of political analysis and behavior by means of mysticism is not to turn one's back on politics, but to open the political to new influences, to new challenges, to new knowledges that may provide unexpected insights and a way to avoid the repetition of past mistakes. "Antipolitics" undertaken by these means remains very much a political practice, although it brings with it the dangers Moulakis aptly describes in his analysis of the aporias of the political *"esprit contre."*

It was precisely Weil's tendency to see force everywhere that allowed her to recognize different aspects of intellectual, political, and spiritual life — despite their apparent (and not merely apparent) fragmentation — as influencing one another in ways of which an exclusively secularized view cannot make sense. Weil could think mysticism as the inner prolongation of war and affirm that political action (emerging from authentic attention) could advance the "cure of the soul," indeed under some circumstances constituted an indispensable requirement for personal spiritual healing (see *E*, 237–380). Precisely Weil's refusal radically to separate physical, political, and spiritual force endowed her thinking about the possible liberative uses of force with bold originality. Weil could show how the crystallization of spiritual force in mystical practice empowered the decreated, "selfless" subject for courageous political engagement. On the other hand, she could argue that true mystical transformation not only revealed itself as compatible with political action, but positively demanded committed action and risk in the political sphere. Spiritual change first becomes real when it engages and expresses itself through the body in public, political action. In the later pages of *The Need for Roots*, Weil argued that, for the Christian, political action is a sacred duty, the concrete means to save one's soul. The souls of individuals and the spiritual heritage of nations are saved by action (240, 250–51). But saving action is rooted in attention — patient waiting for the inspiration of grace — and grace itself is assimilated as energy.

Her doctrine of a polymorphous but still ultimately unified force operative on multiple levels also allowed Weil to discern that "education" in attention and in beauty — while it could not simply substitute for other forms of political action — might nonetheless become an important factor in limiting force and, in the long term, in altering European society and political culture so as to make the resistance to oppressive force a meaningful feature of that culture.

Weil was able to make sense of the aestheticization of politics in the Third Reich and at the same time to show why Nazism was not the final word on relations between aesthetic feeling, "education," and political will.

Much of Weil's provocative freshness as a thinker springs from her gift for applying terms metaphorically in a range of domains where they initially seem to have no business. Force, hunger, and reading provide examples of this phenomenon. Weil's politics were poetic and mystical; her mysticism was warlike and political; she saw even her own bodily hunger in metaphorical terms, as expressive of political solidarity with the oppressed and of all humans' shared subjection to the tragedy of finitude. No mere logical confusion, Weil's telescoping of these categories under the heading of force represented a considered effort to connect areas of experience and practice held separate in modernity. In the face of the bankruptcy of modern Western civilization incarnated by Nazism, Weil judged it an urgent task to seek new links and cross-fertilizations between religion, bodily discipline, cognition (reading), and political practice.

Faced with what appeared to her as the crushing enslavement of the human being to the compounded tyranny of natural and social force, Weil sought to discern a path that would lead not to moral paralysis but to lucid courage, not to despair but to empowerment. By the cultivation of a spiritual attention that could "read" through the shock and countershock of force to the divine order beyond, Weil claimed it was possible to reconcile the passionate struggle for justice on the human level with wonder, gratitude, and love toward the cosmos. Indeed, Weil argued, mystical love, obedience to God, and joyful consent to the "perfectly beautiful order of the universe" (*E*, 364) constituted the surest (perhaps the only reliable) foundation for those determined to overcome the sadistic fanaticism inculcated by leaders like Hitler.

Weil's celebration of Christian love and of the crystalline beauty of a mathematically ordered, harmonious cosmos appears remote indeed from the convulsive, seething, acephalic universe of Georges Bataille. Weil's and Bataille's personal contacts while both were writing for Boris Souvarine's journal *La Critique sociale* (1933–34) appeared to confirm an antithetical opposition of personalities, worldviews, and political principles. Yet in a novel written shortly after *La Critique sociale* ceased publication, Bataille staged a very different relationship between a character closely modeled on Weil and a narrator into whom Bataille put more than a little of himself. *Le Bleu du ciel* displays the disconcerting mutations and inversions to which a politics of the sacred gives rise.

Chapter Three

IF REVOLUTION IS A SICKNESS
Politics and Necrophilia in *Le Bleu du ciel*

¿No es ir contra la razón,
siendo tú tan buen soldado,
andar tan enamorado
en tan extraña ocasión?
—Cervantes, *Numancia*

IN THE NOVEMBER 1933 ISSUE of the dissident leftist journal *La Critique sociale,* Georges Bataille published a flattering *compte-rendu* of André Malraux's *La Condition humaine.* Like many of his contemporaries, Bataille recognized in Malraux's novel an archetypal example of politically conscious fiction. Bataille also found in *La Condition humaine* support for controversial economic and political theories he had been developing in the early 1930s in essays such as "The Notion of Expenditure" and "The Problem of the State." Revolutionary struggle, Bataille had argued, ought primarily to be understood not as a means of achieving utilitarian social transformation, but as an end in itself, an ecstatic "catastrophe" or glorious sacrifice lived passionately by its participants, regardless of its concrete results. Malraux's work confirmed, according to Bataille, how in the "capital hours" of political combat, a "violent convulsion" reveals that the revolution is "not simple utility or means, but *value,*" a value that owes nothing to practical outcomes, but is linked instead to "disinterested states of excitation" (*BOC* I, 373). The revolution itself is a "state of excitation," an unleashing of orgiastic emotions inseparable from torture and death. What matters is not the success or failure of the struggle as measured by an external "criterion of utility" (372), but rather the way in which revolutionary events are experienced by those engaged in them. Bataille finds a model in Malraux's terrorist Chen, "who

82

before being killed by his own bomb has *lived* [the revolution] in a crushing 'downward ecstasy' " (374). This same ecstasy, Bataille tells his readers, is "what we can live, or what we can live from, the only concrete and powerfully human *value* that imposes itself on the avidity of those who refuse to limit their life to an empty exercise" (374).

Like many of Bataille's publications in *La Critique sociale*, the *compte-rendu* of Malraux inspired strong reactions. A particularly vehement response came from one of Bataille's colleagues at the journal, destined, like Bataille himself, for posthumous celebrity: Simone Weil.

Weil found Bataille's comments on *La Condition humaine* galling enough to plan an article of her own in answer. Her article was never completed, but a set of notes outlining its intended subject matter have survived. *La Condition humaine* is, for Weil, a beautiful book, but one that "has its limits." Bataille's review has praised above all the novel's most unsavory aspects. But for Weil much more is at stake than a difference of literary taste. Bataille's attitude raises a fundamental question about the nature and legitimacy of revolutionary activity itself. "We have to know once and for all if the revolutionary spirit must be considered as a sort of sickness" (*WOC* 2.1, 318).

For Weil, the "basis" of Malraux's novel and the "unity of all the characters" lie in their shared, desperate hurling of themselves into the realm of action in the attempt to escape the "nothingness of [their] own existence." Revolutionary action functions for them as religion functioned for Pascal: as a means of flight from the self and its anguished emptiness (*WOC* 2.1, 318). Under these conditions, revolutionary struggle is, like Pascalian religion, essentially an expression of psychological weakness. It is a disease. Weil states:

One must ask oneself seriously if revolutionary action, when it issues from such a source, has any meaning. If it's a matter of fleeing from oneself, it's simpler to gamble or drink. And it's even simpler to die. For that matter, all distraction, including revolutionary action of this order, is a disguised form of suicide. And revolutionary action conceived, as in Kyo's case, as the most radical means of escape from the consciousness of the emptiness of human existence, goes naturally to defeat and death. For an existence whose object is to escape from life constitutes in the final analysis a search for death. [...] One cannot be a revolutionary if one doesn't love life. (318–19)

The revolution in and of itself is not capable of giving meaning to human life. For those who have not discerned a sense in existence already, the revolution will not create one. "The revolution is a struggle against everything that forms an obstacle to life. It has meaning only as a means; if the goal pursued is vain, the means loses its value." For "nothing has value from the moment human life has none" (318–19).

Bataille's and Weil's ideological dispute over Malraux's novel was not an isolated incident. It reflected a conflict ongoing between the two thinkers throughout the period 1932–34, when both were associated with *La Critique sociale* and with Boris Souvarine's Cercle communiste démocratique.[1] Bataille and Weil were two of the most powerful creative personalities linked with Souvarine's group.[2] Yet their views on virtually every topic appeared radically opposed. Weil herself detailed some of the most significant divergences in the draft of a letter to the Cercle, in which she responded coldly to Bataille's invitation to become an official adherent of the organization:

> The revolution is for him [Bataille] the triumph of the irrational, for me of the rational; for him a catastrophe, for me a methodical action in which one must strive to limit the damage; for him the liberation of the instincts, and notably those that are generally considered pathological, for me a superior morality. What is there in common? [...] How is it possible to coexist in the same revolutionary organization when on one side and the other one understands by revolution two contrary things? (*SP* I, 422)

Weil affirmed acerbically that the Cercle was above all a "psychological phenomenon" whose semblance of unity derived in part from "obscure affinities" on the emotional level, but above all from the lack of clarity in its own members' thinking. Bataille himself, she suggested, was the prime source of this intellectual incoherence, which rendered both useful theorizing and effective revolutionary action impossible (422–23).

Weil expressed her thoughts on revolution in a more lyrical vein in a *compte-rendu* of Rosa Luxemburg's *Letters from Prison* published in the same issue of *La Critique sociale* as Bataille's comments on *La Condition humaine*. Yet Weil's review also exhibited a polemical agenda. Weil chose terms expressly calculated to underscore her rejection of the interpretation of revolution as orgiastic sacrifice propounded by Bataille. Weil praised Luxemburg for a revolutionary commitment motivated by "an aspiration to life and not to death, to effective action and not to sacrifice" (*WOC* 2.1, 300). She quoted copiously from Luxemburg's writings on the beauty and joy of life and concluded her review by exhorting all those involved in the revolutionary struggle to imitate Luxemburg's "joy and her pious love of life and the world" (302).

Weil's text clearly aims to refute Bataille's nihilistic theories. That her polemical challenge reached its intended target is also documented. A note in which he quotes the review ironically shows that Bataille read Weil's comments on Luxemburg (and her implicit critique of his own views) with attention (see *BOC* II, 435).

Less than six months after its tension-fraught tenth issue appeared, *La Critique sociale* ceased publication, under the pressure of financial difficulties, dissent within the group, and — not least — the furor unleashed when Bataille began a tortured affair with Colette Peignot (Laure), Boris Souvarine's companion. In the months that followed the dissolution, Simone Weil devoted herself to clarifying and synthesizing her ideas on Marxism and social transformation in the masterpiece of her early career, *Reflections on the Causes of Liberty and Social Oppression*. Bataille started and then abandoned the project of a study of fascism in France, then turned his hand to writing fiction. By May 1935, he had completed a "political" novel of his own, *Le Bleu du ciel*. Not the least interesting aspect of the text was the fact that one of its central characters, the religious revolutionary Lazare, was visibly modeled on Simone Weil.

Unlike Malraux's *La Condition humaine,* Bataille's novel was not destined to garner rapid approbation from the literary public. Once finished, *Le Bleu du ciel* was not offered to the public at all. The first version of the manuscript circulated only among a small group of Bataille's friends. As of 1936, Bataille had "decided not to think about [the book] anymore" (*BOC* III, 382). It was not until 1957, more than twenty years after its completion, that the novel was revised and published. The book has never achieved the celebrity of Malraux's classic staging of virile revolutionary heroism. Yet recent commentators have recognized in *Le Bleu du ciel* one of the twentieth century's most important examinations of the ambiguities of writing, politics, and intellectual *engagement.*[3]

In this chapter, I will argue that Simone Weil's haunting of the text of *Le Bleu du ciel* holds the key to some of the novel's most important political problematics. My reading involves the claim that Weil's ideas from the period of *La Critique sociale* provide the terms for a fruitful interrogation of Bataille's self-censored political fiction. Specifically, I will take as a point of departure Weil's challenge to Bataille's theory of revolutionary struggle, as outlined in her notes on Malraux, her draft letter to the Cercle communiste démocratique, and her review of Rosa Luxemburg. *Le Bleu du ciel* can be read as a response to the question given a characteristically lapidary and percussive form by Weil — whether revolutionary spirit must be thought of as "a kind of sickness" — and as an answer to Weil's claim that "one cannot be a revolutionary if one doesn't love life." In *Le Bleu du ciel,* the revolution is indeed a kind of sickness, or perhaps several kinds that share a common essence: necrophilia. In opposition to the life-loving revolutionary Weil held up as her ideal, Bataille offers a set of characters deeply and incurably in love with death. More provocatively, he casts Simone Weil herself as the most morbidly avid of his novel's necrophiles. With his depiction of Weil as Lazare, Bataille wants to claim that the image of the life-loving revolutionary is based on self-deception. Those who proclaim the ideology of life nourish a secret necrophilia. But since sexual perversion carries for Bataille a potent subversive charge, political commitment tainted with the lust for death is not thereby invalidated. Necrophilia may be the

~~only force that can restore political life.~~ *Le Bleu du ciel* hints ironically that if in 1934–35 any route to political revitalization still lies open, that route will pass through the necrophilic focus on death and expenditure. The revolutionary affirmation of life must recognize itself as entangled with the fascination of sacrificial death in an impure mixture outside of which all political commitment is illusory. Such a claim has — as one suspects — significant implications for the nature of political *engagement* and for the relationship between politics and literature.

Before turning to the details of the novel, it is necessary to clarify further what is at stake for Bataille in giving space and voice to Lazare/Weil in his narrative. Previous commentators on *Le Bleu du ciel*, while acknowledging Lazare's importance, have tended to focus on another female character (Dorothea, nicknamed Dirty) as the central "sacrificial" presence in the book and the woman whose personality most crucially impacts the narrator, Troppmann.[4] I want to show that the character of Lazare serves as the primary vector within the novel of a complex of political and philosophical questions with which Bataille was struggling at the time he wrote *Le Bleu du ciel*. As her comments on Malraux and her draft letter to the Cercle show, Weil's political and philosophical convictions appeared to contradict Bataille's frontally during the period in which they worked together at *La Critique sociale*. Weil defended reason; compassionate solidarity with the oppressed; scrupulous moral reflection; pacifism; and religion. She was associated in Bataille's mind both with Marxism and with Christianity, and her thought on these issues challenged and powerfully affected Bataille. Weil was not among those who read the draft of *Le Bleu du ciel* completed in 1935. In the wake of Bataille's adventure with Colette Peignot, Weil came to shun Bataille completely, dismissing him as "obsessed and sick" (*SP* I, 425). Yet the rupture in their relations makes the central presence of Simone Weil within the text of Bataille's novel all the more remarkable. If Weil did not read *Le Bleu du ciel*, she in a real sense took a hand in writing it. Weil's personality and politics, transcribed in the character of Lazare, molded the book's political content and set many of the questions to which the text sought to respond.

What is at stake for Bataille in the literary prolongation of his dispute with Weil is nothing less than the very concept of revolution, the cornerstone of the leftist politics to which both, in this period, were committed.[5] But beyond this vital ideological issue, the debate with Weil had a personal dimension that for Bataille was equally significant. During the period of their tense collaboration at *La Critique sociale,* Bataille experienced a fascination with Weil the intensity of which was uncommon even in a life marked by more than its share of emotional excess.[6] Nor was Bataille's interest ephemeral. After the war, in his review of her posthumously published *L'Enracinement,* Bataille would note: "I knew Simone Weil earlier. [...] Very few human beings have interested me to the same point. Her uncontestable ugliness was frightening, but personally I claimed she also had, in a sense, a veritable beauty (I still think I was right)" (*BOC* XI, 537). His long review article — in which the physical and psychological descriptions of Simone Weil match, sometimes almost word for word, the descriptions of Lazare in *Le Bleu du ciel* — bears witness to Bataille's sustained concern with the questions raised by Weil's philosophy, questions that Bataille clearly felt as in some way challenges addressed to him. But the most suggestive proof of Weil's importance for Bataille remains the attitude expressed toward the character of Lazare by Bataille's narrator Troppmann: a mixture of revulsion, superstitious veneration, and perhaps even "love" (*BOC* III, 445). Her simultaneous power of "attraction and repulsion" signals Lazare/Weil's association with the sacred.[7]

The sacred stands — along with the revolution — at the center of Bataille's debate with Weil in *Le Bleu du ciel.* The ideological polemic Bataille restages in the novel turns on the role and scope in human life of the "avidity for sacrifice" that characterized Bataille's own thought (in particular his concept of revolution) and that in *Le Bleu du ciel* he ironically ascribes to Weil/Lazare, as well. Bataille saw in this irrational avidity a principle that, reaching beyond (or sinking beneath) conventional politics, might reanimate (by sacrificing) and redirect (through a salutary *dis*-orientation) political resistance to the "tide of murder" (*BOC* III, 487) that potent tyrannies and senile democracies together prepared to unleash across Europe and the world.

Troppmann: Dilemma of a Dolorous Don Juan

The narrator of *Le Bleu du ciel* is Henri Troppmann, a highly ironic Don Juan figure: necrophilic, tortured, and selectively impotent. Troppmann's name foreshadows the problems with which the erotically challenged hero must struggle: those of power versus impotence and rational control versus the sacrifice of rationality in explosive "headlessness." Troppmann is in some sense "trop" mann, too much of a man, though as Susan Suleiman points out, a small shift in pronunciation is all that is required to reduce him to "trop-peu-mann," as well.[8] The historical Troppmann was a celebrated murderer convicted of the brutal killings of the Klinck family in Paris in 1870 and executed by decapitation on the guillotine. The hero's first name, Henri, was among the names of the Klinck children killed by Troppmann, thus making Bataille's narrator both criminal and victim, violator of the law and powerless sacrificial object. This tension in the narrator's identity resonates throughout the novel.[9]

Le Bleu du ciel recounts the story of Troppmann's tortuous relations with three women who in his eyes are "emblematic of certain modes of being":[10] the wildly debauched Dirty (Dorothea), unconcerned with politics and committed to orgiastic excess in all its forms; "simple," tender Xénie, who cares for Troppmann with slightly dull-witted devotion in his moments of moral and bodily collapse; and the austere Lazare, who maintains a cold, rational demeanor and has renounced worldly pleasure in the pursuit of the twin goals of political revolution and spiritual purification. Troppmann is attracted by all these women and the values they represent, yet the women's respective ways of life appear irreconcilable, and Troppmann cannot manage to make a choice. His profound confusion and ambivalence express themselves as hesitation and cynicism on the subject of political engagement and, even more humiliatingly, as sexual impotence with Dirty, the woman he desires most but with whom he is chronically unable to perform sexually.

Among the powerful female figures in the novel, Lazare is particularly striking. She "dominates" the other characters by the force of her personality and the intransigence of her opinions,[11] exercising on them a fascination that is recognized as a form of sainthood (*BOC* III, 442). From her earliest appearance in the text, she is presented in terms that mark her clearly as a sacred figure in the double sense — simultaneously attractive and repulsive — in which Bataille understood the term. ("She was a twenty-five-year-old girl, ugly and visibly dirty. [...] She exercised a fascination, as much by her lucidity as by her hallucinatory thought" [401].) Lazare's character is associated both with religion ("She's a Christian, I thought, obviously!" [424]) and with the rational social analysis of Marxism (Troppmann gives her money to support the publication of a small magazine in which she "defended the principles of a communism very different from the official communism of Moscow" [401]). As the representative of the stony laws of religion and reason, Lazare is linked in the novel to the ambiguous figure of the Commander, the real pivot of the Don Juan legend.[12] Lazare summons Troppmann to give up his self-indulgent pursuit of pleasure and shoulder the burden of political responsibility, by committing himself to stand "beside the oppressed" (424).[13]

Troppmann seeks to deaden the anguish of his dilemma through excesses of drunkenness and debauchery in London and Paris, falling seriously ill as a result. Recovered, he flees to Barcelona, where through a series of coincidences he once again finds himself in the company of Dirty, Xénie, and Lazare. In Barcelona, Troppmann is reluctantly caught up in an uprising of Catalan separatists, in which Lazare seeks to take a leading role. Yet after a marginal and derisory participation in the (itself derisory) rebellion, Troppmann again runs away: this time to Germany, in the company of Dirty. On a muddy hillside overlooking a cemetery in Trier (the birthplace of Karl Marx), Troppmann is at last able to overcome his impotence and make love to Dirty. The event darkly presages the triumphant fusion of eros and death in Nazism, represented by the marching corps of Hitler Youth Troppmann observes in the novel's final scene.

The disorder and fragmentation of Troppmann's existence are reflected in the far-flung geographical scope and fragmented textual structure of *Le Bleu du ciel*. The novel unfolds the chaos of Troppmann's personal life across an entire continent in the throes of political disintegration. The action moves from London (where

Marx is buried) to Trier (where he was born), with intermediate stops in an imposing number of politically charged locations: Paris in the wake of the riots of February 1934; Vienna on the day after the assassination of Dollfuss (Troppmann recounts a somber episode with Dirty in the Austrian capital shortly after the killing); Barcelona in the grip of the separatist uprising; Leningrad (through a dream Troppmann narrates, in which he sees the "edifice" of the revolution destroyed by an explosion); and Frankfurt, where Troppmann contemplates with "black irony" the Nazi march that closes the novel.

The textual structure of the novel is similarly complex, marked by abrupt ruptures and including half-digested fragments of Bataille's earlier works. The calculated disorder of the writing (which Bataille's later revisions sought to accentuate rather than diminish)[14] mirrors Troppmann's uncomfortably self-conscious brand of debauchery and expenditure. Like its narrator, the text works methodically to achieve disorder; and in the midst of irrational explosion, its ironic self-consciousness remains altogether apparent.

In its opening phases, the text exhibits what Leo Bersani terms a "spurting motor structure."[15] It has a good deal of trouble getting started (like sex between Troppmann and Dirty, or the stumbling revolt of the workers in Barcelona). The text comports an "Avant-propos," an "Introduction," and a "First Part" comprising only two pages (in italics), before the beginning of the "Second Part" (in roman type, almost one hundred pages long in the *Oeuvres complètes*) in which the main body of the story is recounted.

In the "Avant-propos" — written for the book's long-delayed publication in 1957 — Bataille describes the origin of his novel in a "spasm of rage," a "suffocating, impossible ordeal" (*BOC* III, 381–82): terms that could, as Bersani points out, describe Troppmann's odyssey as well as Bataille's situation in the period in which the novel was drafted. Thus, the "Avant-propos" establishes not identity, but a close "compositional complicity" between Bataille and his narrator.[16] This effect of an ironic and unstable complicity between autobiography and fiction is reinforced in the "First Part." In this brief italicized text, the nameless narrator enigmatically evokes a visit to a "city that resembled the stage set of a tragedy." In the course of their stay, the narrator and an equally anonymous "second victim" are overwhelmed by the midnight visit of the "Commander." "In the middle of the night, the Commander entered my room: during the afternoon, I passed in front of his tomb, pride had made me invite him ironically. His unexpected arrival terrified me." Since that day, the narrator states, "I have been condemned to this solitude that I refuse, that I no longer have the heart to tolerate" (395).

This brief and elusive text in which Don Juan's nemesis, the Commander, makes his first appearance in the novel was published separately as one of fourteen aphorisms (also grouped under the title "Le Bleu du ciel") in the review *Minotaure* in 1936 and later incorporated into the chapter of Bataille's *Inner Experience* called "Antécédents au supplice." There is evidence that the enigmatic tableau refers to Bataille's flight to the Italian city of Trente with Colette Peignot (Laure), the companion of Boris Souvarine, during the summer of 1934. Bataille and Peignot were together for several desperate days in Trente and other locations after Bataille rushed from Paris to join Laure in Italy, where she had run away from Souvarine in the course of a vacation trip.[17] The figure of the Commander would then be linked to Souvarine and to the political commitments he embodied, as well as to the notion of punishment for sexual transgressions. The Commander's politics are, however, ambiguous. Later it will become clear that he can represent not only the law of Marxist orthodoxy, but also the inflexible authority of totalitarianism.[18] Significantly, the "coincidence of results" between bolshevism and fascism was a theme that had been stressed in the pages of *La Critique sociale,* both in Bataille's texts and those of other contributors, including Souvarine himself. Souvarine was at this time at work on a monumental study of Stalin, and the two figures would inevitably have been linked in Bataille's mind.

The biographical details underscore the connection between Lazare/Weil and the Commander motif. Weil was a devoted friend of Souvarine's, deeply and painfully affected by the rupture in his and Laure's relationship, for which she appears to have held Bataille solely responsible. And Weil was directly involved in the dramatic *rebondissements* of the adventure in Trente. It was in Weil's apartment that Laure spent her first night in Paris after her flight with and dramatic separation from Bataille. Weil's father, Dr. Bernard Weil, put Souvarine in contact with physicians at the St-Mandé clinic, where Laure was placed for a period of recuperation after her return (*ML,* 210).

The tortured autobiographical resonances of the scene tend to support the notion that the "First Part" — constituting in structural terms half the novel[19] — presents a tableau of decisive importance for *Le Bleu du ciel* as a whole: an unidentified "je" (Troppmann and/or Bataille) is surprised in the middle of a guilty night by the "Commander," before whom the narrator "trembles," yet whom he continues to defy. The narrator senses that "happiness" can only lie in an insolent refusal of everything the Commander represents, "a happiness affirmed against all reason" (*BOC* III, 396). Such happiness "exalts" but also "blinds," and in the end it leaves the narrator in an intolerable solitude. (Even though, in a sense, he "triumphs.") The tension between guilty, blinding happiness and the demands of reason and morality (associated with the petrified and petrifying Commander) traces the decisive line of conflict and negotiation along which the action of the novel will unfold.

Troppmann's fundamental dilemma, foreshadowed in the menacing appearance of the Commander, subsequently organizes itself around the two most important women in his life. On the one hand, Troppmann is fascinated by the delirious expenditure and transgressive excess incarnated by Dirty; on the other, he remains haunted by the ideals of moral fortitude and political commitment embodied by Lazare. Troppmann is drawn irresistibly by Dirty's furious and obscene excesses, the unrestrained violence of her behavior, her apparent absence of conscience and utter indifference to political issues. Yet on the other side, he has a "bad conscience toward the workers" (*BOC* III, 448). Many of his friends are involved in political agitation, and Troppmann himself has been active enough in leftist politics that his wife has nightmares he may be killed for writing subversive articles (402–3). Nevertheless, Troppmann's political sentiments are ambivalent and lukewarm. He is sickened by Lazare's and M. Melou's earnest discussion of the "collapse of socialist hopes" (422), yet by the end of the scene he shows a grudging respect for their devotion to a lost cause ("without transition, the absurd, the laughable character became sublime" [425]). Troppmann remains suspended between Dirty and Lazare, between the seduction of irrational excess and the ideal of a disciplined revolutionary engagement guided by rational and religious principles.

This symbolic conflict within the novel reflects Bataille's own central political and philosophical struggles in the period of his work at *La Critique sociale*. Having sought to link the doctrines of Marxism with the concept — developed in such essays as "The Notion of Expenditure" and "The Psychological Structure of Fascism" — of a universe convulsed by violent, irrational expenditure, Bataille was forced to confront anxiously the extreme difficulty of combining these two principles or systems in a coherent worldview.[20] The Marxist emphasis on rational historical analysis and on the unfolding of the modes of production as the motor of economic development clashed sharply with Bataille's fascination with the irrational and his conviction that useless expenditure rather than production and accumulation constituted the key to the functioning of economic systems (including, perhaps, the all-embracing "economy" of the universe itself). While Bataille's essays in *La Critique sociale* never posed directly the possibility that Marxism was in the last analysis irreconcilable with a genuine grasp of *dépense*, Bataille allowed himself to explore this idea in the fictional setting of *Le Bleu du ciel*, where Troppmann grapples with what initially appears as the utter impossibility of reconciling his and Dirty's proclivity for expenditure with the rationalist political program defended by Lazare.[21] However, as the plot progresses and the characterization of Lazare is deepened, this conflict finds — as I will argue — a surprising resolution.

Torn between explosive eroticism and revolutionary *engagement*, Troppmann is a deeply tormented man. Indeed, his insistence on his own misery is so tireless and vehement that he is readable as a parodic, antithetical double of the life-loving revolutionary Weil celebrated during her tenure at *La Critique sociale*, and to which she gave public embodiment in the review of Rosa Luxemburg's prison letters. Point for point, Bataille's narrator ironically inverts Weil's ideal. Weil had written of Luxemburg: "Sadness was for her only a passing weakness to which one must submit in silence and make disappear as fast as possible. Lamentations were odious to her" (*WOC* 2.1, 301). For Troppmann, sadness is the opposite of a momentary *défaillance:* the very substance of his existence. And far from submitting to it in stoic silence, Troppmann positively refuses to shut up on the subject of his gloom and suffering. Weil salutes Luxemburg's "virile attitude toward affliction [*malheur*]" (300). Troppmann rarely loses an opportunity to put his *absence* of virility on display. While Rosa Luxemburg exults, " 'I smile at life in the shadow of my cell' " (301), Troppmann weeps at life in the burning sunlight of the Barcelona streets, where he feels himself as "impotent [*impuissant*] as a young child" (*BOC* III, 449). Criticizing Bataille's notion of the revolution as a value in itself, Weil had stated in her notes on *La Condition humaine* that "Nothing has value from the moment human life has none" (*WOC* 2.1, 319). Describing his own mental condition, Troppmann remarks: "I hoped to finish off my health, maybe even to finish a life with no reason for being. [...] For the moment, nothing had any importance" (*BOC* III, 414).

Troppmann repeatedly and insistently describes himself as "unhappy" [*malheureux*]. Indeed, the noun and adjective *malheur* and *malheureux* return under his pen with obsessive regularity. In the opening sentence of "Le Mauvais Présage," the first chapter of the "Second Part," Troppmann describes the events he is about to relate as having taken place "during the period of my life when I was the most unhappy [*malheureux*]" (*BOC* III, 401). The companion Troppmann seeks out as often as possible in this period, the only person who can stir him from his lethargy and dejection, is Lazare, whom he describes as a "bird of ill omen [*oiseau de malheur*]" (401). Lazare's "absurd aspect" (401) irritates Troppmann but at the same time exerts a compelling power over him.

Troppmann's bombastic language of spiritual and physical suffering has a clear parodic thrust. Bataille plays with the image of a Don Juan as far removed from the luminous insouciance of the Mozartean/Kierkegaardean hero as possible: an impotent and miserable seducer whose "constantly reiterated unhappiness is manifested in Herculean bouts of drinking, crying, and vomiting."[22] Yet Troppmann's misery may also have a more "serious" side.

"Unhappy consciousness" has for Bataille, of course, primarily Hegelian associations. In "The Problem of the State," he suggests that the revolutionary consciousness of the embattled proletariat can be nothing else than *"conscience déchirée* et *conscience malheureuse"* (*BOC* I, 332). Yet the term *malheur* was also central to the mature thought of Simone Weil. When Bataille wrote his original draft of *Le Bleu du ciel* in 1935, the concept (rendered by Weil's English translators as "affliction") had not yet taken on the importance it was to acquire in Weil's later writings. But by the time of his reworking of the novel's manuscript for publication in 1957, Bataille was quite familiar with the prominence of *malheur* in Weil's posthumously published journals and essays, as his 1949 review of *L'Enracinement* makes clear (*BOC* XI, 542–43). Bataille was alert to the distinctive sense that the term had in Weil's lexicon: designating a form of suffering that simultaneously includes physical, psychological, and social components, and whose particular corrosive power derives from the conjunction of these different aspects. Bataille was also aware that for Weil *malheur* possessed a sacred — and thus a double — character. On the one hand, affliction inspires a natural reaction of aversion, horror, and contempt; we are repulsed by others whom it has touched, and we loathe ourselves to the extent that we feel ourselves to be its victims. On the other hand, the confrontation with affliction and the opportunity (impossibly) to embrace intense suffering represent the supreme chance for spiritual development.

It was not lost on Bataille that contact with *malheur* represented in Weil's view the critical moment of a human existence, the moment that calls for a decision on which the whole character of a life depends: the choice either to turn away from suffering or to enter its sphere fully through obedient acceptance and solidarity with the oppressed, thus exposing oneself to the destruction — but also to the possibility of transformation — that affliction represents. To choose the identification with affliction, Weil maintained, was utterly unnatural, indeed impossible for the unaided human will. And yet this is just what is required of those wishing to act in accordance with the highest — the only legitimate — moral ideals.[23] Troppmann's situation is the parodic/anguished image of this impossible choice between self-destructive excess and selfless solidarity, both of which exude a disturbing *"odeur de tombe"* (*BOC* III, 446).[24] In the world of *Le Bleu du ciel,* the theme of *malheur* establishes an initial sense of connection between Troppmann and Lazare, showing them as bound together not by the love of life but — precisely — by affliction: that is, by the sum of those forces that oppose, corrupt, and seek to destroy life.

Troppmann often seems content enough to wallow in his misery. At other moments, however, he longs to escape from suffering and from the morbid "bird of ill omen" whose presence constantly reawakens his sense of guilt. Troppmann's dreams of an explosive escape from unhappiness are organized around the central phantasm of decapitation, the "loss of one's head" (an appropriate image for a character in whose very name transgression and decapitation converge). Escaping from his head would mean escaping from Lazare and the demands of her rigid rationality. (Souvarine had praised Simone Weil, in a significant metonymy, as "the only brain the workers' movement has had for years.")[25] Meanwhile Troppmann notes that Lazare exhibits "the firmness of a man at the head of a movement," while Troppmann himself has not "been able to do anything but lose my head" (*BOC* III, 454). Headlessness becomes, as it were, a capital issue in *Le Bleu du ciel,* mingling desire for a surrender of rational control with images and anxieties of castration.

The expression *perdre la tête* recurs in the text with an almost slapstick frequency. At some moments it describes lost or mutilated states in which Troppmann and the novel's other characters find themselves unwillingly, and whose consequences can be disastrous (e.g., *BOC* III, 478–79). More often, however, "losing one's head" is a coveted goal. The expression points to the ecstatic, explosive self-abandon Troppmann longs for and cannot fully achieve.

The aphorisms Bataille published in *Minotaure* under the title "Le Bleu du ciel" begin with the image of a shattered, opened head linked to Bataille's phantasm of the *oeil pinéal* (*BOC* V, 92; cf. *BOC* II, 13–50). An eye pierces outward at the crown of the skull to contemplate the sun "in its nakedness." Present due to a "strange absurdity," this unnatural eye "is not the effect of my reason: it is a cry that escapes me." Through the shattering penetration of the skull, life spends itself upward into the "infinite void" of the sky (*BOC* V, 92), procuring an annihilating liberation.

In the novel *Le Bleu du ciel,* Dirty — associated with the sun and with the negation of reason — is the high priestess of headlessness. Her significance for Troppmann is inseparable from notions of headlessness and madness (e.g., *BOC* III, 386–88, 408). In the passage in which Troppmann — waiting for news of the planned revolt in Barcelona — has an "epiphanous experience"[26] weaving together the novel's most decisive themes, Dirty is linked with Troppmann's memory of a butcher's truck seen in Paris "under a beautiful sun," and from which "the headless necks of the skinned sheep stuck out through the canvas curtains," providing Troppmann with a decisive revelation of the sun's essential, decapitating violence. "When I was a child, I loved the sun. I closed my eyes, and through my eyelids it was red. The sun was terrible. It made me think of an explosion: was there anything more solar than red blood flowing on the pavement, as if light itself were bursting and killing?" (454–55). The same sunlike violence is the quality Troppmann worships in Dirty, from the moment in the "Introduction" in which, "the blood rising to her face" (388), Dirty urinates and defecates before the stunned hotel employees in her room at the London Savoy, "scarlet and twisted on her chair like a pig under a knife," her urine "form[ing] a growing puddle on the carpet" (389) like the "solar" blood on the Paris pavement.

Troppmann hopes to imitate and share in Dirty's headlessness, as opposed to the unsolar, cerebral rationality of Lazare. However, giving up his head proves difficult for Bataille's narrator. Although he bravely insists to Lazare that Dirty does in fact make him "absolutely lose my head" (*BOC* III, 404), it is clear that his "loss" (which would equal triumphant empowerment through *dépense*) is far from total. The humiliating proof is Troppmann's inability to perform sexually with Dirty.

Dirty herself clearly grasps the nature of Troppmann's problem. The frustrated lovers are in a hotel room in Barcelona together when the gunfire of the separatists' uprising breaks out in the streets below. Despite physical weakness that has brought her to the threshold of death, Dirty is thrown into a paroxysm of passion. Troppmann remains unresponsive. He is able neither to make love to Dirty nor to go down into the street and take part in the fighting. Dirty speculates ironically that it might be "less false" if Troppmann were actually to join in the combat and "get [him]self killed." But Troppmann remains prudently in the hotel room, losing himself neither in sex with Dirty, nor in the bloody struggle raging outside. "If only," Dirty laments, "you could lose your head!" (*BOC* III, 477).

Dirty has accurately diagnosed the fundamental conflict at the root of Troppmann's character. On the one hand, he yearns to abandon himself to the absolute convulsion of pure loss (loss of the head); on the other, he fears this loss and its personal and political consequences. Seduced by Dirty's *dépense,* Troppmann worries about its political implications. The notion of expenditure seems to undermine not only Marxist "science," but the very idea of coherent, goal-oriented political action. On the other hand, as Bataille's essays in *La Critique sociale* had argued, expenditure is more fundamental than production, and rational political programs consistently fail precisely because they lack the capacity to seduce through an appeal to "headless" impulses. Suspended in anguish between these two positions (two aspects of himself), Troppmann remains paralyzed.

As Stoekl argues, Troppmann's misfortune stems from being a Don Juan who has internalized the Commander.[27] Troppmann cannot — like the insouciant hero of Mozart's opera — simply confront the stony image of retribution as an external enemy; rather the Commander's law — the cold statu(t)e of reason and guilt associated with Souvarine and with Lazare/Weil — is inscribed/erected within Bataille's narrator himself. Bataille's seducer is split. The self-conscious Don Juan has — *pour son malheur* — let the Commander "get inside his head." To be liberated, Troppmann would have to resolve himself to a definitive decapitation. As Dirty's challenge implies, mutilation-castration might restore Troppmann's potency, "according to that characteristically Bataillean equation which states that a violent loss of control is the precondition of *jouissance,* a radical letting go."[28] But this liberating loss is precisely what Troppmann cannot pull off.

The theme of decapitation is linked to liberatory castration, but also of course to death. Troppmann's yearning to lose his head announces a lust for annihilation. To the Weilian image of the life-loving revolutionary, Bataille juxtaposes a figure who is — concretely and obscenely — in love with death. In various guises, necrophilia is the defining motif of Troppmann's character.

Bataille's 1957 *prière d'insérer* describes Troppmann as a character who "expends himself until he touches death" through his dissolute excesses (cited in *ML*, 214). His frantic debauchery and subsequent physical collapse are a conscious courting of annihilation under the most degrading possible conditions. From the bed in which he expects to die, Troppmann gleefully croaks to Xénie: "You're here to make my death dirtier. Take off your clothes now. It'll be like I'm dying in the whorehouse" (*BOC* III, 434).

Troppmann's relationship with Dirty is entirely oriented toward death. From her first appearance in the "Introduction," Dirty's character is linked with motifs of sacrifice, obscenity, and expenditure for which death forms the horizon. Urinating and emptying her bowels on a chair in a luxurious suite at the Savoy, under the gaze of a horrified hotel maid and lift operator, Dirty resembles a pig under the butcher's knife (*BOC* III, 389). Later, Troppmann's reflections link Dirty to the sacrificial image of the decapitated, skinned sheep in the butcher's truck, and to the bloody sun, whose light bursts and kills (454–55). In another episode, Dirty plans to simulate death in order to excite Troppmann sexually. The narrator explains: "One day she told me to call a Catholic priest: she wanted to receive extreme unction while simulating agony in front of me" (407). At the airport in Barcelona, Troppmann waits for Dirty "the same way one waits for death" (469).

Troppmann's and Dirty's death-oriented bond finds its apotheosis on the *"jour des morts"* in the mud of a hillside above a German cemetery, where the physical presence of death liberates Troppmann from his impotence. He and Dirty are at last able to experience *jouissance* in an atmosphere saturated with death and corruption:

> We fell on the loose soil, and I drove into her wet body as a well-steered plow drives into the earth. The earth, under this body, was open like a grave, her naked belly opened to me like a fresh grave. We were struck with stupor, making love above a starry cemetery. Each one of the lights announced a

skeleton in a grave. They formed a vacillating sky, as troubled
as the movements of our mingled bodies. (*BOC* III, 481)

Troppmann's and Dirty's relationship culminates in a fusion of sex
and death in which — at last — the promise held out by the image
of the pineal eye is (momentarily) fulfilled: notions of "high" and
"low" lose their meaning, and "I could have believed, marveling,
that we were falling into the void of the sky" (482).

Behind the picture of Dirty's body as a sexualized tomb, however, lurks a necrophilic image that for Troppmann is still more
fundamental. Twice in the course of the novel — once to Lazare
and once to Xénie — Troppmann narrates the incestuous and
necrophilic episode in which he masturbates in front of his
mother's corpse. The body of his dead mother constitutes the definitive erotic object for Troppmann, to the point where he himself
wonders — not quite coherently — whether this obsession might
not be at the root of his inability to perform sexually with Dirty
(*BOC* III, 406–7). Troppmann's erotic obsessions remain permanently focused around this cold and "completely withered"
body, funereal candles burning at its sides, before which he spends
himself, ecstatically shaken *"à en perdre la tête"* (407).

Incest, necrophilia, and the "desecration of the mother" recur
as entwined obsessions at decisive points in Bataille's oeuvre.[29]
(Troppmann's description must notably be connected with Bataille's autobiographical narration of a similar incident in "Le
cadavre maternel" [*BOC* II, 130].) The mother's body represents
the site of a triumphant violation of the most fundamental inter-
dictions, the terrain of transgression par excellence. It is on this
terrain that the law of the Commander-father (the "old man" of
Part I, *BOC* III, 395) can be most toxically contested. But at the
same time, the mother's power awakens dread. The promise of
transgressive ecstasy is also the threat of dissolution, the disintegration of "man's 'unity' confronted with woman."[30] It is only
dead that the mother can be completely and safely enjoyed. As a
source of life, she must be killed, sacrificed, her obliterating embrace courted but simultaneously eluded, so that the proper degree
of tension and anguish can be maintained, and headlessness is not
allowed to become definitive. The same tense relationship with

the maternal is given an elemental or mythic status in Bataille's "Bleu du ciel" aphorisms, in which generic man, who has "den[ied] Mother-Earth [*la Terre-Mère*] who gave birth to him," finds himself torn between nostalgia for the lost maternal and the yearning for a "lacerating fall into the void of the sky." This upward fall requires that men show "defiance to the Earth, to the mud which engenders them and which they are happy to send back to nothingness. Nature giving birth to man was a dying mother: she gave 'being' to him who killed her by coming into the world" (*BOC* V, 94, 93). The sacrificial *mise-à-mort* of the mother is reenacted in the son's masturbation in front of her corpse, in which — as Bataille indicated in a barred note — the erection itself and the "obscene manipulation" of the penis (like a sacrificial weapon) determine the meaning of the comportment (*BOC* II, 429).

Most important for Troppmann (and Bataille), the crime must be confessed. The transgressive act must be reenacted in a discourse that both confirms and contains its shattering force. Troppmann speaks his unspeakable transgression — twice — and then writes a book about it. The mother, reduced to the silence and passivity of inert matter, becomes the lifeless ground against which Troppmann/Bataille pushes off for his written fall into the *bleu du ciel*. Troppmann's incestuous cravings and their translation into writing thus display a pattern similar to Pierre Angélique's in Bataille's *Ma mère*. "After [his] sexual education, which culminates in incest and his mother's suicide, Pierre is at last able to become a writer. The life of the writer is the destined goal of all the initiations and transgressions."[31]

Lazare: Avidity for Sacrifice

The character of Lazare — an immediately recognizable literary portrait of Simone Weil — ought by rights to represent a clear alternative to the necrophilic preoccupations and the fascination with irrational excess that link Troppmann to Dirty. At the time Bataille was close to her, Simone Weil had publicly defended "joy and pious love for life" (*WOC* 2.1, 301–2) as the only legitimate basis of revolutionary engagement. And she had distinguished herself in the Cercle communiste démocratique by her exceptional intellectual powers and uncompromising analytic rigor. In the masterpiece of her early career, *Reflections on the Causes of Liberty and Social Oppression,* researched and written during the period immediately preceding the drafting of *Le Bleu du ciel,* Weil tied all hope for positive political change to the disciplined employment of "methodical thought" (*RCL,* 88–94, 126). She included as an epigraph to *Reflections* a quotation from Spinoza: "In what concerns human things, not to laugh, not to cry, not to become indignant, but to understand" (*RCL,* 7). One could hardly imagine a more succinct formulation of a worldview utterly antithetical to that of Troppmann, to whom laughter, tears, and rage (along with — as Bersani indicates — drinking and vomiting) are the only credible responses to the human condition.

In certain ways, Lazare does offer the expected Apollonian antithesis to the death-oriented Dionysian values that constitute the basis of Troppmann's relationship with Dirty. Lazare displays a clear and penetrating intelligence and a tranquillity of demeanor that captivate Troppmann from their earliest interactions, precisely because they are so radically opposed to his own dissolute habits and disordered mental state (*BOC* III, 399–402). Lazare shows a calm and purposeful devotion to the revolutionary "projects" she and Troppmann meet to discuss; yet she is also compassionate, and when he explains to her that he is "suffering," she seeks to help, interrupting the discussion of the planned actions to listen to Troppmann's account of his difficulties and offer him various forms of assistance. Even with respect to emotional crises she does not fully understand, she feels a strong sense of moral "duty" to aid those in pain (400). In spite of himself, Troppmann is impressed by Lazare's "serenity" and "lucidity" (401). The narrator's language closely echoes Bataille's own statements concerning his recollections of Weil as an idealist who nonetheless "pleased by her lucidity" and displayed a compelling yet "very gentle" form of authority (*BOC* XI, 537).

Lazare, like her model Simone Weil, is deeply opposed to war and horrified by the notion of gratuitous violence. Lazare's reaction to Troppmann's confession of necrophilia is rather unjudgmental and matter of fact (*BOC* III, 406–7); on the other hand, she is outraged when Troppmann unveils to her his obsession with the idea of war as an end in itself, not a means to revolutionary liberation (409–10). This exchange picks up precisely the tenor of Bataille's discussion of revolution as a nonutilitarian "value" in his review of *La Condition humaine* and of Simone Weil's critical response.[32] Troppmann confesses his fascination with war conceived as pure violence, with no thought of utilitarian goals ("I'm talking about war. I'm not talking about what would come after it" [410]). Lazare responds with shock and revulsion to the idea.[33] On the surface, the key to Lazare's worldview is veneration for life. Troppmann draws attention to this fact explicitly, though he characteristically formulates the idea of the love of life in negative terms. Lazare, he notes, claims to feel "horror for what is connected with death" (411). The moral rejection of death — like Rosa Luxemburg's "aspiration to life and not to death" (*WOC* 2.1, 300) — grounds a commitment to revolutionary action that seems to stand in sharp opposition to Troppmann's own necrophilic proclivities.

On the surface, then, the antithesis between the values embodied by Dirty (and worshiped in Dirty by Troppmann) and those defended by Lazare confirms and reinscribes the opposition mapped by Weil in her letter to the Cercle communiste démocratique: on one side (Bataille's), the "triumph of the irrational," the revolution as useless catastrophe, and the liberation of pathological instincts; on the other (Weil's own), rationality, morality, and the revolution as "methodical action" (*SP* I, 422). The contrast between Dirty's irrational excess and Lazare's sober discipline seems to mime this conflict precisely. Stoekl is right to see in this opposition and the dramatic choice it appears to offer Troppmann the central structuring tension of *Le Bleu du ciel*. However, the analysis of this set of alternatives must be taken a step further. My claim is that despite the appearance of an irreconcilable opposition, Bataille wants to suggest there is something in common between Dirty/Troppmann and Lazare (between Bataille himself and Simone Weil), after all. And the presence of this dark force may undermine the seeming antithesis between *dépense* and the values of reason and religion. The central political thrust of Bataille's novel is to set up the tension, and simultaneously to ruin it, by unmasking the ostensibly rational and life-affirming forces as themselves turned toward madness and death.

Lazare's character reveals a deep and significant split. Beneath the rhetoric of a commitment to rationality and to the affirmation of life lurk forces of death that hold the real key to the character. (It is no coincidence that Bataille's portrait of Weil in his critical essay remembers her as "always black," "ominous" [*néfaste*], and at the same time as internally "cracked" [*fêlée*] [*BOC* XI, 537].) In truth, Lazare only *claims* [*prétendait*] to feel horror for death and what is connected to it (*BOC* III, 411). Troppmann insinuates that on this point Lazare/Weil misjudges her own character in the same way that in the early stages of their acquaintance she completely mistakes his (taking him for an *"homme sérieux"* [400]).[34] In reality, her moral outrage against war notwithstanding, Lazare herself has a deep connection to the sphere of violence and death.

Lazare's family name is only the most obvious indicator of this relation. Troppmann pointedly insists on Lazare's physical dirtiness (*BOC* III, 401), emphasizing her connection both to her counterpart Dirty and to the scatological realm of *souillure*, transgression, and physical corruption. Lazare's complexion is "cadaverous" (405). An *"odeur de tombe"* hovers about her person (446). She constantly dresses in black, a fact that — in addition to being simply an accurate reflection of Simone Weil's well-known habits in clothing — has funereal resonances Bataille is happy to exploit. In the end, "Everything about her — her jerky, somnambulistic walk, the tone of her voice, her ability to project around herself a sort of silence, her avidity for sacrifice — contributed to giving the impression she had signed a contract with death" (411–12). Thus, in the world of Bataille's novel, the theorist of the life-loving revolutionary is herself turned into (revealed as) a figure whose political engagement — indeed, whose whole personality — is under the spell of death.

The motif of "blackness" allows Bataille to associate Lazare with the *"banderole noire"* seen by Troppmann outside his hotel room window in Vienna and thus with the figure of the Commander ("I still kept thinking about Lazare, and each time I jumped: through the effect of my fatigue, she had taken on a meaning analogous to the black streamer that had frightened me in Vienna" [*BOC* III, 411]). It is as an aspect of the Commander that Lazare deploys her full, suggestive ambiguity. The life-loving revolutionary is also the one who summons the reprobate to judgment and death. She is the messenger of guilt, the voice of Troppmann's own "bad conscience," whose brutal call is both feared and hungered for precisely because of the threat/promise of fatal punishment it carries. Called from the tomb (whose "odor" still floats around her), Lazare as the Commander now calls Don Juan into the tomb (to annihilation, but also perhaps to that *jouissance* that only becomes possible in death's ecstatic realm, where heads are lost and bodies open like *"une tombe fraîche"* [481]). Moreover, as Suleiman argues, Lazare, assuming the aspect of the Commander, voices a threat that is at once sexual and political and that accuses Troppmann's impotence in both areas, while at the same time associating with Lazare herself an intimidating potency based on her willingness to die.[35]

Troppmann's internalization of the Commander points, among other things, to Bataille's internalization of the commanding and judging voice of Simone Weil: in a splitting of the self, a *déchirement*, a self-mutilation that, on the one hand, petrifies, but, on the other, may set the stage for more explosive *dépense* and a deeper communion between these contrary personalities. The situation complexifies itself further when Troppmann, who had at first declared his relationship with Lazare to be "without the shadow of a sexual attraction" (*BOC* III, 399), realizes that he may be attracted to this otherworldly shadow after all, that he may indeed "love Lazare" (445).

Troppmann narrates a dream in which a female Commander's murderous scimitar threatens him with castration-death (*BOC* III, 418–20). This mutilation may be just what Troppmann needs, or at any rate yearns for. As Denis Hollier suggests, the Commander in Bataille's novel is no longer the traditional personage whose simple and unequivocal function is to represent the realm of law and interdiction in opposition to Don Juan's transgressive exuberance, to embody the "world of seriousness, work, savings, and salvation."[36] Bataille's Commander certainly does continue to unite the force of law and the menace of death; but the traditional *"dispositif interdit-transgression"* of the Don Juan legend is challenged and complicated in Bataille's version. Bataille's Commander — who can appear in both masculine and feminine guises, and of whom Lazare represents one face — is him/herself troublingly "sexualized."[37] As an aspect of the Commander, Lazare is linked to death, but to a death that promises perverse pleasure, to a death that demands to be enjoyed.

The central strand of Lazare's connection to death lies in what Troppmann terms her "avidity for sacrifice" (*BOC* III, 411–12). This delirious hunger is linked with themes of bloody (self-) expenditure that radically complicate the Apollonian rationality that constitutes the official facade of Lazare's political program. Dirty is *Le Bleu du ciel*'s designated representative of violent expenditure and loss. Yet Lazare, too, yearns to spend herself. Her chosen vehicle is different, of course: sacrificial engagement in the cause of the oppressed. Lazare's avidity repels and disconcerts Troppmann, but also holds him fascinated. "What interested me the most was the sickly avidity that pushed her to give her life and her blood for the cause of the disinherited. I thought about it: it would be the thin blood of a dirty virgin" (402).

Lazare's ostensibly rational, productive, and life-affirming revolutionary program is infected with the sickness of expenditure. Lazare herself cannot acknowledge this fact. But the deep and unacknowledged hunger for violence bursts into the open through her efforts to participate in the separatists' uprising in Barcelona. In Spain, Lazare — for all her vaunted "sang-froid" (*BOC* III, 445) — seeks in turn to lose her head in an act of sacrifice that will fuse the personal spasm with the revolutionary political act.[38]

Lazare's active courting of sacrificial death is shown in the story (told to Troppmann by her fellow activist Michel) of Lazare's interaction with the young Catalan revolutionary Antonio. Lazare convinces Antonio to sign a document without looking at it, then tricks him into believing it was a statement of adherence to fascism, challenging him to kill her in vengeance. In an elaborately staged interaction at the edge of the sea, endowed with all the solemnity of a sacrificial ritual, Lazare stands without resistance while Antonio holds the muzzle of his revolver against her chest, trying to decide whether or not to kill her. In the end, he is unable to do so, since for him Lazare is — and remains — a "saint" (*BOC* III, 442). Lazare, seemingly thrilled by the experience, asks to keep as a souvenir the bullet that was in the firing chamber of the revolver at the moment in which her life hung in the balance (443). Simone Fraisse indicates that this incident, seemingly one of the more implausible and "romanesque" in Bataille's novel, is in fact based largely on actual events that occurred during Simone Weil's visit to Barcelona in 1933.[39]

What is for Troppmann the most powerful indication of Lazare's secret complicity with death comes earlier, however, in Paris. At the lowest point of the life-threatening illness brought on by Troppmann's debauchery and relentless self-expenditure, Lazare visits him unexpectedly at his home. In an inverted reenactment of Troppmann's necrophilic visit to his dead mother's mortuary chamber, Lazare creeps into Troppmann's room on tiptoe to gaze at his presumably unconscious body on what she believes (as does Troppmann himself at this juncture) is destined to be his *lit de mort*.

Troppmann, drunk and highly emotional, later narrates the ensuing scene to Michel in the Barcelona bar La Criolla. He relates that Lazare's entry into his sickroom caused him to slip out of his stupor. "When I saw her in the middle of my room, she stayed on tiptoe, immobile. [. . .] She was three feet away, as pale as if she had looked at a corpse. There was sunlight in the room, but she, Lazare, she was black, as black as a prison." Sunlight, that Bataillean emblem of excess and bloody expenditure, saturates the atmosphere. Enveloped by this light, Lazare remains at the same time "black": as black as ink, as black as the banderole that announces the Commander, as black as the prison that Lazare will shortly urge the Catalan workers to squander their lives (and her own) in the useless effort to seize. A blackness irradiated with deadly sunlight, Lazare is at this moment the perfect image of the perversely sexualized Commander that Hollier detects in *Le Bleu du ciel*: the Commander who arrives not to "put an end to the orgy, [but] to take part in it," and whose stone-cold law both forbids and inculcates "necrophilic perversion."[40] Lazare's visit to Troppmann's sickroom has nothing to do with the compassionate love of life. Rather, Lazare obeys her own libidinous love of death. "It was death that attracted her," Troppmann declares to Michel, "do you understand me?" (*BOC* III, 445). Lazare's life-affirming protestations notwithstanding, it is death that fascinates the *"oiseau de malheur,"* whom Troppmann has also earlier compared to a scavenger or carrion bird (*"avaleur de déchets"* [405]). Lazare stands before Troppmann — "as pale as if she had looked at a corpse [*aussi pâle que si elle avait regardé un mort*]" — precisely as Troppmann stood before his mother's body, experiencing his liberating spasm *"de loin, en regardant"* (407). The gaze is once again the instrument of necrophilic pleasure, the mark of a sexual mastery that has shifted unexpectedly from Don Juan to the Commander (disguised as a "dirty virgin"). Lazare is not merely the recipient of Troppmann's necrophilic confession; she is herself a potent and perverse death-lover, who takes Troppmann as her unwilling partner/victim. The inversion picks up a recurrent theme in Bataille's refiguring of the Don Juan legend. At crucial moments in the Bataillean version(s) of Don Juan, the seducer and the Commander exchange attributes and positions; Don Juan "occupies 'the cadaver's place,' "[41] while the stony representative of the law is moved by transgressive lusts.

Lazare's necrophilic incursion casts Troppmann in the role of his own mother's corpse, further volatilizing his already doubtful virility. The destabilization of gender positions at work in the scene is rendered still more troubling by the fact that La Criolla, the setting in which Troppmann narrates the sickroom incident to Michel, is a notorious drag bar, in which the sight of a "boy dressed as a girl" on the dance floor in a low-cut evening gown fills Troppmann with a "deep discomfort" as he and Michel begin their drunken conversation about Lazare (*BOC* III, 440). Troppmann's discomfort turns abruptly to violent rage when Michel informs him that Lazare herself, during her previous stay in Barcelona, "often spent the night at La Criolla" (440); it is as if by preceding Troppmann in this quintessentially decadent setting, Lazare has once again turned the tables, taken a perverse erotic initiative at the impotent Don Juan's expense. (Fraisse, citing the personal recollections of Aimé Patri, confirms that Simone Weil was fascinated by the stories she had heard about the transvestite subculture at La Criolla and visited the bar during her stay in Barcelona in the summer of 1933, staying there on at least one occasion until two in the morning.)[42]

In Troppmann's sickroom, the Commander in drag seems ready to make good the castration-murder threat hurled by his earlier cross-dressing incarnation (as the mad, scimitar-wielding goddess of Troppmann's dream). Lazare's uninvited penetration threatens to turn Troppmann not only into a woman, but into a dead woman (and not only a dead woman, but the dead mother: the sacrificed source of an impossible life). But this transformation is not one Troppmann is prepared to take lying down. In this necrophilic interlude, the supposed corpse refuses to cooperate. The formerly inert body reacts with sudden, spasmodic violence. The erotic charge of this response is unmistakable. When he sees Lazare, Troppmann lets out an uncontrollable cry (*BOC* III, 445). "I insulted her. I called her a dirty cunt. I called her a priest. [. . .] I was shaking all over [*je tremblais de tous mes membres*]. I was stammering. [. . .] I wanted my bedpan to be full, I would have thrown shit in her face" (445). At this point in his recounting of the story to Michel, Troppmann breaks into explosive laughter. "I laughed. I laughed. I was seeing double, and I was losing my head" (446). The ecstatic headlessness that he cannot fully achieve with Dirty comes palpably closer for Troppmann in the moment in which he narrates his own necrophilic violation by Lazare. But in this particular instance of necrophilia, it appears to be the corpse who comes. In fact, even though (or because) he is "dead," Troppmann's habitual erotic torpor is transmuted into convulsive ecstasy that finds a suitably liquid conclusion: "I soaked my sheets with sweat [*J'ai mouillé mes draps de transpiration*]," Troppmann states. "I thought I would die at that very moment" (446).

The necrophilic interaction with Lazare procures for Troppmann an explosive erotic sensation. But it does more. It is Lazare's visit that resurrects the narrator from the brink of death. Seeing Lazare, Troppmann tells Michel, he assumed he would die. But shortly thereafter, thanks to the violent emotions her presence stirred in him, "I was better. I felt I was saved' " (*BOC* III, 446). Xénie's tender solicitude and the dutiful care of his mother-in-law had done nothing to improve Troppmann's condition. But Lazare's visit and the surge of scatological-erotic energies the interaction awakens in Troppmann propel the narrator back into the realm of the living. Lazare (the name indicates one who has herself passed through death and reemerged) reanimates Troppmann, not by sharing the love of life preached by her prototype, but by communing with him in a contagious lust for death.

The event confirms Lazare's status as a sacred figure. She inspires love, terror, and revulsion, but never indifference. She is above all — to borrow the key term of Bataille's analysis in "The Psychological Structure of Fascism" — *hétérogène:* foreign to the realm of profane reality (*BOC* I, 339–40; cf. *BOC* III, 442: "Lazare mesmerizes people who listen to her. She seems to be from another world [*Elle leur semble hors de terre*]"). Like all avatars of sacred or heterogeneous forces, she possesses both death-dealing and life-giving attributes, which reciprocally nourish and unstably metamorphose into one another. A woman with the name of a dead man, she puts Troppmann in the place of a dead woman and seduces him back to life.[43]

It should be noted that the association of Lazare with necrophilic perversion by no means automatically negates the importance of the political commitments she embodies. Just the opposite may in fact be the case. In the Bataillean economy, sexual perversion and political subversion have significant points of contact. Bataille's first contribution to *La Critique sociale* had been a review of Kraft-Ebing's *Psychopathia Sexualis,* in which Bataille attributed to sexual deviance a durable power of social destabilization and critique. For Bataille, the perversions signal a "grave discord opposing the individual to society," marking the limit of the ability of any collective order to impose its values (*BOC* I, 276). Jean-Michel Besnier interprets perversion in Bataille's sense as "an objection of the heterogeneous to the social homogenization that is always ruinous for humanity." Perversion is thus intimately related to revolution, which in Bataille's writings at *La Critique sociale* takes the form of the "offensive positing of an *outside*" irreducibly opposed to the totalizing structures of the state.[44] Far from disqualifying Lazare as a revolutionary, the lust for death may be her only legitimation.

Troppmann and Lazare: Complicity in Uselessness

As befits her sacred status, the reactions Lazare's personality and actions awaken in Troppmann are complex. Troppmann claims at times to be repulsed by Lazare, indeed at certain moments to hate her to the point of wanting to kill her (another echo of the Commander motif) (*BOC* III, 441, 445). Yet as *Le Bleu du ciel* moves toward its grim conclusion it becomes clear to Troppmann himself and to the reader that among the women in the novel it is not Dirty but Lazare with whom Troppmann has the deepest bond.[45]

The basis of the connection between Troppmann and Lazare is precisely the "avidity for sacrifice" both characters share. Troppmann's hunger for self-destruction expresses itself in debauchery, Lazare's in selfless revolutionary agitation. Yet Bataille clearly wants to suggest that the impulses that animate the two characters spring from the same source, a hunger for pure expenditure prior to and deeper than any particular form of excess, whether "private" or political. Despite their disparate rhetorics, the forms of action in which these characters engage are identical in being oriented toward violent loss and ultimately toward death. In Lazare's case, this expenditure is superficially subordinated to utilitarian goals. At bottom, however, it is useless: an operation of loss with no realistic productive aims beyond the intensity of the experience itself, precisely as in Bataille's model of *dépense* (see *BOC* I, 305–8).

This becomes clear at the moment during the planning of the separatist uprising when the workers' group with which Lazare is associated must decide between attacking an arms depot and a prison. The arms depot clearly constitutes the more reasonable target. As Lazare's fellow revolutionary Michel insists to Troppmann, attacking the prison "serves no purpose [*ne sert à rien*]" (*BOC* III, 457). But Lazare is obsessed with the notion of mounting an assault on the prison: perhaps, we are given to suspect, precisely because the operation would be a completely useless one, a spectacular sacrificial gesture, a sovereign act in the sense in which Bataille will come to use the term (designating that which "does not serve"). The plan to attack the prison becomes the emblem of Lazare's entire revolutionary program. What presents itself as a sober, rational, and carefully worked out strategy is in the final analysis oriented toward an utterly useless sacrificial expenditure. On another level, Lazare was described earlier as being "black as a prison" (445). Thus, in attacking a prison she will be attacking herself, seeking her own destruction, seeking a liberation from herself: precisely the attitude Simone Weil had criticized in Malraux's heroes.

Not altogether surprisingly, Troppmann is seized with enthusiasm when he learns about Lazare's plan, so much so that he proposes to participate actively in the prison assault. The idea that the assault may be "impossible" (*BOC* III, 458) and is certainly without utility does not daunt Troppmann. In fact the madness and complete impracticality of Lazare's scheme reveal to Troppmann the deeper affinity that links him to the "macabre" revolutionary and that his anger and sense of guilt had momentarily obscured. "Basically, I was fascinated by the idea of a prison being attacked, and I thought it was good the workers should listen to Lazare. All at once the horror that Lazare inspired in me had fallen away. I thought: she's macabre, but she's the only one who understands" (457). The "understanding" Lazare shows in her plan to attack the prison is an intuitive grasp of the paradox of useless expenditure in pure loss. The fact that an operation will bring no gains at all on the practical level is not necessarily a reason not to perform that operation; it may indeed be the best reason to do so. And in any case, where the seduction of an impossible project is involved, reasons and justifications are superfluous. The language of Bataille's review of *L'Enracinement* is once again revealing. In the essay, Bataille writes of Weil's "extreme courage that the impossible attracted" (*BOC* XI, 537), placing Weil (as he had placed her double, Lazare) under the sign of the impossible, the master category of Bataille's own thought.

In addition to their accord on the useless revolutionary "*coup de main*" against the prison, the affinity between Troppmann and Lazare finds expression in connection with another useless and "impossible" activity, as well: that of writing, closely connected in Troppmann's mind (and in Bataille's) with notions of self-mutilation, torture, and sacrifice. Troppmann, we know, is a writer of sorts; the only even faintly productive activity in which we see him engage is "typing a report" at four in the morning after an extended drinking bout (*BOC* III, 414). His wife, meanwhile, worries about the possibility of reprisals for his "political articles" (402–3). At the same time, one of the first pieces of information

Troppmann furnishes concerning Lazare links her to the work of writing and publishing. "I gave her the money necessary for the printing of a minuscule monthly magazine to which she attached a great deal of importance. In it, she defended the principles of a communism very different from the official communism of Moscow" (401).[46] Lazare is associated symbolically with the physical materials of writing, in particular ink. She has for Troppmann "a meaning analogous to that of the black streamer" in Vienna (411), which is also compared with "a stream of ink flowing in the clouds" (409). As Simone Weil could be seen in public with "spots of ink on her hands and sometimes even on her face" (*SP* I, 424), in *Le Bleu du ciel* Troppmann emphasizes Lazare's dirtiness and the filthy condition of her hands in particular (405). Later, Lazare's hands are the focus of an evocation of her yearning for self-torture, in an incident that precisely matches an episode from Weil's biography.[47] Simultaneously awed, sarcastically amused, and infuriated by Lazare's hunger for suffering, the drunken Michel exclaims to Troppmann:

> —I wanted to break her wrist. [. . .] You don't know her! She asked me to stick pins in her skin! You don't know her! She's intolerable. . . .
> —Why pins?
> —She wanted to train herself . . .
> I yelled:
> —Train herself for what?
> Michel laughed even harder.
> —To endure torture . . . (*BOC* III, 442; Bataille's punctuation; unbracketed ellipses in original)

Outside the house where the revolutionary workers are meeting with Lazare, Troppmann waits with his car for news of the revolutionary action being planned and the part he may be called on to play. His thoughts drift, and memories surface that in his mind link Troppmann to Lazare through the united themes of pollution-degradation, mutilation, and writing:

> I remembered: like Lazare I had been dirty when I was a child. It was a painful memory. In particular, I recalled this

depressing episode. I had been a boarder at a lycée. I was bored during study hours; I stayed there, almost immobile, often with my mouth open. One evening, by gaslight, I raised my desktop in front of me. No one could see me. I seized my fountain pen. Holding it in my closed right fist like a knife, I stabbed myself with the steel pen nib on the back of my left hand and my forearm. To see. . . . To see, and then too: *I wanted to harden myself against pain.* I had given myself a certain number of dirty wounds, less red than blackish (because of the ink). These small wounds had the form of a crescent, the form of the nib in cross section. (*BOC* III, 454; ellipsis in original)

The perverse complicity Tròppmann senses between himself and Lazare has its root here: in this wielding of the pen that lacerates and mutilates the writer, marking him or her with "dirty wounds": bloody, but at the same time blackish, "because of the ink." The impure and troubling color picks up again Lazare's *"sang pauvre de vierge sale,"* as well as the inky blackness consistently associated with Lazare and with the summons of the Commander: the summons to judgment, to death. The crescent shape of the child automutilator's wounds meanwhile recalls the scimitar brandished by the marble goddess/Commander in Troppmann's nightmare. The pen and the sword both inflict "dirty wounds"; both are tools of (self-)torture. Linked to death, they awaken fear and deep ambivalence. Yet sword and pen can also be instruments of liberation and emblems of potency. To wield one or the other may be the best way to "harden oneself" ("Je voulais m'endurcir contre la douleur" [454]). But in order to experience the hardness, one must turn the weapons against oneself, lacerate and violate oneself, submit to a spasm of violence in which the notion of purposeful activity threatens to dissolve.

Writing is self-mutilation, a gratuitous and "black" act. The act of sacrificial violence shatters the framework of utility, and as such it brings with it an infinite guilt. If it serves a purpose, it is an "impossible" purpose (like the storming of a prison; perhaps like the revolution itself): and this is the same as serving no purpose at all. Troppmann sees this connection explicitly as he waits for Lazare, Michel, and the workers to complete the plans for their participation in the doomed uprising to take place the next day: "I got out of the car, and so I saw the starry sky above my head. After twenty years, the child who stabbed himself with the fountain pen was waiting — standing under the sky, in a foreign street to which he had never come — for something unknown and impossible. There were stars, an infinite number of stars. It was absurd, screamingly absurd" (*BOC* III, 454). The doomed revolution is absurd; the self-mutilation of writing is absurd. Under the "hostile" (454) stars, the activities that bind Troppmann and Lazare together reveal the full depth of their violence, irrelevance, and tragic risibility.

The unnatural and ambivalent community Troppmann and Lazare form is one based on uselessness (*communauté désoeuvrée*, sacred group, heterogeneous ensemble of elements rejected by the dominant society "either as waste matter or as superior transcendent value" [*BOC* I, 346]). It is the unlikely alliance of antithetical personalities drawn together by a common hunger for "something unknown and impossible." The aspiration to the impossible is expressed in Troppmann's frantic, excessive debauchery and in Lazare's determination to carry through a suicidal guerrilla assault on a target without military use. In both cases the horizon is death, and the driving passion is necrophilic: the most sterile, unnatural, and "useless" drive of all. In the face of the crushing political events in which they are caught up (and of the "hostile" universe that forms the backdrop to these events), their shared uselessness links Troppmann and Lazare on a level deeper and more significant than the plane of official ideologies. Through their avidity for the impossible (inseparably intertwined with the lust for death), the two figures are joined in a common sickness, tainted by an inky poison to which there appears to be no antidote but the *pharmakon* itself.

Bataille and Weil in the 1930s: Politics and Pathology

When he abandoned his project of a book-length study of fascism in France and instead set out in early 1935 to write a novel, there was no a priori reason why Bataille should have included a character clearly modeled on Simone Weil. None of Bataille's other associates from the period were given a comparable treatment.[48] In the period of the troubled liaison with Laure, relations between Bataille and Weil degenerated and eventually ceased altogether. Why, then, did Bataille assign Weil such a prominent place in *Le Bleu du ciel*?

Weil's presence as a haunting "apparition" (*BOC* III, 442) in the pages of the novel shows that she crystallized decisive ideological and personal issues for Bataille. Bataille evidently felt compelled to address these questions, to justify himself before the figure of the Commander, incarnated for him in Simone Weil (and reincarnated, resurrected textually, in Lazare). As Troppmann acknowledges, "I was shamefully afraid of Lazare. As if I had had to give an account of myself to her [*Comme si j'avais eu des comptes à lui rendre*]" (447).

As their appreciations of Malraux and Weil's letter to the Cercle communiste démocratique demonstrate, the philosophical and political positions Bataille and Weil officially defended during their time together at *La Critique sociale* were often diametrically opposed. In 1935, Weil represented for Bataille the values of rational, methodical thought; selfless solidarity with the oppressed; pacifism; and Christianity. A more dramatic inversion of Bataille's own values could hardly be imagined. Yet the very radicality of the perceived contrast between the two thinkers makes the treatment of their counterpart characters in *Le Bleu du ciel* remarkable. In the novel, Bataille is concerned to suggest that deeper, unacknowledged affinities lie beneath the appearance of irreconcilable opposition.

To Weil's ideal of the joyful revolutionary who "smiles at life from the shadow of her cell," Bataille juxtaposes the figure of the radical necrophile: the debauched antihero in love with death, oriented toward violent expenditure, and haunted by incurable guilt. Yet Bataille does not simply juxtapose; he unmasks Weil's life-loving insurgent as a secret devotee of death and excess. In the character of Lazare, Simone Weil herself — the spokeswoman of a "pious love of life and the world" — is transformed into/revealed as a necrophile whose avidity for sacrifice is, if anything, more feverish than Troppmann's own.

In Weil, Bataille seems to have seen Marxism pushed to its logical limit, metamorphosing under the pressures of history into a mode of action beyond conventional rationality, expressive instead of a *"conscience déchirée"* driven by the hunger for sacrificial expenditure. This perception is rendered in the novel by Lazare's plea for the storming of a prison. Here, reason argues against itself, sublates and sacrifices itself. Whatever her official ideological commitments, and whether or not she can acknowledge the fact, Lazare/Weil's political practice has already left instrumental reason behind, is already sacrificial. It is based on violence as an end in itself rather than as a means to a utilitarian goal. Her attitudes reflect a tacit acceptance of the primacy of the intense, sacrificial moment and a renunciation of the principle that the revolution possesses only an instrumental value.

It is clear, then, that Bataille is not trying to "prove Weil wrong" with his representation of her thought and personality in the figure of Lazare. On the contrary, Bataille is concerned to show how *right* Weil is, that is to say, how closely her views actually agree with his own. Bataille is anxious to demonstrate this secret agreement or complicity despite — or rather perhaps because of — the fact that Weil herself remained unwilling to acknowledge the common ground between them. Her "hallucinatory" aspect (the combination of spiritual purity and physical filth, meticulous lucidity and madness) conferred on Weil a sacred aura and prestige in Bataille's eyes. The negative judgment of this transgendered Commander weighed on Bataille, as Troppmann's anxious comments concerning Lazare reveal: "She must have thought that I was unbearable" (*BOC* III, 400); "In such a moment, I saw it, my life was not justifiable. I was ashamed of it" (448). Bataille accorded to Simone Weil a right he gave to *"bien peu d'êtres humains"* (*BOC* XI, 537): the right to interrogate and judge him, the authority to demand a moral accounting of his actions. But Bataille reserved the right to cross-examine Weil in his turn. And he claimed to discern more clearly than Weil herself the ultimate springs of her own thinking. *Le Bleu du ciel* tries to settle accounts with Weil not (only) by ridiculing her, but by displaying-enacting the deeper connection between Weil's worldview and Bataille's own: a connection he perceived but Weil had been unable or unwilling to recognize. In his essay on *L'Enracinement,* Bataille formulates his intention explicitly: "It is good method to draw from an author a truth which escaped him: from her who affirmed the immutability of laws, the evidence of a feeling in disaccord with this principle" (539).

Bataille channels through Troppmann's pen this direct avowal: "At bottom, I was obsessed by Lazare; in my stupidity I wanted to see her again; I felt then an insurmountable need to embrace my entire life at once: all the extravagance of my life" (*BOC* III, 453). Lazare/Weil is not merely an intellectual adversary; she is an obsessive element of the narrator's (and the author's) own life, a part of himself that he must simultaneously embrace and mutilate, honor and defy.

In Weil as Bataille paints her in *Le Bleu du ciel,* the concern with immutable laws (the aspect of the Commander) is inextricably tied to (violating and violated by) the explosive principle of useless expenditure. Despite their differences, Lazare and Troppmann (Weil and Bataille) are seen as joined. The love of life opposes them, but at a deeper level they commune in the lust for death. They are linked in the revolutionary sickness that is orientation toward death, avidity for the violence of useless sacrifice.

For Bataille there is no such thing as a life-loving revolutionary in the sense Weil wanted to maintain. The first step toward a realistic assessment of political prospects is the recognition that under present circumstances the revolutionary spirit *is* an aberration and a sickness, a death-driven avidity. What presents itself as love of life and desire to stand beside the oppressed is in reality necrophilic fascination.

Bataille's aim is not simply to unmask the supposed hypocrisy of the love of life so that this false concept can be discarded. The point is to recognize that to genuinely love life, one must have "signed a contract with death." The love of life — to the extent that it is something other than naiveté, delusion, or cynical manipulation — will (ambiguously) emerge from, nourish, and incorporate necrophilia. A "love of life" that seeks to exclude or refuse death is not, in fact, a love of *life* at all, but the worship of an idealistic myth whose inevitable effect will be a devaluing of life in its real and tragic fullness. The fascinating but "sinister" and "hallucinatory" quality of Lazare's personality stems from her existence being informed by a necrophilic avidity whose scope and depth she cannot allow herself to acknowledge consciously.

Such avidity does not invalidate the revolutionary struggle. It may be precisely what the struggle requires. As Bataille had argued in "The Problem of the State," an objectively hopeless political situation may generate transformation, on the condition that those involved allow themselves to be fully inhabited by the anguish that the impasse provokes and "get used to considering death" (*BOC* I, 332). In the same way that, in *Le Bleu du ciel*, it is Lazare's necrophilia that reanimates Troppmann on his deathbed, a necrophilic politics of despair, *dépense*, and tragedy might have been the only force capable of reviving Europe's fragmented and moribund revolutionary movements. Only a summons from one who is herself steeped in death can resurrect and recall to life. Only the ambiguous and terrifying contact of the sacred can energize and transform. But it does, or would do, so precisely by abolishing all calculations of utility and health, by acknowledging its own aimlessness and perverse "sickness." The struggle thus engaged would be a struggle moved by the love of death, a necrophilic revolution celebrating the anguish of its own impossibility. Its goal would be nothing other than its own catastrophic *"forme vécue"* (372), the form in which it offers itself to those who have learned "to belong in ecstasy *to death*" (*BOC* II, 213).[49]

But such a politics of death and ecstasy involved serious equivocations. Had the worship of death not received its most perfect political expression already in fascism? Was this ambiguous, death-oriented sacrificial ecstasy not precisely the energy the Nazis had harnessed to drive their machinery of conquest? And by offering the love of death as a literary, philosophical, and political principle, is Bataille not acknowledging a community of "value" and spirit with the fascists? This was the judgment of Boris Souvarine, who labeled *Le Bleu du ciel* "Nazi prose."[50]

If ambiguity and irony are to be understood as "Nazi" traits, then Souvarine's assessment may be correct. If not, the picture is more complicated. The novel certainly offers no unambiguous suggestions about how the threat of fascism ought best to be combated. It holds out no hope that any of the main characters have found a strategy that will permit them to resist fascism effectively or to disentangle themselves from the guilt of implied complicity. The dark ambiguity of the sexualized Commander condenses this confusion. His/her "law" signifies the stern rationality of Marxist analysis *and* the monolithic force of totalitarianism and underscores the disturbing "coincidence" (*BOC* I, 332) between the two. On the other hand, Troppmann's debauchery cannot engineer an effective escape from political categories, much less an effective subversion.

The closing segments of the novel offer no one a genuine escape from impotence and guilt. The uprising in which Lazare hoped to invest herself aborts abjectly. (Lazare is not permitted to play her coveted sacrificial role.) The struggle against oppression by political means is utterly without effect. Does this imply that Troppmann's and Dirty's apolitical, dyadic expenditure is the "correct" option? Clearly not. The closing passages of the novel do not exculpate the morbid pair. On the contrary, Troppmann underlines their guilt. He notes that Dirty's dress has the red color of "swastikaed flags" (*BOC* III, 484). And he suggests his own conflicted complicity with the marching Hitlerjugend of the novel's final scene:

> I looked into the distance . . . an army of children ranked for battle [*rangée en bataille*]. Meanwhile they were still, but in a trance. I saw them, not far from me, spellbound by the desire to go to death. Hallucinated by the endless fields where, one day, they would advance, laughing in the sun: they would leave behind them the dying and the dead. (487; ellipsis in original)

The participants in the Nazi parade are "not far" from Troppmann in any sense, spatially or politically. The murderous children who will one day laugh as they sow death across the continent mirror the "happy insolence" of Troppmann's own childhood self at the moment in which he knew it was his destiny to *"tout renverser, de toute nécessité tout renverser"* (455). The bloody sun that will incite and accompany them in their murderous march is the same one Troppmann himself has worshiped. Seeing the "hallucinated" Nazi children and imagining their laughter when they unleash their tide of murder, Troppmann himself feels overcome by an irresistible "hilarity," a "black irony" that seems to mingle the convulsions of sex and death. It is the emotion "that accompanies the spasms in the moments where one cannot keep oneself from screaming" (487). Troppmann's reactions, as Bersani argues, "irreversibly implicate him in the murderous solar laugh of his fantasized Nazi butchers."[51]

But as Bersani also rightly suggests, Troppmann's consciousness of this complicity may be the mark of a (faint and ambiguous) hope. "Black irony can be thought of in terms of a pervasive self-consciousness"; and it is just this quality that allows Le Bleu du ciel to subvert the self-righteous "ethos of political engagement" founded on the "illusion that we have not produced the violence against which we struggle."[52]

In the blackness of the irony that overwhelms Bataille's narrator we see once again the trace of Lazare within Troppmann himself, the blackish "dirty wound" of the interrogations she imposes on him, the unreconciled tension of a mutual infection (communication) between the rational and the explosive-ecstatic. Precisely this wound, this split of irony, may be the only hope. What separates Troppmann from the Nazi butchers may be only the self-consciousness of his love of death, marked within him by the black trace. The trace is the ironic self-consciousness of Troppmann's/Bataille's writing itself, the hopelessly written staging of effervescence,[53] in which rationality and explosive expenditure are brought together, inhabit and reciprocally mutilate (sacrifice) one another. Bataille's writing of the triumph of fascism does not "redeem" that triumph. For Bataille it is certainly not the function of art to repair and make good the losses of the political realm. Yet at the same time, one must observe that Bataille's implicit denial of a redemptive power to art by no means signifies that his writing detaches itself from the political to pursue its rituals of excess independent of a political reality in which it would no longer understand itself as irrevocably implicated. In Le Bleu du ciel, nothing is healed or liberated, except partially, ironically, and necrophilically. Bataille's text ruins both the purity of revolutionary engagement and the simplistic transgressive play of individualistic aestheticism. The extinguishing of the idea of redemption leaves writing and politics not freed from each other, but bound together even more closely by the strand of a shared "sickness": impotence, infinite guilt, and the fascination with death.

From the pathological condition common to Troppmann and Lazare, there is no possibility of a return to purity and integrity. Revolution is a sickness, but the disease is not curable. Yet this acknowledgment is itself the beginning of an (ironic and interminable) treatment. The alternative to political sickness is not wellness. The choice is rather between different kinds of disease: between an illness that acknowledges itself as such and one that proclaims itself as health; a necrophilia that confesses its crime and a death-lust that parades in a laughing mask of innocence.

Chapter Four

EXERCISES IN INUTILITY
War, Mysticism, and Bataille's Writing

One will recognize here the abusive use that lazy epoch made of the
vocabulary of religion, sometimes applying it to the strangest domains.
— Robert Brasillach, *Notre avant-guerre*

"THE DATE ON WHICH I begin to write (September 5, 1939) is
not a coincidence. I am beginning because of the events, but not
in order to talk about them" (*BOC* V, 245). The first lines of
Bataille's *Guilty* (*Le Coupable*) signal both a linkage and a disjunction between the text and the historical setting in which Bataille
writes. *Guilty,* Bataille tells us, is born with, out of, and against
World War II. On September 2, Hitler's troops had invaded Poland;
France and England declared war on Germany the following day.
As Europe plunged into what would be the most murderous armed
conflict in human history, Bataille, living in the tranquil Paris suburb of Saint-Germain-en-Laye, affirmed: "I will not talk about
war, but about mystical experience"; "I began to read, standing in
a crowded train, the *Book of Visions* of Angela of Foligno [...]"
(246, 245).

The early years of World War II marked a crucial transition
in Bataille's life and authorship. After the hiatus of the *"drôle de
guerre,"* German armies stormed through the Netherlands and
Belgium into France in May 1940. Pétain, judging the military
situation hopeless, sued for and obtained an armistice, even as
de Gaulle, in his famous June 18 radio address from London,
vowed to fight on. The first Resistance networks began to form
in the partitioned French territory in the months that followed.
Meanwhile Bataille — known in the 1930s as a militant leftist
intellectual prepared to fight political oppression "in the street"
(*BOC* I, 402–12) — appeared to turn his back on politics. Living

quietly in occupied Paris and in a series of remote provincial set-tings, he devoted himself to a program of yoga and meditation, to which a series of romantic involvements formed a counterpoint.

Health problems (Bataille was diagnosed with a mild case of tuberculosis) did not prevent the period from being an extraor-dinarily productive one in literary terms. Written in 1941–42 and issued by Gallimard in 1943, *Inner Experience* was the first book to appear with a major publisher under Bataille's name (and remains the one often cited as his masterwork).[1] Other important publications followed in quick succession.[2] Overall, Bataille's lit-erary output during the war years was striking in quantity, range, and boldness, and his wartime writings brought Bataille a level of public attention he had not previously enjoyed. It is scarcely an exaggeration to say that the war corresponds to Bataille's birth as a writer. But was it also his demise as a political and ethical thinker?

The tension between sacrificial violence and the ethical, between mysticism and the "demands of history," has inspired some of the most promising recent studies of Bataille's work.[3] This chapter will pursue such questions by examining the complex relation-ship between war, mysticism, and writing in Bataille. Bataille's apparent disengagement from politics at the time of the war has been attributed to unflattering and perhaps sinister motives. From those — like Jean-Paul Sartre and Gabriel Marcel — who de-nounced *Inner Experience* on its publication through some more recent commentators, Bataille's mysticism has been represented as an ignoble escape from the harsh realities of war and politics, a demobilization that may have masked leanings toward Nazism.[4] Carolyn Dean has challenged the arguments of critics friendly to Bataille who would cast his inaction and performative renunci-ation of "phallic virtue" as in themselves an "ethical position." Seeking to justify Bataille's "perpetual sacrifice" of stable mean-ings, his friends "now transform aporia into the aim and summit of analysis." But by glorifying equivocation, they may be disguis-ing mechanisms by which Bataille avoided "hard decisions" in the political realm.[5] Uncertainty lingers over what — if any — politi-cal sense is to be made of Bataille's turn to "inner experience" at a historical moment that would seem to have called, if any moment ever has, for outward-directed activism and a sober shouldering of political responsibility. How ought Bataille's mystical turn to be interpreted *if not* as the expression of a profound political demobilization and a deep indifference to the fate of a world at war, in effect a capitulation to the inhuman forces that had crystallized in fascism and propagated themselves through military violence?

In a political discussion, few accusations are more damning than that of "mysticism." "A New Mystic," Sartre's mordant 1943 review of *Inner Experience*, uses the term as one of unalloyed scorn (*NM*, 146, 151). But the charge of mysticism was one Bataille had quite consciously brought on himself. In his attempt to bridge the gap between "mystical life" (*BOC* VII, 251) and the political, Bataille staged mystical retreat as a public provocation. He performed inner experience as a literary spectacle within earshot of the falling bombs. In this chapter, I want to show that the relationship between mysticism and war in Bataille's texts is the key to his political attitude in the period 1939–45. I will argue that Bataille's literary mysticism can best be read not as a retreat from war and politics, but as a provocative response to war's political, psychological, and philosophical challenges in a context in which standard modes of political reflection had been rendered largely inoperative. Bataille was sensitive to the seductions of catastrophic violence and made no secret of the fact. His texts, both literary and theoretical, overflowed with sanguinary images, and his writings in the 1930s frequently celebrated violence as a fundamental human drive. But precisely by means of the model of sacrificial violence developed in the 1930s and internalized in his mystical practice, Bataille was also able to frame an original critique of the abuses of power and violence in war. Death, Bataille maintained, is the key to meaning in human existence (a self-contesting, self-lacerating "meaning" equivalent to "supplication without response" [*BOC* V, 25]). Paradoxically, however, it is not war but inner experience that most effectively catalyzes intimacy with death. Bataille rejects war not in the name of pacifism, but in the name of a purified and heightened violence: that of sacrifice internalized in mysticism and writing. Praising the sovereign, useless inner violence of a mysticism aimed at the shattering of the self, Bataille positioned himself to critique war's servile, instrumental violence, entirely directed toward the destruction of the other.

For Bataille, writing is the practice/medium in which violence and consciousness are (impossibly) brought together. Sacrificial writing opens a space of communication in which the violence of war — like the tyranny of hegemonic Hegelian reason — can be focused and "mimed," not to celebrate the military order, but to model its radical contestation. Vital questions, however, remain in play: To what extent does Bataille's textual performance of himself as mystical sage establish a position on the basis of which ethical and political choices could be made? In what measure does Bataille's textualized violence still implicitly legitimize violence and oppression perpetrated against real bodies? I read Bataille's mysticism as a move beyond "principled equivocation,"[6] though surely not beyond ambiguity. Bataille's claim that the summit of human life is realized in the impossible coincidence of consciousness and death is not in itself an act of resistance against political tyranny. Yet to the extent Bataille sought to teach (through a certain mode of self-enactment) "exercises" by which this summit could be attained, I will argue that Bataille worked against the forces destructive of human dignity and sovereignty. Bataille's mystical texts aimed (though this projective "aiming" perpetually undid itself) to teach people how to be sacred. Bataille proposed a method, a training regimen, a technique, in the form of an exemplary life-pattern: no Kierkegaardian "training in Christianity,"[7] needless to say, but a course in an anti-Christian holiness hostile to all forms of authoritarian domination.

War as a Stimulant of the Imagination

To grasp the meaning of Bataille's mysticism at the outbreak of World War II, it is necessary to trace in some of Bataille's earlier texts his attitude toward war and his figuring of the relationship between military violence and religious experience.

Martin Jay has argued that Bataille's own war experiences deserve a more central place than they have generally been accorded in attempts to map his intellectual development.[8] Carolyn Dean also insists on the importance of the "trauma" of the Great War for Bataille's subsequent career.[9] Details of Bataille's exposure to the realities of military life during his brief service in World War I are difficult to reconstruct. In general, it is not always possible (and perhaps not necessary) to distinguish truth from fiction in Bataille's various recountings of his youthful experiences. (As Amy Hollywood argues, Bataille's seemingly "transparent" confessional gestures pointedly subvert the trustworthiness of the "autobiographical subject.")[10] There is in any case no doubt that events connected with the war of 1914–18 decisively informed Bataille's later writing, in particular his elaboration of his own pedigree as a heterogeneous figure.

More important than Bataille's official army service were a series of personal crises apparently provoked by the war, notably a passionate adolescent conversion to Catholicism on the eve of the conflict and the death of Bataille's father in Reims, a city bombarded and overrun by the German army, in November 1915 (*ML*, 29–31). According to his later accounts, Bataille and his mother were evacuated from Reims along with most of the city's civilian population in August 1914. They left behind, under the care of a cleaning woman, Bataille's father, Joseph-Aristide Bataille: blind, partially paralyzed, and mentally disturbed through the effects of advanced syphilis. Joseph-Aristide Bataille may himself have urged his wife and son to escape the looming German offensive (*ML*, 31). Yet the young Bataille experienced this departure in retrospect as a betrayal. "On November 6, 1915, in a bombarded city, four or five kilometers from the German lines, my father died abandoned" (*BOC* III, 60). According to biographer Michel Surya, his father's death became for Bataille the self-sacrifice of an "abandoned and betrayed god" (*ML*, 32): a blind, impotent, yet triumphantly mad deity toward whom Bataille would continue to experience complex feelings of loathing and passionate identification. For the remainder of his career, his writing would reflect the tensions set up in the Oedipal drama of war and treachery, from which Bataille emerged convinced that "so much horror" predestined him for an extraordinary fate (*BOC* III, 61).

On one level, Bataille rejected the "paternal order that spawned [war], an order represented by his own father."[11] Yet Bataille remained avowedly fascinated by the extremes of violence war unleashed. Through the 1930s, Bataille routinely associated the uncontrolled violence of war and revolution with the assertion of a genuine "virility."[12] As the drift to war accelerated and French and English political authorities struggled to avert military confrontation with Germany, Bataille echoed Nietzsche in praising violence as the expression of health. His Acéphale program (1936) proclaimed the ambition: "To take on the function of destruction and decomposition, but as the completion, not the negation, of being." The program concluded with the vow: "To affirm the value of violence and of the will to aggression insofar as they are the basis of all power [*puissance*]" (*BOC* II, 273).

Bataille found in the drive to "give" or sacrifice the self for a "dangerous cause" (*BOC* II, 393) a common denominator linking war, revolutionary struggle, and the religious fervor of earlier civilizations. War and religion are historically among the most potent channels of expenditure, catalyzing violent ecstasies whose essence is a "loss of substance" (395). The Aztec civilization was Bataille's favored example of a society in which sacrificial religion functioned as the dominant vehicle of expenditure. But in the modern West, the transgressive value of religious sacrifice had failed. Wars and revolutions now emerged as the only "immense *wounds*" still capable of exercising a triumphant "seduction" (392). Quoting Nietzsche, Bataille affirmed: " 'WARS ARE FOR THE MOMENT THE STRONGEST STIMULANTS OF THE IMAGINATION, NOW THAT THE ECSTASIES AND TERRORS OF CHRISTIANITY HAVE LOST THEIR VIRTUE' " (392). It was axiomatic for Bataille that individuals and societies required such "stimulants" in order to remain viable. Lack of appetite for "ecstasies and terrors" was the symptom of a personality or a culture in decline. Absorbing the sacred values institutional religion could no longer mobilize, war became the privileged locus of a sacrificial drama in which the collective drive for expenditure fused with the individual's lust to transcend, by violence, the imprisoning limits of the self.

The Joy of Dying

From the early 1930s, Bataille tended to interrogate war, sacrifice, and religious ecstasy together, as closely allied phenomena. In his unpublished essay on war as a stimulant, Bataille had claimed to discern an underlying affective structure shared by combat and ecstatic religion. In 1939, in one of the first published texts in which he made a positive use of the term "mysticism," Bataille developed this conjunction of war and religious experience in an unexpected direction, proposing it as the basis of a meditative "practice" capable of yielding states of "ecstatic contemplation" (*BOC* I, 553).

"The Practice of Joy before Death" appeared in the fourth and final issue of *Acéphale* (June 1939). The essay consists of an introduction followed by six short texts that recall spiritual "exercises" in the Ignatian style, though Bataille notes that the texts are "less *exercises* properly speaking than simple descriptions of a contemplative state" (*BOC* I, 553–54). In this period, Bataille considered the project of founding a "religion" or a "Church" (cf. *BOC* VI, 485–86). In "The Practice of Joy," he clearly and ironically positions himself as a mystical authority or spiritual teacher, the representative of an "indecent saintliness" (*BOC* I, 554) who seeks to convert others to his godless "Church" (550). The recipients of his message will be those who have "seen that [they] cannot accomplish life without abandoning [themselves] to an inexorable movement" welling within them as a terrifying "inner violence" (552–53). The texts mark the intensity of the joy this violence summons: the "tragic jubilation that man 'is,' from the moment he ceases acting like an invalid [. . .] and letting himself be emasculated by the fear of tomorrow" (554).

Spiritual ecstasy springs from sanguinary visions of violence and asserts the supreme virility and " 'spiritual power' " (*BOC* I, 550) of the "mystic of joy before death." The mystic faces destruction fearlessly, regarding suffering, anguish, and death itself as "gifts":

> I picture the gift of an infinite suffering, blood and opened bodies, in the image of an ejaculation, crushing the one that it shakes and abandoning him to an exhaustion charged with nausea.
>
> I picture the Earth hurled through space like a woman screaming, her head in flames.
>
> Before the terrestrial world whose summer and winter order the agony of all that lives, [. . .] I see nothing but a

succession of cruel splendors whose very movement demands that I die. [...]

I picture myself covered with blood, broken but transfigured and in accord with the world, at once as the prey and as a jaw of TIME which kills without ceasing and without ceasing is killed. (557–58)

Internalizing death, the mystic forges an "accord with the world," whose rhythm of cyclical transformation — "summer and winter" — demands the constant annihilation of existing beings (*"explosive* consumption of all that was") to make way for new life ("joy in existence of all that comes into the world" [557]). Ecstasy surges through a savage but celebratory fusion in which the person dissolves into this vast impersonal movement. The depiction brings together (unstably yet grippingly) Hegelian-Kojèvian visions of a grand historical struggle absorbing individual destinies in its dialectical advance and Nietzschean notions of exuberant violence, cyclical return, and heroic *amor fati*.[13]

Bataille insists that "if there is reason to employ the word 'mysticism' on the subject of 'joy before death,' " one must not infer that the practice he describes shares more than a "resemblance of the affective order" with the mystical traditions of established religions. " 'Joy before death' belongs only to him for whom there is no *beyond"* (*BOC* I, 554). The "timid saintliness" of the traditional religions, "which had first of all to be sheltered from erotic excesses," has lost its power irrevocably. "It is only a shameless, indecent [*impudique*] saintliness that brings a sufficiently happy *loss of self"* (554). Paradoxically, the embrace of death means the end of fear and suspicion of the body, a new and passionate affirmation of life. Joy before death "means that life can be glorified from the root to the summit. It denies meaning to all that is intellectual or moral *beyond,* substance, God, immutable order, or salvation. It is the apotheosis of what is perishable, apotheosis of the flesh and alcohol as well as the trances of mysticism" (554).

The self-annihilation of the Heraclitean meditator has the dithyrambic exuberance of a Dionysian festival, a "great festival of blood" in which the meditator contemplates "myself destroying and consuming myself ceaselessly within myself" (*BOC* I, 556).

Death is not craven surrender, powerlessness, collapse, but an apotheosis, a luminous explosion, a surge of energy in which the meditator's own "violent decision" becomes "act and power [*puissance*]" (553). Death is an act of virile triumph, barely (if at all) distinguishable from "erotic excesses" (554). Martin Jay has pointed to the way in which the images of Bataille's "Heraclitean Meditation" recall the shattered landscapes and sensory chaos of the First World War.[14] The ravaged battlefield and its violence are actively internalized in Bataille's meditation. The landscape of war forms the theater for a sacrificial destruction of the self, a "practice" rehearsing the "frozen instant of my own death" (556), in anticipation of the real death promised to millions in the apocalypse only months away.

In "The Practice of Joy before Death," mystical sacrifice and war appear inseparably intertwined, if not simply identical. The meditator employs war consciously as a "stimulant of the imagination," summoning within himself the destructive energies that will soon be unleashed across Europe in real combat. "I picture a human movement and excitation whose possibilities are without limit: this movement and this excitation can only be *appeased* by *war*" (*BOC* I, 557). But simply to contemplate war is not enough. Even to "undertake" a war (443) no longer seems sufficient. As the Heraclitean meditator, Bataille declares: "I MYSELF AM WAR" (557).

It would seem hard to imagine a more enthusiastic and unlimited embrace of war than the total identification Bataille proclaims. Yet the stance adopted in "The Practice of Joy before Death" is in reality hardly unequivocal. Bataille revels in a deployment of sanguinary images, offering violence and destruction as themes for "ecstatic contemplation" (*BOC* I, 553). But the violence Bataille speaks of seems not to exclude but to embrace a strange, "annihilating" peace: "I abandon myself to peace to the point of annihilation. [...] / I enter into peace as into an obscure unknown. / I fall into that obscure unknown" (555). Bataille extols aggressive action, seeing "ecstatic contemplation and lucid knowledge *accomplishing themselves in an action* that cannot fail to become risk" (553). Yet the nature of this action is mysterious: "The power [*puissance*] of combat is accomplished in the silence of all action" (555). War is the ostensible setting (and substance) of the mystic's bliss. Yet the Heraclitean meditator never imagines attacking and killing others. It is himself he envisions "covered with blood, broken but transfigured" (557). The meditative warrior is his own only victim. ("I picture myself destroying and consuming myself ceaselessly within myself in a great festival of blood" [556].) The objectives of this mystical struggle seem out of line with those of ordinary military campaigns. The meditator's war aims not at the sadistic exuberance of triumph and conquest, but at the "frozen instant of my own death" (556). But isn't war supposed to be about winning? And doesn't winning mean killing *other* people? Perhaps not. Bataille cautions that war is too complex to be "reduced to an expression and a means of development for some ideology, even bellicist." On the contrary, "A war overflows [*dépasse*] in all directions the contradictory 'slogans' that are pronounced concerning it" (550–51). War is too important to be entrusted to the warriors.

The Limit of the Useful

Three months after the appearance of the final issue of *Acéphale*, the conflict the world had awaited at last exploded. In June, in an article entitled "The Threat of War," Bataille had seen the threat as a promise: "Combat is the same thing as life. A man's value depends on his aggressive force." He had praised the "tonic value" of looming destruction (*BOC* I, 550). In September, the war he joyfully envisaged broke out. Abruptly, however, Bataille seemed to have lost interest.

"I will not speak of war, but of mystical experience" (*BOC* V, 246). From 1939 to 1945, Bataille's "aggressive force" would be deployed primarily in meditative practice, the pleasures of the flesh, and copious writing centered not around the political and military events, but around his own inner states. While millions died on battlefields and in concentration camps, the bloodiest event depicted in Bataille's confessional prose was a painful tooth extraction (310–11).

Bataille's attitude during the war has been a source of confusion to his admirers. One of the clearest signs of this discomfiture, as

Carolyn Dean indicates, is the "defensiveness" evident in some recent writings and the amount of ink that has been spent by Bataille's friends to justify his comportment.[15] Those who judge Bataille's work negatively, meanwhile, have read his apparent political demobilization in 1939 as proof of intellectual and moral weakness, if not indeed something darker. The issue remains troubling, despite skillful efforts to clarify its stakes. Dean has formulated the problem with refreshing directness, challenging commentators to find less evasive answers to the questions: "What, after all, Bataille was for? What he was against?"[16] Why would a thinker who had spent the preceding decade glorifying headless sacrificial expenditure and the thirst for liberty turn away conspicuously from the war in which liberty seemed to be radically at stake? A war that would present, moreover, a potent and prolonged explosion of the sacrificial violence to which Bataille had noisily attributed such "tonic" effects?

Bataille himself was not unaware of the irony. In fact, in his mystical writings, he insisted heavily on it. Bataille claimed unique insight into war's mysterious truth: "No one takes war as madly: I am *alone* in being able to do so" (*BOC* V, 246). Yet he suggested that war, from which so much was expected, had revealed itself quickly as lacking in power and grandeur, a kind of *pétard mouillé*. "A war cannot light up [the] perfect night" of Bataille's self-constructed metaphysical "tomb" (246). "The war left me cold" (*BOC* VI, 474). Bataille used his text to stage in as ostentatious a manner as possible his own turning away from war toward the "burning love" modeled by mystics like Angela of Foligno (*BOC* V, 245).

In *Guilty* as in *Inner Experience*, Bataille paraded the irony and indignity of his mystical retreat so insistently in front of the reader that the retreat begins to feel distinctly like an attack. Mystical demobilization seems determined to present itself as an action, or at the very least as a genuine "position"[17] with respect to the war. I believe Bataille's intellectual opponents, including Sartre and Souvarine, were right in concluding that the appearance of mystical writings like *Inner Experience* under the German Occupation and at the height of the military conflict was not fortuitous. Bataille's mystical work articulated a message in and for this specific historical context. But the content of this message may be neither the nombrilistic cynicism nor the discreet assent to Nazi ideals these critics have seen. I want to argue that, though it had other aspects, Bataille's mysticism was a critical/communicative device through which Bataille staged a challenge to the war and to the values and assumptions that underlay its conduct. Enacted as a public (written) performance, Bataille's mystical practice went beyond "principled equivocation" to embody attitudes in which fundamental political commitments are evidenced.

But what kind of political commitments? Bataille's mysticism proclaimed itself useless and lavishly trumpeted its own orientation toward death. Is such a message — even if it can be shown to be "political" — receivable?

To better understand Bataille's mystical withdrawal and to assess the political importance (or otherwise) of the gesture, we must look further at the relationship Bataille's texts establish between war and mystical experience. The most systematic discussions of the topic in Bataille's wartime writings figure, not in the major confessional/mystical texts (*Guilty, Inner Experience, On Nietzsche*), but in theoretical writings on which Bataille was also at work in this period. The draft chapter titled "War" in Bataille's sprawling, never-completed project *The Limit of the Useful* (*La Limite de l'utile*) offers the most revealing site of this interrogation. "War" (1939–40) reflects the oscillations and tensions in Bataille's effort to theorize the relationship between the violence of the battlefield and the inner torture that catalyzes mystical ecstasy. Precisely because of its unresolved contradictions and structural awkwardnesses, this text reflects better than some of Bataille's more polished writings the back-and-forth movement of Bataille's intense self-questioning on the issue of the relationship between war and the destructive sacred. As a draft text, clearly rushed in passages, "War" directly exhibits tensions in Bataille's thought that will ultimately lead to a significant shift in his mode of literary self-production.

Initially, however, the draft chapter may simply give the reader of "The Practice of Joy before Death" a sense of déjà vu. The text begins with the claim that mysticism and war are, if not identical, then at the very least functionally equivalent. Bataille opens his discussion with the following thesis: "I want to show that an equivalence exists between *war, ritual sacrifice,* and the *mystical life.*" All these forms of behavior reflect "the same play of 'ecstasies' and 'terrors' in which man joins in the games of heaven" (*BOC* VII, 251).

Bataille draws his central references on war from the morbidly rhapsodic combat descriptions of Ernst Jünger. Bataille praises Jünger for having "avoid[ed] nothing" in his accounts of war's "glory and disgust" (*BOC* VII, 251). The early pages of the "War" chapter consist in large part of passages copied verbatim from Jünger's *Der Kampf als inneres Erlebnis,* in its French translation as *La Guerre, notre mère:*

> "The blood," Jünger writes, "leaps in the arteries in divine sparks when a man advances on the battlefield with the full consciousness of his bravery. [. . .] What is more sacred than a fighter? A God???..."
>
> He adds: "Courage is the unlimited staking [*enjeu*] of one's own person.... If one ... perceives the combat's true reason for being, one cannot fail to honor heroism, above all in one's enemy.... The warrior defends his cause as fiercely as he can, and we proved it on either side of the barricade, we, fighters of the whole world.... We shattered the petrified vessel of the world ... we chiseled the new face of the earth ... *the immense sum of consented sacrifices forms a single holocaust which unites us all!*" (253; Bataille's punctuation; unbracketed ellipses in original)

Bataille is clearly enraptured by this account. The ecstatic communion in death Jünger evokes, using the language of sacrifice explicitly ("consented sacrifices," "a single holocaust"), strikes the same deep chord in Bataille as the writings of mystics like Angela of Foligno. On Jünger's battlefield as in the mystics' combat with sin, doubt, and temptation, unleashed violence attains an intensity that blurs the distinction between ecstasy and torture. After transcribing a long citation in which Jünger portrays living soldiers crouching for cover among the worm-gnawed, putrefying bodies of the fallen, Bataille exclaims: "This is the language of mysticism.

This great concern with horror is not vice or depression. It is the threshold of a church" (253-54).

Bataille seems to have concluded that combat and mystical ecstasy are the same thing, after all. So does the claimed "equivalence" between war and "mystical life" mean that Bataille saw no essential difference between them and was prepared to endorse both? Did Bataille wish to justify war as a means of achieving transgressive mystical *jouissance*? Was he persuaded by Jünger's portrayal of combat as a heroic "consented sacrifice" that divinized its participants? Did he accept Jünger's inference that the political ends pursued in war were unimportant, because fundamentally irrelevant to the *inneres Erlebnis* that was the fight's real reason for being? Or again, looking at the situation from a different angle, was the cultivation of inner experience simply a recuperation of war's savagery for the meditator's private (and protected) pleasure, a means to absorb the thrill of combat without risk?

Taken in isolation,[18] Bataille's remark on the "equivalence" among war, sacrifice, and "mystical life" suggests that Bataille in fact supposed these modes of practice to be interchangeable. One could then legitimately interpret Bataille's mysticism of inner violence as an endorsement of war's external violence. The inner sacrifice of the mystic would emerge as a form of vicarious participation in the military "holocaust." Essentially, inner experience would constitute a parasitic miming of the bloody expenditure of warfare, a perverse simulacrum and celebration of real torture and killing.

A number of commentators seem to have accepted this equation (war = sacrifice = mystical experience) as representing something like Bataille's definitive view. And more than one critic has gone on to claim that the linking of mystical transcendence with military violence places Bataille dangerously close to the ideology propagated by Hitler. Such charges must of course be taken seriously. By withdrawing from overt political action and celebrating a mystical sacrifice fueled by exultant representations of violence, Bataille might have signaled an (conscious or unconscious) endorsement, if not of the letter of Nazism, then at least of its spirit. This was the judgment of Souvarine, who denounced Bataillean inner experience as "pseudo-Nietzschean onanism" intended to allow its

practitioner to intoxicate himself with the sadomasochistic pleasures authorized by the Nazi *Weltanschauung,* while avoiding
the imprudence of a public adherence to fascism.[19] Conclusions
scarcely less severe have been reached not only by Bataille's intellectual enemies, but also by a number of his personal friends. Pierre
Klossowski believes Bataille's spirit had been sapped more profoundly than Bataille himself was aware by the "deep temptations
of fascist cynicism."[20] For Klossowski, Bataille's mysticism veered
dangerously close to the demonic cult of violence exemplified by
"Jünger, that false Mephisto."[21]

Simply to state that Bataille's notion of inner or mystical experience has little to do with Jünger's *inneres Erlebnis* is, I think,
too hasty.[22] As usual with Bataille, the situation is more complex. The opening pages of "War" make clear that Bataille does
perceive a form of continuity between the unleashing of mortal
violence on the battlefield and the inner violence of mysticism.
And Bataille believes Jünger offers a "testimony" [*témoignage*] on
warfare that is more "intelligible" [*lisible*] than those of writers
who refuse to envisage the mystical dimension of combat (*BOC*
VII, 254). However, the clarity of Bataille's opening thesis —
that of an "equivalence" between war, sacrifice, and mysticism —
clouds rapidly as the "War" chapter unfolds. In a series of abrupt
forward-and-back shifts, Bataille's text ends by distancing itself
from Jünger's position, while continuing to honor Jünger for having revealed a hidden aspect of war's "deep mechanism" [*jeu
profond*] (254). My claim is that it is precisely because he is initially seduced by Jünger's view, because he senses a suggestive link
between this account of mystical experience and his own, that
Bataille's ultimate move away from Jünger's conception has significance. It is only on the basis of the initial coincidence between
war and mysticism that the opposition Bataille later exposes can
reveal something important about both combat and religious life,
rather than simply echoing what is taken to be the commonsense
point that they are unrelated.

Bataille will not disavow Jünger entirely, as he will not — in
The Limit of the Useful or elsewhere — disavow the fascination
of unleashed violence. But Bataille qualifies his own initially enthusiastic reaction to Jünger from several important angles. Bataille's

first criticism of Jünger's description of warfare concerns an epistemological "privilege" that the author of *La Guerre, notre mère,*
has failed to acknowledge. Jünger's mystico-aesthetic contemplation was only made possible by the "horrible 'slow motion' of
the War of 1914." The stasis of combat in the trenches "alone
permitted [Jünger's] 'contemplation' of horror and of himself —
and this mysticism" (*BOC* VII, 253). Most soldiers in "classic
wars" have no opportunity, even if they had the desire, to savor
the quasi-religious aspects of combat evoked in Jünger's narrative. The "too rapid rhythm" of war prevents the participants, in
all but the most exceptional circumstances, from "deepening" the
experience (253).

Behind the historically idiosyncratic nature of Jünger's self-
contemplation lurks a conflict that Bataille considers more fundamental. This concerns the relationship between war, mysticism,
and the categories of action and utility. The military is and must
be dominated by the principle of action, by the mode of behavior that in *Inner Experience* Bataille will designate as the project
(*BOC* V, 59–60). "The army has only an active life. And one does
not imagine 'contemplative' soldiers" (*BOC* VII, 251). "Action
and decision spur the rapid rhythm of wars and the immediate
forgetting of all horror. The conqueror must go quickly: he subor-
dinates what he does to the result." And in war, Jünger's rapturous
proclamations notwithstanding, it is the result that matters, not
the intensity of the participants' experiences. "Terror and horror
increase ecstasy, but they reduce the chances of destroying the enemy" (254–55). Powerful emotions are of interest in a military
context never as ends in themselves, but only insofar as they fa-
cilitate or hinder the attainment of strategic objectives, insofar as
they render men more or less efficient as fighting machines.

The subordination of all efforts to a defined goal endows war
with a globally rational, purposive structure, despite the irrational
violence that seethes in combat on a moment-by-moment basis.
Wars are fought to be won. The overarching objective gives a sense
to the sacrifices demanded of individuals and dulls the horror that
would otherwise envelope them. "[I]n battle one approaches horror
with a movement that overcomes it: action and the project linked
to action permit one to *go beyond* [*dépasser*] horror. This going be-

yond gives to action, to the project a captivating grandeur, but the horror in itself is denied" (*BOC* V, 58). This denial, Bataille wants to claim, belongs inevitably to the modern practice (if not to the "idea" [*ML*, 290]) of war. War functions in the modern world by presenting itself precisely not as unlimited horror, but as a necessary instrument for the attainment of practical ends (the continuation of politics by other means, in Clausewitz's formula). Only under the most anomalous circumstances is war's claim to utility unmasked, and then only fleetingly. This is why Bataille addresses to Jünger a rather stunning reproach: "Nothing can stand against a natural law of things: *war does not want to be deepened* and the lyricism of horror suits it badly [*la guerre ne veut pas être approfondie et le lyrisme de l'horreur lui convient mal*]" (*BOC* VII, 253–54).

To find the author of "The Practice of Joy before Death" scolding another writer for abuses of the "lyricism of horror" seems at least incongruous. But Bataille clearly takes this to be a point of importance. Jünger extols war as the real equivalent of mystical ecstasy, the literal source of an "intoxication that surpasses all intoxications, an unleashing of force that tears loose all bonds" (cited in *BOC* VII, 254). Bataille, at this stage in his draft chapter, has decided that this claim involves very serious distortions.

Essentially, what Bataille objects to in Jünger is a version of the modernist strategy of literary "redemption" analyzed by Leo Bersani.[23] By writing war in the mode of lyrical horror, Jünger redeems war's violence, "deepens" it, endows it with a nightmarish but heroic beauty and thus with a kind of higher, quasi-metaphysical purpose.[24] Bataille certainly does not believe there is anything wrong with "writing" violence. He himself perhaps never had any other literary goal. But there are different ways in which this writing can be carried through, and Jünger's involves several crucial errors.

From Bataille's remarks, it is possible to see that he interprets war as unfolding on three distinct levels. Jünger's error springs from his (possibly intentional) conflation of these planes. The most basic stratum is the pure, wordless violence of combat and death. On this level, beneath discursivity and individual identity, it is possible to speculate that there is in fact a subterranean "equivalence" between mystical experience and the paroxystic moments of combat. This idea remains entirely hypothetical, however, because on the battlefield the level of pure horror can never be "known." Those who completely enter its darkness do not come back. Above this level is the plane of the "project," of ends-and-means action, on which the majority of soldiers — like most other people — spend virtually the whole of their time. This is the plane on which war is conducted as a series of interlocking and hierarchically ordered rational operations: efforts individually and collectively to mobilize effective means for the attainment of objectives (e.g., victory or simple survival). On this level, "action and the project" reign, repressing horror, which is an obstacle to efficient performance. The third level is the contemplative, on which Jünger operates as a writer steeped in the "lyricism of horror." Like the first plane, but even more radically, this degree is inaccessible to soldiers under the immediate pressures of combat. Bataille asserts that the condition for reaching this upper level is a "certain distance from the too terrible reality" (*BOC* VII, 255).

From the standpoint he adopts as a writer, Jünger is able to reexperience and transfigure the war in which he participated. Imaginatively, he returns to the battlefield and can illuminate the events that took place there through a poetic language that brings out their ecstatic, sacrificial dimension. This in itself would not necessarily be objectionable (at least not to Bataille) if Jünger acknowledged the particularity of his stance, the combination of anomalous historical and personal circumstances that allow him to "contemplate" war as he does. But Jünger fails to qualify his account in this way. In the effusions of his lyrical prose he attributes the mystical consciousness of war's inner nature that he himself has gained retrospectively through writing to the soldiers actually fighting the battles. He projects his own sovereignty as a writer (able to "deepen" the experience of war because he finds himself at a "distance from the too terrible reality") onto the men who struggled and died in the trenches, not for the most part "sovereignly," but abjectly, under conditions of fear, humiliation, constraint, and bestial suffering. Jünger writes of war as unleashing an intoxication that "tears loose all bonds." But it is evident that all bonds have *not* been loosened from soldiers under the command of a hierarchy that threatens them with summary execution if they fail to obey orders. Thus, Jünger's language of "consented sacrifice" cynically masks the real workings of power in war. It portrays as sovereign freedom what is in fact servility.[25] It attributes to "consent" what is in the majority of cases the result of brute coercion.

Jünger has gained knowledge of war's horror by writing. This in itself is an important "conquest" (cf. *BOC* V, 76). But Jünger falsely ascribes this mystical-sacrificial illumination to the "fighters of the whole world." Whereas in reality war can never genuinely know its own horror. Soldiers in combat, if they want to survive, must in fact make it their business to *avoid at all costs* consciousness of war's "lyrical" or mystical truth, which would compromise and perhaps suppress altogether their efficacy in "destroy[ing] the enemy." War can know itself only if it is not fought, but written. To "deepen" the experience of horror that combat offers him, the soldier would have to stop being a soldier and become, like Jünger, a writer. Perhaps all soldiers *should* become writers (or mystics). But until they do, to treat actual warfare lyrically, as an affair of depth, is to indulge in an irresponsible literary redemption or recuperation of human pain.

Having begun his chapter with the claim of an underlying "equivalence" between war, sacrifice, and mysticism, Bataille closes his text on a very different view. Ultimately, Bataille now argues, action and mystical contemplation do not mix (or if they do, then not on the battlefield, but only on the page, in the texts of an author like Jünger). A *prise de conscience* of the mystical dimension of war from within is rendered impossible in all but the most extraordinary circumstances by the structure of war itself. This is to say that action — of which war constitutes the most potent expression — cannot absorb contemplation. "[O]ne does not imagine 'contemplative' soldiers" (*BOC* VII, 251). The reverse, however, does not hold. Contemplation — two other names for which might be inner experience and writing — can and does comprehend, absorb, and transfigure the violent action that is the essence of war.[26]

Sacrifice and the Height of Death

But why, one might wonder, does Bataille spend so much time wrestling with the nuances of a view like Jünger's, which to most right-thinking people appears absurd from the very beginning? The answer is that Bataille was not a right-thinking person, and he did not find Jünger's view absurd at all. Jünger was correct on a large number of decisive points. He was right to affirm that war was fascinating. He was right to salute death as the central and defining fact of human existence. He was right to claim that the proximity of death was the obligatory setting for the most decisive forms of experience and the most intense bonds of community. He was right to argue that a conscious, consented entry into death was the summit of ecstasy, a moment in which the human being attained a type of divinity. Jünger in fact was wrong only in portraying this ecstatic, divinizing knowledge of horror and death as the common property of the "fighters of the world."

Horror can be "known," Bataille believes. But not — as Jünger's own example in fact unwittingly shows — by the soldier, as soldier. By whom, then? *La guerre, notre mère,* presents the answer in the person of its author: the writer exalted by mystical consciousness.

In exploring the ramifications of this idea in the "War" chapter, Bataille draws again on the distinction between the military and religious orders that had helped him clarify his opposition to fascism in the mid-1930s. In "War" Bataille suggests it is the "religious," the priest, more specifically "the sacrificer," who attains knowledge of the depths of horror: through participation in the sacrificial ritual in which horror is "fabricate[d]" (*BOC* VII, 255). Sacrifice is "a sort of mimetism" (255). Precisely its mimetic, "fabricating," one might say its literary side permits it to attain the contemplative depth that is unreachable for those involved in active life and a fortiori for those caught up in war. For its mimetic aspect means that sacrifice is a form of play, "a free activity" (255) that can liberate consciousness (see *HDS,* 19–20).

The "paradoxical" (*BOC* VII, 255) freedom of the sacrifice manifests itself in a certain form of attention, of patience, a sense of "dramatization" (*BOC* V, 22–23) that stands in contrast to the blunt, utilitarian modes of operation that characterize the "military spirit" (*BOC* VII, 258). The conqueror must "go quickly" (254) to crush the enemy as efficiently as possible. The sacrificial priest "lingers over the victim, he shows it, he glorifies it, then he eats it to make himself drunk with it" (255). It is only in such patient, tortured "lingering," Bataille maintains, that one touches the meaning — the perpetual *glissement* or "sliding" of meaning[27] — in human existence. Sacrifice and its heir, writing, can be thought of as the ceaseless production and impossible pursuit of a meaning whose essence resides in its elusiveness, its ability to resist capture while continuing to summon violent desire.[28]

The sacrificer's renunciation of utility determines a changed relationship to time and opens the way to an experience of/as loss that may, Rebecca Comay notes, be "closer to Benjamin's notion of *Erfahrung*" than to Jünger's *Erlebnis*.[29] This implies nothing less than a transfiguration of "the whole of life" in the light of an intimate experience of death. In sacrifice, "Man places himself at the rhythm of the Universe," "miming" the slow and inscrutable operations of the cosmos. In the sacrificial ritual, one can (and must) "linger" in such a way as to "accentuate the anguish." "Since one must pass, and there is no hurry, one has only to push things to the end, to linger in such a way that the laceration affects [*retentisse sur*] the whole of life" (*BOC* VII, 255). Sacrifice permits a patient cultivation of anguish, without which there can be no deep experience of horror and no lacerating ecstasy. War does not want to be deepened. Depth emerges with the layering, the multiple ruses of the sacrificial mimesis. "Religious life is a deepening of the conditions of our life and our spasm" (255).

Death lies at the heart of war, sacrifice, and mysticism (which is sacrifice internalized). In this sense, the "equivalence" announced at the beginning of the "War" chapter remains valid. Yet sacrifice and the inner sacrifice of mysticism in fact mediate a more potent intimacy with death than does war. Confrontation with death, "upholding" death's "work," is the human being's most difficult and important task. Yet mere physical presence on the battlefield is not enough to guarantee that one has entered into authentic contact with death. It is possible, Bataille argues, to be in the presence of death, to inflict death, even to die oneself without ever rising to the "height of death" [*à hauteur de mort*] (*BOC* VII, 245; cf. *BOC* II, 244; *HDS*, 13). In order to be transformed by the truth of death, one must experience death profoundly, "consciously" (*HDS*, 19–20), or as Bataille phrased it in a number of passages, *religiously*.

Those who know "religious death" (*BOC* II, 238) are those who "live" death in full consciousness and full anguish, who — through a "deepening" — rise to death's paradoxical "height." The "height of death" is primarily the death of the other being, but a death in which one participates fully, experiencing its "lacerating force" to the point of being oneself "deprive[d] of reality" (*BOC* VII, 245). One who genuinely "sees his fellow die" in this manner can from that moment "only subsist *outside himself* [*hors de soi*]" (245). The height of death destabilizes, decenters, de-selves the witnesses who live the death of a fellow being as the revelation of their own absolute contingency and vulnerability.

The height of death, then, contests the very separations and polarizations on which military logic depends: the division between friend and enemy, victor and vanquished, slayer and slain. The sacrificial vertigo of the height of death erases boundaries, signaling a profound participation, a communication of wounded beings in which all are exposed to a solvent *mise en question*. "Each of us is driven out of the narrowness of his person and loses himself as fully as he can in the community of his fellows" (*BOC* VII, 245). Thus, while death in one sense introduces a "consciousness of [the] inevitable separation" among human beings, at the same time the awareness of "death's terrifying reality" mediated by inner experience constitutes the basis of powerful human communication. "The recognition of others' finitude is an essential limit-experience, generative of community."[30] War is hostile to such recognition. Sacrifice, inner experience, and writing demand it. Access to the "height of death" requires not martial bravery, but tragic anguish. It is a recognition of shared impotence more than a celebration of individual or collective power.[31]

The fundamental conditions of war, above all the very imminence of the threat of physical destruction, make it paradoxically difficult for those participating in combat to sustain themselves "*à hauteur de mort.*" For the ordinary soldier, death is not something to be mystically participated in, but something to be fended off at any cost. It is not a force one wishes to internalize, but an external violence one inflicts on others while striving to avoid succumbing to it oneself. When one exposes oneself to death on the battlefield, one does so blindly, "without thinking" (*BOC* II, 238), because reflection would paralyze the capacity for ruthless action on which military success depends. Thus the soldier, remaining on a level of "animality" (239), never reaches the height of death, even if he dies. "Soldiers die and sacrifice themselves without complication and without 'mystery,' as if in a sudden accident." The absence of ceremony, of attention, of careful mental and physical preparation (*apprêt*) leaves their death empty of "deep meaning" (*BOC* VII, 258).

What distinguishes the height of death from mere physical destruction is consciousness. Or more precisely the sacrificial coincidence of consciousness with its own annihilation (*HDS*, 19–20). The sacrificial priest's "lingering" over the victim opens the space (the gap or wound) of this abyssal knowledge. In the fury of battle, the warrior cannot and must not be genuinely conscious of the violence he gives and receives, of the truth of death that presides over the combat. It is only with distance that consciousness can deploy itself, embrace and *know* the truth of violence and death. To "die entirely" (*BOC* V, 17) for Bataille means to die atheistically — without the comfort of a "God" or a "beyond" — but also to die consciously, aware of the anguished movement in which one disappears. Bataille's reading of Hegel convinces him that human being can only find fulfillment in the interpenetration of consciousness and the radical negativity of death. As Bataille would formulate the problem in an important postwar text: "In order for Man to reveal himself ultimately to himself, he would have to die, but he would have to do it while still living — watching himself ceasing to be" (*HDS*, 19).

Uniting death and consciousness, the height of death is linked to Bataillean eroticism, in which, as Suzanne Guerlac has shown, it is above all (for the male subject) "a question of losing oneself *knowingly*."[32] Mysticism, the sacrificial violence of inner experience, is understood as a conscious entry into death, in the same way that "Bataille defines eroticism as the *conscious* activity of the sexual animal, thereby placing an emphasis on lucidity."[33] Consciousness or "lucidity" separates the human from the animal realm in sexuality. The same principle delineates the "religious" from the "military" approaches to death.[34]

The Comedy of Sacrifice

Certain ethical consequences of Bataille's attitude are already clear. First, Bataille does not condemn war or violence as such. He does not — and will not — affirm that the destructive impulses that find expression in combat are bad in themselves. As Bataille will later assert in direct response to Simone Weil, a morality that "curses" human violence is both futile and dishonest, being itself an expression of the aggressive drive it condemns (*BOC* XI, 532–49). What Bataille finds unacceptable about war is not that it is too violent, but on the contrary that it is in most cases not violent (or "evil") *enough:* meaning that it does not *know* its own violence, know itself as unpardonable transgression or, as Bataille will eventually say, as "sin" (*BOC* V, 305–9; cf. *BOC* VI, 315–358). The challenge is to combine violence with consciousness pushed to the point at which it exceeds itself. But this extremity of consciousness depends on *religious* anguish.

What, then, is Bataille suggesting? Is he skulking back, as Sartre concluded, toward the fold of Christianity? Is he toying again with Acéphale's project of a renewal of human sacrifice? Neither option offers a way out. Organized religion in its desiccated modern forms cannot be infused with new vitality. And the notion of staging an actual physical sacrifice appears dwarfish and preposterous in a world where each day thousands are hurled into annihilation on the battlefields.

In the last pages of his "War" chapter, Bataille speculated on a solution to the problem. What would be required, Bataille affirms, is a way of life (and of death) that would be neither military nor religious in the anemic modern sense, but that would somehow combine the virtues of religion and combat. This mode of being would unite the conscious "deepening" associated with the religious existence with the hallucinatory intensity of violence exhibited in war. The possibility Bataille glimpses is a transformed sacrifice that would orient violence not outward against others, but inward, against the sacrificer's own being. It would be, Bataille suggests, a form of "religious suicide":

> [Sacrifice] is the effect of a violent need to lose. As such it threatens in the first place the sacrificer. Possessed by the

need to lose, a priest incarnating the god could, like this god himself, from sacrificer make himself victim. But [the priest] rarely demands from himself what the myths demand from the gods. [...] Only a religious suicide could answer the demands that give themselves free rein in a bloody sacrifice. (*BOC* VII, 257)

Of such "religious suicides," Bataille notes, "there are more examples than one imagines." Yet these acts remain rare (257). But might there not be a way in which a conscious form of suicide could express the "violent need to lose" outside of war, without seeking to revive faded religious systems? In a sense Jünger himself has thrown the question open: "What is more sacred than a fighter?" (cited on 253). Until an answer to this question is found, war will retain its status as the defining human activity.

In closing the "War" chapter of *The Limit of the Useful*, Bataille answers not with a theoretical declaration, but with a literary tableau.

Instead of Jünger's frenzied soldiers, Bataille invites the reader to imagine a Tibetan monk "withdrawing in solitude, in the midst of overwhelming mountains," to meditate at the edge of the site where corpses are exposed to the wolves and vultures. The hermit "gives himself over to a 'comedy' of sacrifice":

He does not die, but a long meditation shows him with growing acuity his own body as "a dead, plump prey, with a succulent appearance, enormous — filling the universe." Then his vision begins to move. He "sees" his own radiant intelligence in the form of an "Angry Goddess" holding a skull and a knife: she cuts off the head of his corpse. In her anger, this "Goddess" that he himself is tears off his skin, heaps on top of it the bones and the flesh, rolls it together, and "tying it using snakes' intestines as rope, she swings it over her head and hurls it to the ground with force." [...]

Nothing real accompanies this exercise. The body treated in this way remains intact. But the ascetic possesses — without doubt — the faculty to render as sensible as the real world what an inner contemplation shows him. And in the ecstasy of this anguished vision, it is really as if the old man were ground up: the life of the narrow person loses itself in a much vaster reality, as the breaking wave loses itself falling back into the water that surrounds it. (*BOC* VII, 258–59)

Through the sacrificial "comedy," the "Tibetan ascetic" lives his own death (259). He "dies in seeing himself die" — that is, consciously — "and even, in a certain way, by his own will" (*HDS*, 19). Meditation creates the conditions for an inner confrontation with death in no way less potent than death in the "real world." Moreover, Bataille explains, the ascetic's ecstasy does not differ from "what it is possible for each one of us to attain" using similar methods (*BOC* VII, 259).

The comedy of sacrifice gives form to Bataille's notion of a "religious suicide." The ascetic *is* the "Angry Goddess" who decapitates his own corpse (while the Goddess, wielding a knife and a skull, recalls the iconography of the Acéphale emblem, and thus suggests a female image of Bataille himself, Bataille in macabre divine drag).[35] Sublimated and turned inward, shifted from external action to the realm of contemplation, sacrifice liberates "an excess of joy" springing from the unleashing within the self of a "movement of completely interior violence" (*BOC* VII, 259). In the world of imagined, fictioned savagery, one kills, one is "morally cruel," one dies in unspeakable torture: yet without damage to physical bodies. This "comedy," these "simulacra" (258), are the way to a deeper truth. They initiate a genuine "accord with death." A "feeling of excessive victory" raises the mystic who "places himself under the mask of a dead man." The feeling "is not drunkenness, since it is lucid, nor is it terror, since it is happy. It partakes at the same time of mad laughter — which hurts — and of the sob one can no longer contain" (259).

Violence *Rentré*

The ascetic enacting a comedic sacrifice at the edge of the corpse-littered field is Bataille himself, staging his mystical journey on the margins of the world war. The tableau — in addition to putting into play an impressive array of characteristic Bataillean phantasms — offers a fictional, yet nonetheless (or rather, thereby) precise, representation of Bataille's own tragicomic posture with respect to the war and its hecatombs. Bataille represents (writes) himself as the Tibetan ascetic representing himself as the decapitating Goddess who mutilates his own corpse. With this self-staging Bataille appears to have placed himself clearly and definitively beyond "the limit of the useful." Yet Bataille insists that something — indeed, something crucially important — has been "discovered" here.[36]

But it is not immediately obvious what, beyond an ironic literary self-portrait "under the mask of a dead man," Bataille offers. Is there anything in this " 'comedy' of sacrifice" that could help us get a better grip on the "hard decisions" Dean calls for? Surely Bataille does not mean to suggest that practicing imaginary meditational sacrifices is an adequate response to the moral and political challenges raised by war?

While sharing Dean's discomfort with Bataille scholars' routine fallback to "principled equivocation," I want to argue that the answer to this question is: no, and yes. No, in the sense that Bataille makes no claim that the cultivation of mystical experience is an ethical position that can be compellingly justified on rational grounds, in wartime or at any other time. (In fact, he fairly frequently says the opposite.) Yes, however, in the sense that Bataille wants people — some people at any rate — to see that the stance and the practice he models are political in the sense that they have implications for "the whole of life" (*BOC* VII, 255) and that he thinks even though this stance is rationally unjustified, indeed precisely because it *is* rationally unjustified and unjustifiable, some people will want to follow his example, to accept his "teaching,"[37] in adopting it. This "sovereign," that is, rationally unmasterable, stance is that of the mystic, the practitioner of Bataillean inner experience.

Bataille went against the discreet advice of his friends (later the bitter protestations of his enemies) in publishing, while the war was still at its height and France still under the domination of Hitler's occupation force, the literary records of his mystical experiences (*ML*, 332).[38] To publish, amid the national humiliation of defeat and occupation by a hostile foreign army, books that declared these grandiose events less interesting than one's own mystical visions of being transformed into a tree (or alternately into a "monstrous penis, naked and injected with blood" [*BOC*

V, 517])³⁹ was an act of disrespect and provocation that involved real professional risks. Bataille could be certain that the appearance of *Inner Experience,* his first signed book, in the midst of war and under the German occupation would mark the remainder of his intellectual career indelibly.⁴⁰ *Inner Experience* was no artistic prank from a juvenile Surrealist in the giddy 1920s, but the work of a mature man writing in the darkest days of war. And it was a work that transgressed and mocked standards of political seriousness and intellectual decorum that seemed to many — surely not without reason — to impose themselves at this historical moment more powerfully than at any time in generations. There is reason to believe that the choice to publish *Inner Experience* at the time he did so was for Bataille in itself something of a "hard decision."⁴¹ But perhaps in this case Bataille's taste for scandal and provocation harmonized with his Nietzschean ethic of harsh "loyalty" (*BOC* XI, 541–44). Bataille's mystical confessions — precisely through their performative turning away from the war — engaged ethical and political questions the military conflict had thrown open.

In order to gauge more precisely what political sense can be made of Bataille's mystical texts against the background of the war, we must look at aspects of both the content and style of inner experience as a project of writing. While the subject is vast, for present purposes I will focus on five aspects of the pursuit of inner experience as Bataille describes and models it in his major mystical writings of the war years.

1. *Inner experience is a form of sacrifice.* In his 1961 preface to the reedition of *Guilty,* Bataille described his mysticism as "essentially internalized violence" [*violence rentrée*] (*BOC* V, 493). For Bataille, the mystic is the heir of the ancient sacrificial priest, a connection Bataille underscores by attributing *Guilty* to "Dianus," the criminal priest-king of Frazer's *Golden Bough* (see above, chapter 1). Mystical contemplation is nothing other than sacrificial violence taken within and wielded against the self. Internalized violence tears the boundaries of the ego and opens the isolated subject to "communication": the "inhuman joy" — inseparable from "despair and madness" — in which subject and object fuse and dissolve in an ecstatic spasm (49, 74).

As the example of the "Tibetan ascetic" suggests, anguish and the visionary confrontation with one's own death provide the emotional force that fuels the experience. In *Guilty,* Bataille makes this program explicit when he outlines his meditational method. "I am going to say how I gained access to ecstasy so intense. On the wall of appearance, I projected images of explosion, of laceration. [...] Obscene, risible, funereal representations followed one another. I imagined the depths of a volcano, war, my own death" (*BOC* V, 269). Turning "the fury of sacrifice" against himself, the meditator is transformed into the pure violence of an inner "combat": "I decided to attack myself [*m'en prendre à moi-même*]. Seated on the edge of the bed, facing the window and the night, I worked, struggled to become a *combat.* The fury to sacrifice, the fury of sacrifice opposed each other in me like the teeth of two gears, if they snag at the moment when the drive shaft begins to move" (250).

In inner experience, sacrificial violence is sublimated but at the same time, Bataille insists, radicalized. In the moment of mystical ecstasy, "I open my eyes on a world where I have meaning only as wounded, lacerated, *sacrificed,* where in the same way divinity is only laceration, putting to death, sacrifice" (*BOC* V, 282). The human being imitates and becomes God in the gesture of self-expenditure, in the *"lama sabachtani?"* of pure abandonment, in the spasm of spiritual death. Taking a cue from the Nietzsche of *Beyond Good and Evil,* the mystic kills God in a mental ceremony of the " 'final cruelty' " (152) in which the human subject (the sacrificer) is sanctified and annihilated along with the (imaginary) divine "victim." *"Laughter in tears.* — The killing of God is a sacrifice that, making me tremble, nevertheless lets me laugh, for in it I succumb no less than the victim" (178). Dying with God, the mystic becomes God, that is, lays claim to an absolute sovereignty: the pure, tragic (and laughing) freedom imparted by death.

2. *The principle of the experience is infinite contestation.* Bataille understands mystical practice as a radical questioning not only of specific contents of knowledge, but of the fundamental structures and operations that make claims to "knowledge" possible: including the ordering structures of language and the coherent identity of the knowing subject. The contestation or calling into question linked to the experience is not circumscribed, but all-encompassing and interminable. Inner experience corresponds to

"the necessity where I am — human existence along with me — to put everything at issue (call everything into question) with no rest allowed" (*BOC* V, 15). Dissolving not "particular items of knowledge" [*connaissances particulières*] but their underlying "ground," inner experience plunges into an "intolerable unknowing [*non-savoir*]" in which "I grasp as I fall that the only truth of man [...] is to be a supplication without response" (25).

Denying all "existing values and authorities," the experience itself becomes "positively the value and *the authority*" (*BOC* V, 19). But the authority residing in the experience is necessarily paradoxical: "founded on questioning [*sur la mise en question*]," this authority is itself constituted by the "questioning of authority." As a "positive questioning" it becomes the "authority of man defining himself as the calling into question of himself [*se définissant comme mise en question de lui-même*]" (19, note 1). With this paradox at its heart, inner experience reveals itself as the "site par excellence" of the Bataillean "impossible."[42] The experience defines the conflicted field of a practice "in which the subject, putting himself into play, experiences his limits, that is to say the beyond of his possible, 'to the point where death is laughable.' "[43] In inner experience, "I enter a dead end" in which "all possibility is exhausted, the possible slips away, and the impossible rages [*sévit*]. To face the impossible — exorbitant, indubitable — when nothing is possible any more is in my eyes to have an experience of the divine; it is analogous to torture" (45).

3. *Inner experience turns reason and utility against themselves.* The experience refuses the mode of existence associated with the "project": a term with which Bataille encompasses all forms of rationally structured, goal-oriented thought and action. The project sets a horizon of aims, then directs attention and effort toward attaining them, thus providing life with meaning and coherence, but at the same time constantly abolishing the present moment in the service of a perpetually receding future. The projective consciousness is for Bataille "a paradoxical way of being in time": the perpetual "deferment of existence until later" (*BOC* V, 59). Inner experience suspends the operations of instrumental reason and crystallizes existence in the violent immediacy of an ecstatic present, initiating "being without delay" (60).

But the roots of projective consciousness lie in the very structure of discursive thought. Thus, inner experience must attack not only specific propositions but language itself. Through a disciplining of attention related to Eastern practices of meditation and yoga, the adept of inner experience learns to "contest [. . .] the law of language" (*BOC* V, 27) within him/herself, working free from the "quicksand" of discursive thought (26). At the highest stages, discursive categories dissolve in an ecstatic unknowing that Bataille evokes with images of violence, erotic frenzy, crime, vertiginous falls, and death. The experience moves beyond the "limit of the useful" into the region of purely useless, sumptuary behaviors, the realm of the sacred.

Bataille must face the fact, however, that escape from the domain of utility is, to the mystic, a useful idea. That is, the intention to suspend projective thinking is itself a project. Thus, the escape from discursivity and the realm of the project cannot itself do otherwise than adopt, initially, the form of what it rejects. Inner experience must be "led by discursive reason," for "only reason has the power to undo its own work" (*BOC* V, 60). The experience turns orderly thought and rational method against themselves, using discursive reason transgressively, autosacrificially, to move beyond the frontiers of reason. Thus, as it mimes sacrificial violence to push forward a mystical economy based on anguish and radical contestation, inner experience "mimes" Hegelian Absolute Knowledge (127) to map and transgress the limits of the system, reaching, "beyond the limits attained, no longer an unknown, but an unknowable" (127).

(4). *Inner experience is a written performance of the self.* As commentators since Sartre have pointed out, it is not the slightest paradox of Bataille's inner experience that the effort to escape from discursivity produces itself as a sprawling body of writing. But like the writings of more orthodox mystics, Bataille's atheological texts are strewn with disclaimers about the inadequacy of language to convey the power of the ecstatic states they purport to evoke. Much of the tension and electricity of Bataille's texts (as with those of other mystical authors) spring precisely from the gap between the "surface" language and the mysterious reserve of the "experience" that the text announces (repeatedly) its incapacity to re-create or satisfactorily describe, yet desire for which it never ceases to tease, stoke, and stimulate.

But if inner experience is not in any simple sense captured or produced in the text entitled *Inner Experience* (though the text may seek by elaborate means to "elicit" such experience in readers),[44] then what *is* produced there? (What, or rather, whom?) On this point, reliable information comes not only from the texts themselves, but from Bataille's most prominent and unforgiving contemporary critic, Sartre. The lengthy review essay Sartre devoted to *Inner Experience* on the book's appearance in 1943 is partial, pedantic, and unfair in many respects. But Sartre discerned certain stakes of Bataille's mystical antiproject with lucidity. Sartre saw that the crucial content of the book was neither philosophical nor literary, but human — or in Sartre's happily chosen term, "carnal" (*NM*, 145). That content is Bataille himself. Bataille in the character and costume of the *"nouveau mystique."*

Bataille is the ironic "Gospel" (*NM*, 150) his mystical text brings. He is his own prophetic "message" (152). "There [Bataille] is in front of us," Sartre writes, "funereal and comic, like an inconsolable widower who abandons himself, clad all in black, to the solitary vice in memory of the deceased" (154): the dear departed who is in this case not Bataille's mother, but God.[45] "For M. Bataille refuses to reconcile these two unshakable and opposed exigencies: God is silent [...]; everything in me demands God" (154). It is Bataille's impossible desire — and above all his impossible self, fissured by that unfulfillable desire — that his book gives us. When we read *Inner Experience,* Sartre affirms, we are not interested in the "unutilizable experience" (187) the book describes. Rather, we are fascinated, repelled, held in suspense by "the man who offers himself up [*se livre*] in these pages, by his 'sumptuous and bitter' soul, his sickly pride, his self-disgust, his eroticism, [...] his vain quest for an impossible escape" (187). "It is a man who is before us, a man alone and naked, who disarms all deductions [...], an unpleasant and 'absorbing' [*'prenant'*] man — like Pascal" (151).

The author of *Inner Experience* absorbs because he is himself absorbed in the anguished contemplation of death. What Bataille offers in his mystical text, Sartre tells us, is Bataille's own "passion," his self-inflicted "crucifixion" (*NM*, 176, 175).[46] The text which enacts this literary self-sacrifice can only be described as a "book-martyrdom" [*essai-martyre*] (144). *Inner Experience* is Bataille. A mystical method "cannot be communicated in writing" (*BOC* V, 265). But it can be embodied in and as the anguished substance of a human life: a life that produces itself (and enacts — repeatedly — its own violent end) as writing. In staging himself as executioner and victim in a mystical martyrdom (a comedy of sacrifice), Bataille performed his own death and lived to write about it.

5. *Bataille's mystical texts are "spiritual exercises."* Bataille's literary self-enactment as mystic rebel generally represents itself as purely gratuitous. Yet Bataille's writing — and above all publication — of his mystical texts clearly aims at certain concrete and (in a sense) useful results. One of these intended results has been touched on relatively little by Bataille's scholarly commentators (for some of whom Bataille's mysticism in general seems to be a rather queasy subject): this is the fact that Bataille wanted to convert people. Bataille himself acknowledged the "*conversion* side [*le côté conversion*]" of his enterprise (*BOC* VII, 519). He published his mystical confessions in part in order to share with the public a set of techniques — or more accurately and importantly the vision of a style of existence[47] — that he believed certain self-selected individuals could and should adopt in order to lead better lives: better, more beautiful, more intense, or — if one prefers — more evil. "Inner experience is conquest," Bataille declares, "and, as such, *for others!*" (*BOC* V, 76). On this question, too, Sartre assessed the situation with little sympathy but considerable insight. "It is for the apprentice mystic that M. Bataille writes, for him who, in solitude, makes his way to the scaffold [*s'achemine au supplice*] in laughter and disgust" (*NM*, 151). But by describing Bataille as a "preacher"[48] in search of "converts" or "disciple[s]" (151–52), Sartre is saying little more than Bataille himself has already acknowledged when he states that his "effort" in pursuing mysticism "will be vain if it does not force conviction" (*BOC* V, 51) from the readers of his book. As we have seen, the communication by means of writing of an experience that contests the foundations of language can hardly proceed without paradoxes.

Yet this shattering *partage* of an exorbitant experience is indeed Bataille's desire. Mere description or philosophical/psychological analysis cannot suffice. "Bataille's text itself attempts [...] to engender in writing and in the reader the dissolution of subject and object that is inner experience."[49] Bataille aims to " 'teach the art of turning anguish into delight' " (47). But this art must be *practiced* to be understood. The (non-)sense of mystical experience can only be grasped "from within" the experience itself (20). A discursive treatment of the experience's epistemological foundations presents "an obscure theoretical appearance." The solution is to recognize that " 'One must seize their meaning from within.' They are not logically demonstrable." Put still more forcefully: "One must *live* the experience" (20–21). Bataille's writing fails if it does not awaken in readers the hunger to live "in its totality" the "dazzling dissolution" (*BOC* VI, 22) Bataille describes.

Guilty makes even clearer Bataille's intention for his book to function as a practical initiatory text, the outline of a spiritual "method" (*BOC* V, 265):

> I wanted and found ecstasy. [...] This *desert* to which I have gained access, I desire that it should be accessible to others, who no doubt *lack* it.
>
> As simply as I can, I will speak of the ways in which I found ecstasy, in the desire that others find it in the same fashion. (264)

Jean-Michel Heimonet has compared Bataille's mystical writings to the *Spiritual Exercises* of Loyola.[50] The warrant is given in Bataille's texts themselves, in which Loyola is evoked repeatedly (e.g., 26, 141), and spiritual exercises and techniques analyzed and compared in detail. Contrasting the "rigor" demanded by inner experience with the self-indulgence of certain " 'poets' " (Breton and the Surrealists), Bataille writes: "Is it a matter of exercises? Concerted? Willed? It is in effect a matter of exercises, of *constraints.*" To refuse constraint, to want to be "a man drifting with the current [*un homme au fil de l'eau*]," is to "make oneself the accomplice of inertia" (50). Bataille asserts, "The desire for ecstasy cannot refuse method" (265).

The methods Bataille proposes include various forms of spiritual "dramatization" (*BOC* V, 22–23) whose intended effects are comparable — but, Bataille claims, superior — to those of the Ignatian exercises. The technique Bataille discusses most frequently is his meditation on one of a series of photographs representing a young Chinese prisoner undergoing torture.[51] Bataille found in the "mad" violence of the image an "infinite value of reversal" opening the way to spiritual "ecstasy" (*BOC* X, 627). The excess of horror focused in the tortured body constitutes a "sign" of the world's sovereign truth (*BOC* V, 141), humans' tragic powerlessness before death, our shared condemnation to ineluctable "ruin." "It was to signs of this kind that the author of the *Exercises* turned," Bataille notes, "wanting to 'disturb' his disciples" (141). But where Loyola taught his followers to "curse the world," Bataille offers his own excessive practice as the way to a deeper "love" for existence (140–41).

In Bataille's meditation, the image of an omnipotent God is replaced "humanly" (*BOC* V, 283) by the photograph of the Chinese prisoner, "streaming with blood, while the executioner tortures him." To this afflicted being, Bataille is "bound by ties of horror and friendship" (283). Contemplating the image *"to the point of accord [jusqu'à l'accord],"* Bataille is propelled into a dark ecstasy in which the excess of pain "suppress[es] in me the need to be only myself" (283). The abyss of horror, Bataille wants to show his readers, is at the same time a height, the height of death at which the meditator experiences, with the irrecusable force of a wound to his/her own body, that "what ties existence to all the *rest* is death." To enter into this accord is to experience dissolution in a "storm of pain" (283) that is at the same time love: a convulsive "love in which the sadistic instinct [has] no part" (140). In this love, *"compassion,* pain, and ecstasy blend [*se composent*]" (273). Love embraces the dying human victim and the whole world, cherished "to the dregs and without hope" (141).

The Politics of Uselessness

Bataille's staging of himself as mystical teacher begins to provide a clearer sense of "what Bataille was for, and what he was against," in the political context of the war years (and beyond). That the message is not wholly comforting will come as little surprise.

Bataille was for violence, and he was against war only because and to the extent that war failed to be the kind of violence he considered most extreme and liberating. Bataille never renounced his conviction that "radical evil" constitutes "the point of departure and the unsurpassable point of reference for any morality 'that escapes the evident servility of conventions' ([*BOC*] XI, 246)."[52] One would search in vain, in Bataille's writings after 1939, for indications that he seriously regretted or wished to disown his incendiary language of the Acéphale period. Bataille was not against war in principle. He believed efforts to banish cruelty from human life were as doomed as they were naive (or disingenuous). It seems certain that if real combat could have generated, reliably and for all its participants, the types of ecstasies portrayed in Jünger, Bataille would have urged people into battle — any battle — and would have been in the front ranks himself. War, however, failed to live up to its advertising. *La Guerre, notre mère,* was not a war but a book. And if Bataille was not against the idea of war — if he was indeed "fascinated" by the idea (*ML,* 290) — he was opposed to mass brutality that stripped death of its grandeur and its terror. It was precisely *because* he was fascinated by violence and convinced that death held the key to all deep meaning, all beauty, all forms of sovereign experience in human life that Bataille turned away from war to pursue a different path. It was for the same reason that he tried — as Sartre sarcastically but accurately noted — to "draw us along with him" toward the "unknown region" he had begun to explore (*NM,* 150).

For Bataille, war was to be condemned not because it brought death, but because it brought a false, incomplete, inhuman death. It forced men and women to disappear in the mode of "animality" (*BOC* II, 239), "without complication and without 'mystery' " (*BOC* VII, 258). War engendered mass death stripped of the "deep meaning" that could only be given to death (and therefore to life) through the work of consciousness, the long and patient labor of sacrifice. True death was not a "sudden accident" (258), but a task, an (artistic) achievement, a (literary) work. This "task" — humans' highest task, maintaining the "work of death"[53] — demanded not war, but "the detachment from action and the infinite attention of religious procedures" (258). Having taken as a point of departure the hypothesis that war and sacrifice were equivalent, Bataille came in the end to the conclusion that, linked on one level, on a deeper plane they were opposed. Indeed, that "Nothing is more opposed to the military spirit than religious sacrifice" (258). Both the equivalence and the opposition were in a sense "true." But in the context of actual warfare, it was the opposition and not the equivalence that had to be stressed by thinkers committed to "contestation." For in this context the official powers could be expected to — and did — tirelessly put forward versions of the notion that war and heroic sacrifice are identical.

War and its underlying logic, then, were to be contested, in the name not of pacifism or resignation, but of a higher violence. But how was this protest to be articulated, and who was going to listen to it?

To analyze the opposition between sacrifice or inner experience and war discursively was certainly a possible response to the confusion. In a number of his theoretical writings, including *The Limit of the Useful,* Bataille did just that. Yet it is significant that Bataille abandoned the project of *The Limit of the Useful* during the war and renounced publishing the results of his more theoretical researches until after the conflict was over. What he insisted on putting before the public while the war raged were not scientific studies but obscene novels (*Madame Edwarda, Le Petit*) and the lacerated confessional texts that proffered not a coherent theory of inner experience, war, or anything else, but rather the "friendship" of an ironic "saint": "*Saintliness* demands the complicity of the being with lubricity, cruelty, mockery. To the lubricious, cruel, and mocking man the *saint* brings friendship, the laughter of connivance" (*BOC* V, 278). Bataille does not advance theses (or does so only unwillingly). Above all, he offers himself, "a man alone and naked" (*NM*, 151): shattered mystic, voyager to the end of the possible, bearing in his own body the grotesque and glorious wounds of inner experience, and anxious to put those wounds on display (144).

It would be wrong to infer that this displaying of (textual) wounds and the communication it seeks to initiate had no political reach or that they said nothing meaningful about the processes by which real wounds were being inflicted on real bodies as Bataille wrote. The basis of effective resistance to political tyranny, Bataille believed, was not a theory or a political doctrine, but an *experience* of radical sovereignty, an experience of the self as sacred. It was this experience Bataille's mystical texts sought to describe, model, and elicit. "The reasons to write a book," Bataille had observed, "can be traced back to the desire to modify the relations that exist between a man and his fellow beings" (*BOC* II, 143). Bataille asserted his desire to change these relations by causing *people* to change: not merely their minds, but more importantly their "conduct." His aim was to initiate people quite literally into "another existence":

> Even the simple difference I describe — I describe uncontrollable laughter as if it were serious — supposes that one pass to another existence — no longer human but divine. Naturally a man can think in many ways, but a new reflex would introduce a veritable divinity.
>
> This is meanwhile what I am trying to introduce, and it is for that reason that my attitude is comparable to that of a sacrificer, not of a simple scholar. (*BOC* VII, 519)

For, Bataille affirmed, his effort was to introduce this human divinity "not on the level of thought but of conduct" (519).

To bring about the divinizing transformation — the passage to "another existence" — promised by sacrificial communication, Bataille's writing mobilized two interwoven approaches. One was the presentation of a method of mystical practice: specific techniques or spiritual exercises that could catalyze a direct experience of the sacred. The other was Bataille's self-representation as a mystical "saint." The second of these two strategies in a sense absorbed the other. It was above all by symbolizing the mystical path in the form of a sacrificial, sacred personage (himself) that Bataille could make this mode of existence compelling to his readers (could hope to convert them). Not dry theoretical analyses but the spectacular tragicomic enactment of his own "sainthood and sovereignty of Evil" (*BOC* IX, 291) was the way the mystic saint could lure readers to "fall into the hole" (*BOC* V, 135) of his *Inner Expe-*

rience. This falling, this surrender, was required if the experience was to be (un)known "from within." As Sartre rightly discerned, Bataille used himself—his "ulcers and wounds," his "'sumptuous and bitter' soul," his "eroticism"—as the bait in this literary trap (*NM*, 144, 187). Angela of Foligno and the "seductive" (*BOC* V, 140) young Chinese torture victim had served as "objects onto which Bataille [could] project his own dissolution" and so achieve ecstasy. Now Bataille in turn, stepping into the place of the saint, offered himself as an analogous "[projective] figure for readers of his text."[54]

As a political thesis, the contestation of war in the name of a higher, interior violence was confusing at best. The idea's intellectual parentage was shady and its implications hard to spell out. Yet despite its difficulties the notion could seduce, if it were embodied in a human life. In order to reach the public, though, life had to be transformed into text. It is in this sense that Bataille's claim to have written *On Nietzsche* (and his other mystical works) *"with my life"* (*BOC* VI, 17) needs to be understood. Writing was the instrument that allowed Bataille to keep the sacrificial laceration of consciousness open and agonized in himself (*"Cruellement, j'étire la déchirure* [...]" [*BOC* V, 273]), and to offer his wound to others, as the basis of an obscene and "intoxicating" communication.

This *parti pris* of responding to a brutal political and military situation with a mystico-literary self-stylization constitutes the force and originality, but also, for some, the deeply unsatisfying ambiguity of Bataille's mystical subversion. Understanding Bataille's concerns in this way shows, in any event, why Bataille's position with respect to the violence of the war could only be enacted/ communicated performatively. What Bataille sought to present was not a set of ethical propositions or rationally coordinated political theses, but rather a *style of life* that, considered as a (lacerated but living) whole, offered an alternative to the values and forms of existence that had found their culmination in totalitarian oppression and war. The life of mysticism and expenditure Bataille proposed could not, he claimed, be adequately described in the language of philosophical, social scientific, or political discourse. This mode of life could only be grasped in its realization (performance) in the existence of an exemplary being: the mystical writer, Bataille himself. Distancing himself from the "professorial" attitude of academic philosophers like Heidegger, whose "method remains *glued* to results," Bataille affirmed: "what counts in my eyes is the moment of *ungluing* [*décollement*]. What I teach (if it is true that...) is an intoxication, not a philosophy. I am not a philosopher, but a *saint*, maybe a madman" (*BOC* V, 218 note; ellipsis in original).

Bataille was convinced that the meditational method and more broadly the mystical style of existence he made available through his writings opened the route to a concrete experience of the heterogeneity and sovereignty of the self and thus laid the groundwork for genuine freedom. The inner experience of freedom remains the precondition of any meaningful deployment of freedom in the public, political world. And if freedom can be understood in Kantian terms as autolegislation, then mystical writing initiates autonomy by showing people that they carry the supreme law within themselves, by teaching them to experience themselves as their own law (a law constituted through endless contestation). "Man is his own law if he strips himself naked before himself. The mystic before God had the attitude of a *subject*. Whoever places being before himself has the attitude of a *sovereign*" (*BOC* V, 278). The "naked" sovereign of inner experience, "knowing that he will die" (278), finds freedom tempered with the awareness of radical vulnerability and contingency, thus making freedom inseparable from "compassion" (273), or as Bataille will later write, from a tragic "loyalty" (*BOC* XI, 541–45). Without the sacrificial knowledge of its own penetration by death, the self's exercise of freedom would inevitably become an "exercise of power" *over* others (*BOC* V, 221). Instead, inner experience is a sacrificial "conquest" of the self *"for others"* (76). Sovereignty is not static governance but tireless "revolt" (221).

Through an unruly mixture of steamy confession, dense philosophical analysis, histrionic bluster, parodic prayers, lachrymose lamentation, "mimicry," and irony, Bataille's textual mysticism undermines or overflows the conceptual structures on which the logic of domination relies. It attacks utility, rationality, hierarchical order, and identity. By affirming a useless inner experience as in itself "sole authority, sole value" (*BOC* V, 18), mysticism challenges the right of coercive political systems to claim ultimate value and unlimited authority for themselves. By introducing — through "autosacrificial"[55] writing — the toxin of the impossible into calculations of human meaning, Bataille sought to reach the "underside" of language and human experience, to uncover the "nakedness" of irreducible anguish that philosophy and political theory had sought to conceal, and to "annul the effects of totalizing discourse," both in the philosophical and in the political realms.[56] For better or worse (for better *and* worse), Bataille's writing not only reveals but *is* the heart of his politics. The impossible practice of this writing puts on display the forces that made Bataille momentarily sensitive to fascism's seductions, but that also propelled him irresistibly away from the fascist orbit: his "monstrosities in the end rebellious toward all political camps."[57]

It was this spiritual and political monstrosity — irreducible heterogeneity, death-obsessed sacredness, ironic "sainthood" — that Bataille hoped to make contagious. Not by analyzing it, but by being it. The content of Bataille's message was himself: himself as mystic, as one who speaks of death from within death. In his mystical texts Bataille produces himself as one who lives and writes *à hauteur de mort*. He demonstrates the confrontation with death in a context that is precisely *not* that of the battlefield, in order to show that death's impossible and necessary truth belongs not to the soldiers plunged in the "vain noise of combat," but to the " 'men of religious death' or sacrifice" who raise up death's "bloody but wholly resplendent image" in the midst of a "sacred silence" (*BOC* II, 238). This is the point Bataille considers it urgent to drive home: that in war or peace human life only begins to deploy its richness when death is internalized and when life can be affirmed and loved in and through death. Bataille as the mystic of *"la joie suppliciante"* embodies this affirmation. Bataille does not merely articulate the claim, he *is* the claim that a life lived in the mad intensity of the *hauteur de mort* is the only life worth having. One can only "have" such a life when one sacrifices it. And one can only sacrifice it if one loses life consciously: through what Bataille variously terms "dramatization," "comedy," "mimetism." By writing his own mystical dissolution, Bataille shows how it is possible to "watch [one]self ceasing to be" (*HDS*, 19). He models the process through which, like the Tibetan monk in the burial ground, one can be penetrated by the secrets of death, while "the body thus treated remains intact" (*BOC* VII, 259). What arises in the experience of Bataille's writing is not an irremediable *mise-à-mort*, but instead a better way of encountering death's power, an endless, anguished *mise-en-jeu* in which mystical unknowing "drains [...] the life of the subject" and holds him/her suspended at the "point of death," but without killing.[58]

After the war, Bataille would expand and systematize this vision of the mystical mediation of death and consciousness in a manifesto-like description of the sacred functions of the writer. Here, Bataille turns to his own account Sartre's portrayal of him as a florid mystical preacher. In his "Letter to René Char on the Incompatibilities of the Writer" (1950), Bataille asserts that every authentic writer is a messenger (and martyr) of love, the bearer of a "Gospel" (*LRC*, 38) that is, however, "diabolical," in the sense that it preaches the refusal of all forms of servility. The reward of this stance of permanent refusal is isolation, but also an ecstatically intensified relationship to existence:

> It is in [the writer] and through him that man learns how he himself remains forever elusive, being essentially unpredictable, and how knowledge must finally be resolved into the simplicity of emotion. It is in and through the writer that existence, in a general way, is what a girl is to the man who desires her, whether she love or spurn him, bring him pleasure or despair. (37–38)

Writers mediate between human beings and "existence," seeking to model, stir, and nourish a love of life that sustains itself at the height of death. Writers carry out this mediation not by presenting philosophical or political lessons in literary guise (a procedure that could produce nothing but "platitudes" [38]), but, more mysteriously, by offering a writing that draws as close as possible to "silence." The obsession with constructive action that distorts the modern worldview can only be contested, Bataille claims, "through silence — or through poetry, which opens, as it were, a window onto silence" (32–33).

Challenging the tyranny of action and production (the hallmark of "homogeneous" society [*BOC* I, 339–40]), the mystical writer shows people how to become "silent," inactive, and unproductive, that is, useless, that is, sacred. To Jünger's decisive question, "What could be more sacred than a fighter?" Bataille brings — incarnates — his answer. The sacred being is not the fighter, but the writer. Not the warrior bravely obeying the order to advance, but an irreducibly insubordinate figure who questions all orders and challenges not just particular institutions (fascism, Christianity), but the general "tendency of humanity to submit to authority."[59]

By staging himself, through writing, as a sacrificial mystic, Bataille eluded the categories through which "political action" is usually understood and its effects assessed. Bataille himself claimed not to act out of political motives, but in response to an unreasoning passion (*LRC*, 38).[60] Yet by presenting a paradoxical writing hungry to become silence, and by displaying his own written self as a tortured text, a pointless verbal sacrifice on the margins of war's mass manufacture of "useful" death, Bataille took a position with regard to power. He did so not by commenting on or seeking to intervene in political and military events per se, but by reasserting in opposition to the realm of power and useful violence as a whole the existence of another mode of being whose "fullest expression" came not in a deployment of might, but "only in man's powerlessness and death" (35). It was this sacred powerlessness, the opposite of the virtues required by war, that Bataille sought to embody — provocatively, grotesquely, madly — in his written martyrdom. His task as a writer was to communicate a refusal of the logic of power that found its supreme expression in war and to affirm a sovereignty based not on the domination of others, but on the sacrificial calling-into-question of the self. "From the very start, the dialectic [of the ego and the totality] is in an impasse. The one who questions [*interroge*], the one who speaks, eliminates himself by questioning. But the one who sinks in that absence — and in that silence — , from the depths of that silence, is the *prophet* of what is lost in absence . . . " (*BOC* V, 364; Bataille's punctuation).[61] Such a "prophetic" attitude demands, Bataille will suggest, "indifference, or rather the maturity of a dead man" (*LRC*, 42). The writer's patient, courageous, knowing embrace of death (of his/her own absence) is the exemplary exercise of freedom. It is a training in that renunciation (*askesis* through excess) that, though hardly proclaimable as the law of the polity, may be a surer defense than many such laws against our urge to turn violence against our fellow beings.

Yet this solemn praise of Bataille's folly risks leaving fundamental objections imperfectly addressed and indeed renders the problems more acute. The challenges articulated by Carolyn Dean and others move us back unforgivingly from Bataille's literary-mystical performance to the events of the war out of and against which the performance was born. And here the questions take on all their urgency. When men and women are really dying — not under the constraint of poetic inspiration, but under falling bombs or in concentration camp gas chambers — is "indifference," even rebaptized as "maturity," defensible? When people are losing their real lives in the struggle against a totalitarian oppressor, aren't there more urgent tasks at hand than the staging of a "comedy of sacrifice"? Surely there are moments, and surely the war against Hitler was one of them, when "comedic" contestation is a drastically inadequate response, whether or not inaction can be styled in retrospect as a "renunciation of phallic virtue." One cannot fail to agree with Dean that certain situations demand real hardness.[62]

Bataille of course never imagined that his mystical teachings would be of use to those bearing the direct brunt of Nazi violence. Bataille wrote not for the present, but for a future about which he had only *Unwissenheit,* beyond the certainty of his own death. "Far beyond the failures of *close* friends and readers, I search now for the friends, the readers that a dead man can find" (*BOC V,* 299). Yet this orientation toward the future, in the midst of the *malheurs du temps présent,* has the ring of an evasion.

If we believe that freedom is not *only* an inner experience or spiritual attitude, but that freedom (our own and others') concerns vulnerable bodies and must under certain circumstances be defended bodily against the powers that would abolish it, then Bataille's written sacrifice cannot permanently elude Dean's charge that a literary performance is not in itself an adequate position, much less a sufficient political action. There are indeed moments when we want to, when we must, say there exists a sovereign duty to renounce sovereignty, to make oneself — one's intelligence, one's writing, one's "blood and exhaustion" (*BOC* V, 246) — an instrument in the defense of tangibly threatened human lives. With his failure to enlist himself actively in this cause or even clearly to acknowledge its importance, we have perhaps reached what for some will be the "limit of the useful" in Bataille: the point beyond which we cannot and should not follow him. Yet this is a limit where we, too, must tread carefully and avoid speaking of "what is infernal" with the indiscretion and the false bravado (*BOC* I, 551) that are easily engendered by distance from the "too terrible reality."

Carolyn Dean's problematization of "principled equivocation" and the hypostasizing of aporia, and her challenge to a politics that would remain on the level of textual performance, echo in an intriguing fashion the critique of Bataille's attitude formulated by Simone Weil in 1933–34 (*SP* I, 422–24). Weil resembled Bataille in her conviction that death reveals truth, in politics as in the spiritual realm. In sharp contrast to Bataille, however, Weil believed death's truth could only be absorbed through committed action undertaken in a situation where real, bodily destruction loomed as an imminent threat (*E*, 378). The sacrificial violence of inner experience pulled Bataille away from the battlefield. Weil's mystical consciousness drove her toward it.

Chapter Five

THE SPECTACLE OF SACRIFICE
War and Performance in Simone Weil

Now, the problem is this. Have we found a positive foundation, instead
of self-sacrifice, for the hermeneutics of the self? I cannot say this, no.
We have tried, at least from the humanistic period of the Renaissance till
now. And we can't find it.
— Michel Foucault, speaking in Berkeley, 1980

FROM 1939 TO 1943, as Bataille chronicled his "mad experience of
the divine" (*BOC* V, 45) in *Guilty* and *Inner Experience*, Simone
Weil was also exploring the boundaries of violence, mysticism,
and communication. Like Bataille's, Weil's mystical turn coincided
with the beginning of World War II. For Weil as for Bataille, the war
was a period of anguish, deep spiritual experience, and feverish
literary productivity.

In contrast to Bataille, however, Simone Weil did not view her
mystical explorations as precluding engagement in the war effort.
The last years of Weil's life, during which her mysticism flourished,
were marked by repeated attempts to involve herself actively in the
military struggle against Hitler. Weil tirelessly solicited a mission
on the front lines of battle, and it is generally accepted that her
despair at not being allowed to carry out such a mission played
a significant role in the physical decline that led to her death in
England in August 1943, of tuberculosis complicated by the effects
of self-starvation.

This chapter explores the relationship between war, mystical
religion, and writing in Simone Weil. Influenced by her philosophical mentor Alain, Weil began the 1930s as a pacifist. Yet when
she renounced pacifism in 1939, Weil resolved not merely to support the military struggle against Hitler in principle, but to take an
active role in the fight. Political and spiritual motives lay behind

this decision. Convinced that the "consent to die" as an isolated ego is the essence of mystical wisdom and that spiritual truths are empty unless realized through bodily action, Weil came to believe her spiritual quest would find its fulfillment in the ordeal of combat. With her plan to lead a formation of battlefield nurses directly under enemy fire, Weil aimed both to complete a process of religious purification and to transform herself into a sacrificial symbol, uniting politics, art, and spirituality in the crucible of violence. Recent commentators have criticized Weil's war projects as pathological attempts to erase her Jewishness and her identity as a woman.[1] Such a reading is perceptive and important. Yet, as with Bataille's literary self-sacrifice, Weil's war program was no mere quirk of individual psychopathology. Weil's attempt to enact spiritual "decreation" in the midst of war opens a new interface between politics and performance and foregrounds urgent questions about how those struggling against an apparatus of political violence can avoid reproducing that apparatus's own logics.

Pacifism and the Specter of War

Simone Weil was concerned with war from her early youth. During Weil's student days, under the influence of Alain, this preoccupation expressed itself as a resolute pacifism. Weil worked as a volunteer for the pacifist organization Volonté de paix, and many of her early writings developed pacifist themes. In an article published in *La Critique sociale* in 1933 (in the same issue containing Bataille's *compte-rendu* of Malraux and Weil's text on Rosa Luxemburg), Weil argued that war constitutes the culmination of the process by which modern industrial capitalism inverts the relationship between human beings and things (*WOC* 2.1, 293). War can never be — for the workers and ordinary citizens forced to bear the brunt of the violence — a victory. The triumph of the opposing army signifies death and dispossession; yet the victory of one's own side only strengthens the tyrannizing masters and reinforces workers' slavery. On this basis, Weil rejected the arguments of those who in 1933 called for preemptive military intervention against Germany to suppress the Nazi forces gaining power there. Once the reality of modern warfare has been grasped, Weil argued, "the absurdity of an anti-fascist struggle that would take war as a means of action" is clear. By constraining millions of men to submit to the tyrannical domination of an apparatus of military command, one would simply be "extend[ing] in another form" the fascist regime one ostensibly hoped to abolish (297).

Weil's attitude changed as the savagery of Hitler's policies emerged more clearly in the second half of the 1930s. Somewhat paradoxically, Weil's explicit turn to Christianity in 1938 played a significant role in detaching her from pacifist commitments. Increasing concern with religious questions reinforced Weil's sense of the vulnerability of the human spirit to military might and social force. Far from rendering her indifferent to conflicts played out on the temporal plane, Weil's Christianity sharpened her awareness of human suffering and permitted her to analyze the mechanisms and effects of war with greater precision.[2] It became clear to Weil that the Nazi threat demanded relentless resistance using all available means and that the pacifist movement had been misguided and naive in its response to fascism. In "Réflexions en vue d'un bilan" (spring-summer 1939), Weil broke with the pacifism she had maintained throughout the preceding decade.[3]

Typically, having reached the decision to support the use of armed force against the Nazis, Weil had no intention of affirming this idea merely as an abstract principle, leaving to others the task of putting the theory into practice. Weil determined to engage herself bodily in the struggle.

Mystical Rebirth as Inner Violence

Weil left Paris with her family in June 1940, as the French leadership under Pétain surrendered the capital to Hitler's troops. Joining the stream of refugees headed south toward Marseilles, Weil planned to sail to New York with her parents, then cross to London and enroll in de Gaulle's Free French force (attempts to reach London by a more direct route had failed). In Marseilles, Weil involved herself actively in the local Resistance network. Her apartment was searched, and she underwent several police interrogations.[4] Weil arrived in New York with her parents in June 1942. From there, she wrote urgently to her former classmate

Maurice Schumann, a Gaullist official in London, asking him to use his influence to bring her to England and assign her a mission, "preferably dangerous" (*EL,* 186–87), with the Resistance. Weil's aim was to be sent back onto French soil, either with the special corps of battlefield nurses she hoped to organize or on a reconnaissance or sabotage mission against the German occupation force (*SP* II, 425–29).

The months in which she waited for answers to her requests constituted a period of anguish for Weil. She came to suspect that her decision to accompany her parents to New York, though well-intentioned, was in reality a betrayal of France and an act of disobedience toward God.[5] Her sense of guilt and helplessness propelled her into a crushing depression. Yet perhaps as a result of this suffering the months in America also brought an intensification of Weil's spirituality and a deepening of her mystical theology.[6] Weil's American notebooks, the bulk written during October 1942, contain bold metaphysical theses and accounts of mystical experiences that are among the most powerful and disturbing pages in Weil's authorship.

Weil's situation was in certain respects ironically similar to Bataille's at the same moment (though neither was aware of the parallels). Like Bataille, Weil found herself in isolation on the margins of the war, observing its unfolding from a distance and meanwhile gripped by mystical experiences that mirrored the violence of the military conflict. However, where Bataille had chosen his retreat to solitude and mystical nonaction, Weil was forced into inactivity against her desires.

Weil's mystical theology is probably the best known, but also for many commentators the most problematic, aspect of her work.[7] Weil's thought is assuredly not for the tender-minded. Hers is a mysticism in which suffering and violence play central roles and whose ultimate aim is the brutal eradication of the human ego.

The foundation of Weil's mystical program consists in the view that the sinful, self-asserting human ego is a barrier between God and the impersonal purity of God's material creation. Mystical discipline aims to remove this barrier by suppressing human personality. Thus, while Weil is sometimes disparaged as a modern gnostic, a hater of the flesh and the material world, this characterization is mistaken. It is neither the material world nor the human body that Weil believes must be rejected. The source of defilement is the ego. Matter as such and the body as such are creations of God and partake of cosmic beauty. Perfection is attained when pure matter and pure spirit (the divine) are able to unite and "exchange their secrets" (*PG*, 53). But in order for this union of matter and spirit to take place, the degraded, sinful form of spirit (the human self) must disappear. At the height of mystical awareness, the human surrenders her separate identity to God, consenting to a supreme violence that literally destroys the personality.

According to Weil, the deity created the material universe and human beings through an act of renunciation, abdication, withdrawal, or sacrifice (see, e.g., *PSO*, 35; *CS*, 168–70). The human task is to reenact this original divine sacrifice in reverse, willingly giving up the separate existence God has accorded us. "God abdicated by creating, and [. . .] we give back to him by destroying. God's sacrifice is creation, man's is destruction" (*CS*, 168). To designate the spiritual process by which human beings reenact and invert God's creative sacrifice, accepting their own annihilation as autonomous personalities, Weil adopted the term "decreation."[8]

In practice, the process of decreative transformation Weil describes foregrounds and capitalizes upon precisely those aspects of human life that ordinarily appear most negative: intense physical suffering; psychological humiliation and despair; the experiences of anguish that arise when urgent desires go unfulfilled or cherished hopes are dashed. The value of such experiences for Simone Weil lies precisely in their capacity to inflict violence on the ego. The violation, wounding, and finally killing of the self are the necessary means to liberation.

To analyze the mechanics of decreation, Weil uses a vocabulary adopted in part from ancient Greek science. She describes the human self as constituted by the interplay between the "vegetative" dimension — the life of the body — and the "supplementary energies," which fund the personality. Supplementary energies include our desire for power and pleasure, but also fuel those faculties often (wrongly) understood to constitute what is highest in human life: imagination, will, rational thought. The supplementary energies shape individual selfhood, which includes what Weil terms the "carnal part" of the soul. Beyond the carnal soul lies the soul's "uncreated" part: a tiny divine spark of which we only become clearly conscious at the paradoxical decreative moment when "we" cease to exist.

Two phases are discernible in Weil's theorization of the inner struggle that leads to decreation, though the transition between the two is less a matter of abrupt rupture than of a gradual shift in emphasis. Weil's first model was discussed in chapter 2. Comparing the "supplementary energy" of the human will to an "armed force" (C2, 175–76), Weil theorized that the will should impose a quasi-military discipline on the other aspects of the personality. Through ongoing efforts of renunciation and attention (the "training of the animal in oneself"), energy could be progressively withdrawn from worldly objects and oriented toward the divine. This model of ascetic spirituality is in many ways rather conventional, blending results of Weil's own experiments in prayer and meditation with her readings of texts from Christian and Indian mystical traditions.

Weil's writings in New York and London, however, reveal a different approach. Weil moved increasingly toward a model of religious purification emphasizing receptivity and waiting (*attente*) over agency and will. The obstacles Weil's own will encountered in these months played a catalyzing role, helping — forcing — her to reconceive the ends and means of her spiritual practice. Weil experienced the pain of exile, as well as crushing frustration at the Allied military authorities' reluctance to assign her an active mission. At the same time, she confronted the ongoing physical torture of severe migraine headaches. Since she was powerless to change these circumstances, Weil struggled to *use* them.[9] Instead of trying to deny or ignore the physical and emotional torment she experienced, she explored this torment to its farthest limits, making the pain the center of her practice of meditation and prayer, surrendering to the dissolution of the personality provoked by these multiple forms of anguish. Weil continued in her notebooks to employ the vocabulary of "vegetative" and "supplementary" energies, but characterized their interaction in a new way. Her focus shifted from ascetic discipline and the requirement to master one's "animal" nature to the essential passivity of the human spirit in its relation to the divine.

Weil now suggested that the true role of the supplementary energy is not to "train" the somatic energies and lead them upward, but simply to expend itself in anguished, unfulfilled desire, at last leaving the vegetative level of purely somatic life "naked" (*CS*, 193). Transformation comes through the shattering, unmediated contact of the vegetative level of existence with the divine, when the imaginary cravings and compensations of the ego have been depleted. This contact is equivalent to the genuine death of the person undergoing the experience.

Weil's experiences convinced her that sustained physical pain was the most potent catalyst of spiritual transformation. Yet, she notes, "one can make the same use of hunger, fatigue, fear," or of any other shattering experience that constrains the "carnal" part of the soul to cry out in despair: "I can't stand it anymore!" (*CS*, 177). The terrestrial or carnal portion of the soul includes all aspects of "what one feels to be the self" (178). In a situation of sustained physical pain or emotional torment, the carnal self quickly rebels. Yet against the whole of her own suffering personality, the mystic "takes the part of the other interlocutor," that minute, higher portion of the soul that continues to consent to the torture, understanding it as willed by God. To consent spiritually to intense pain is literally to "step outside oneself [*sortir de soi*]" (178). Under these conditions, "a quarter of an hour is like a perpetual duration." "[T]he very sap flows out, and the still living man becomes dead wood" (178). Yet if, at the end of the quarter-hour of trial, a tiny part of the soul has refused to shout "Enough!" that part of the soul "has crossed the indefinite length of time and has passed to the other side of time, in eternity" (178). Spiritual death, the abolition of that in the subject that is specifically human, makes way for a "new creation" (182).[10]

In contrast to Weil's earlier theory of spiritual transformation as a process of controlled, disciplined "training of the animal," the emphasis in these passages is on an explosive *loss of control* that bankrupts the human being's volition and rational faculties. Thus, in her New York notebooks, Weil focuses her most detailed account of the decreative process around a reading of the biblical parable of the prodigal son. The fascination of the parable for Weil lies in its suggestion that spiritual transformation *begins* where human will *ends*. In the parable's terms, the prodigal's fortune — which Weil identifies with the supplementary energies of the personality — must be utterly dissipated, spent without reserve as a precondition for repentance and change. The wayward son must expend his fortune (his ego) totally and sink to the lowest level of despair and humiliation. Only then will he turn back — naked, empty-handed, abject — to his father's house. "The supplementary energy [. . .] is the portion of the inheritance taken away by the prodigal son." This energy must be "totally expended before the soul can take a single step in the direction of eternity" (CS, 179).

Weil's notion of the prodigal dispersal of the very energies that make up the self has been compared — not inappropriately — to Bataille's doctrine of liberative expenditure.[11] Both models point to the decisive moment in human existence as a violent opening/shattering of the self: a hemorrhage of desiring energies whose explosion destroys the ego's (semblance of) stability, integrity, identity. Both Weil's decreation and Bataille's *dépense* draw their power from a loss of control. The person is no longer the self-centered, self-mastering subject but the site of his/her own violent overthrow. Moreover, this overthrow erupts *against the will* of the ego struggling for self-preservation. Neither decreation (equivalent to death [CS, 181–82]) nor expenditure (whose horizon is death and horror [e.g., BOC I, 152–58, 305–7]) can be chosen. Decreation and Bataillean sacrificial excess seize us "despite ourselves" (BOC III, 11). Weil insists that the whole of the personality, the whole of our "carnal" nature, cries out against the torture of decreation and is right to do so. Decreation proves its authenticity by overcoming the will's resistance. "One cannot escape from the self by will. The more one wants to, the more one is in the self. One can only desire and supplicate" (CS, 224). Indeed, Weil was convinced that decreation cannot even sincerely be asked for by the ego (204–5). Even the genuine desire for spiritual liberation comes from beyond the self. Weil related the sacrificial destruction of the personality to her notion of affliction [*malheur*]. Used properly, affliction can catalyze decreative transformation. But like affliction itself, decreation cannot be produced by volitional acts. One does not *will* this ultimate violence; one *submits* to it and does so only when there is no possibility of escape.

The simultaneous aspects of violence, desperate resistance, and ultimate surrender link decreation to the Weilian archetype of the prisoner of war kneeling at the feet of his conqueror. In a passage from the New York notebooks Weil adopts the kneeling captive (in the essay on the *Iliad*, her central emblem of war's power to dehumanize) as a symbol of the proper spiritual posture of the soul before God:

> To supplicate is to wait for life or death from outside. Kneeling, head bent, in the most convenient position for the conqueror to sever the neck with a sword blow; hand touching his knees. [...] The heart empties itself of all its attachments, frozen by the imminent contact of death. [...] One should pray to God in this way. (*CS,* 44)

The savagery to which war's captives and victims are subjected, and which in "The Poem of Force" Weil had shown as the nadir of dehumanizing abjection, becomes the model of the posture that makes possible the subject's spiritual transformation and rebirth. The condition of unthinking, lifeless matter into which the condemned captive sinks is an image of the spiritual state to which the mystic aspires. Spiritual "perfection [...] is the direct union of the divine spirit with inert matter." This is why, "if a man is transformed into a perfect being, and his thought replaced by the divine thought, his flesh, beneath the appearance of living flesh, has become in a sense a cadaver" (*CS,* 260–61). In a characteristically Weilian inversion, only by sinking below the human can one finally rise above it.

As Georges Bataille had also observed, such a reversal of "high" and "low" in spirituality constitutes a persistent though often repressed aspect of Christianity. Weil for her part was convinced human beings should aspire to "resemble God, but God crucified" (*C2,* 110). Actively and purposefully to seek crucifixion would be a "perversion." Yet what one should not only accept but "love," Weil maintained, was the ever-present "possibility of affliction" that can at any moment reduce one's self — in its physical, psychological, and social aspects — to ruins (*PSO,* 108–9). Revealing our radical vulnerability, affliction tears us loose from ourselves and points us toward the supernatural good we can only attain by ceasing to *be* human selves. One does not consent to this decreative transformation, Weil states, with joyful "abandon." Rather, one "consents to it with a violence enacted by the entire soul upon the entire soul" (*CS*, 205).

War as Spiritual Opportunity

The decreated human being becomes "in a sense a cadaver." Ultimately, to renounce the self means to accept death. Facing this implication squarely, Weil identified the consent to death as the essence of mystical wisdom.[12] In one of her notes from London, among her last writings, Weil equated the consent to death directly with sainthood. "Total humility is consent to death, which makes of us inert nothingness [*du néant inerte*]. The saints are those who while still alive have really consented to death." In Greek, Weil added the formula: "Give me this, Lord" (*CS*, 325).

Along with birth, Weil theorized, the passage into death represented one of only two instants of "nakedness and perfect purity" in human life (*C3*, 87). Thus the moment of death might be "the instant in which, for an infinitesimal fraction of time, the pure, naked, certain, eternal truth enters into the soul" (*AD*, 33). In this sense, "Death is the most precious gift that has been given to man." And this is why, by the same token, "the supreme impiety is to use [death] badly."[13] If authentic, the consent to death could itself be said to constitute "salvation" (*CS*, 169), insofar as this consent to vanish as an isolated ego both symbolizes and enacts the self's total surrender to God.

Yet authentic consent must not be merely theoretical.[14] "The consent to death cannot be fully real unless death is present" (*E*, 378). Nowhere, clearly, does death loom more powerfully than in war. Thus, Weil came to interpret war both as a human disaster and as a spiritual opportunity. On the surface, war is the antithesis of the atmosphere of contemplative attention where religion would be expected to flourish. Yet precisely because of the violence and terror it unleashes, the situation of battle could represent a crucial opportunity for the fulfillment of a mystical vocation aiming at the decreative liquidation of the ego. The possible spiritual "uses" of war became a dominant theme in Weil's writing in the last year of her life.

Weil argued that the concrete events of war itself might be vectors of religious meaning and that participation in combat could function as a form of spiritual discipline. In a sense, she found in this topic the culmination of her entire intellectual and spiritual project. In a letter to Maurice Schumann, Weil wrote that through the course of a lifetime she had "always felt" her destiny would bring her the obligation to explore, not just in thought but by direct experience, the connection she "confusedly" sensed between her religious convictions and the extreme forms of human experience catalyzed in war (*EL*, 203). Only by facing war's violence "physically" would Weil be enabled to "think together in truth the affliction of human beings, the perfection of God, and the link between the two" (213).

While furnishing a laboratory for the investigation of affliction, war also presented a uniquely appropriate context in which to work out another crucial issue connected with the notion of decreation. This was the question of whether and how a spiritually transformed or decreated person (or one drawing close to this ideal state) would *act* in the world. Weil was convinced the decreated human being would not withdraw into aloof seclusion but would continue to participate in historical struggles. Yet the thorny problem was immediately raised of how a being with no self could possibly "act." What would motivate an entity emptied of desire and will to undertake action? What principles would guide her interventions? On what basis would she judge one political outcome preferable to another?

Weil addressed these problems by appealing to a concept drawn from the Bhagavad Gita. As she prepared to risk her life in the struggle against Hitler, Weil nourished her thought with the Sanskrit classic's teachings on cosmic order, spiritual transformation, war, and duty. Weil found a pivotal resource in the Gita's concept of "non-acting action" [*action non-agissante*]. In the margins of Weil's Sanskrit copy of the poem, she transcribed verses that provide a key to the idea of a form of action without ego-involvement: "He who can see inaction in action and action in inaction, he among all men is wise; he remains in balance even as he pursues action"; "As busy as [the wise man] may be, in reality he does not act; accomplishing actions only with the body, he contracts no defilement."[15]

Non-acting action is undertaken with no attachment to its fruits or consequences, out of pure obedience to dharma, the cosmic ordering principle that in a Christian context would be called the will of God. Following the Gita's descriptions of the true sage, Weil theorized that the decreated human being would indeed continue to act, but that his/her action would be utterly impersonal: pure obedience to the commands of God, of whom the spiritually purified human has become a passive instrument. "Emptied of its personal elements," action under these conditions is nothing but "a certain succession of physical movements" accomplished with a mathematical necessity as rigorous as that exhibited by inanimate objects responding to natural laws.[16] Liberated from personal cravings and aversions, the decreated being is free to submit fully to the dharma whose commands are oriented to "the good of all beings."[17]

That the "action" of the decreated being would be in a deeper sense equal to pure passivity by no means implied that this action would not be dramatic and possibly violent. The Bhagavad Gita's case study of non-acting action is the saintly king Arjuna, who, counseled by Krishna, proves his obedience to the dharma precisely by going to war and engaging in a combat that, out of misplaced compassion, he had hoped to avoid. The example of Arjuna, on which Simone Weil meditated steadily in this period, showed that "non-acting action" could include human activity in its apparently most extreme and savage forms. Indeed, the story of Arjuna, Krishna, and the battle at Kurukshetra suggests that war may be, paradoxically, a singularly appropriate matrix for the testing and purification of a spiritual vocation. Obedience to God may come too cheaply in other settings; on the battlefield, where one's own physical survival is at stake, the degree of one's authentic consent to God emerges undisguised.

Weil believed war could transform not just individuals, but communities and whole countries. In the last months of her life, contemplating the situation of France under Nazi domination,

Weil sought to show how war's horror, since it could not be escaped, might be used to catalyze a national spiritual renewal.

The very bleakness of France's situation as a conquered province of the German Reich seemed to Weil to offer a ray of hope. France's disarray and subjection, she claimed, simultaneously rendered indifference impossible and precluded recourse to the idolatrous worship of the nation itself as a motivation for struggle (*EL,* 107). If the French could find the strength to fight for freedom without falling prey to nationalist fanaticism and the lust for revenge, the nation's spiritual vocation and authentic "genius" — incarnated historically by figures like Joan of Arc — might reemerge at the moment of greatest peril (*E,* 271).

The country's spiritual regeneration would be a long process. Yet Weil insisted the renewal had to begin with dramatic, defining actions during the military conflict itself, not afterward. The nation's spiritual transformation had to be catalyzed not through a collective inward turn or nombrilistic withdrawal, but on the contrary through an "act of war [*action guerrière*]":

> The unique source of salvation and greatness for France is to reestablish contact with her genius in the depths of her affliction. This must be done now, immediately, while the affliction is still crushing, while France still has before her, in the future, the possibility to realize [*rendre réelle*] the first glimmer of the consciousness of her rediscovered genius, by expressing it through an act of war.
>
> After the victory, this possibility would be past, and peace would present no equivalents. For it is infinitely more difficult [. . .] to conceive of a peaceful action than an act of war; to pass by way of a peaceful action, an inspiration must already have a high degree of consciousness, of light, of reality. This will be the case for France when peace comes only if the last period of the war has produced this effect. *War must be the teacher who develops and nourishes this inspiration; for that, a deep, authentic inspiration, a true light, must surge up in the very midst of war.* (*E,* 271–72; emphasis added)

Where in previous writings Weil had emphasized war and education as radically opposed means of exerting an influence over people's ways of "reading" reality (*NB*, 24; see above, chapter 2), she now used the language of teaching and education to discuss the effects of war itself. Precisely because of the threat it posed to national survival, the war offered an occasion for France to relearn spiritual truths lost during the nation's long process of historical uprooting and alienation (*E*, 129–234). War could "develop and nourish" authentic virtues more effectively than could the less acute challenges of peacetime. Summoning up and focusing its energies in an effort of war, the nation had the chance not only to reconquer its lost political sovereignty, but to rediscover the deep sources of its moral inspiration. Thus Weil enjoined not only individuals but the whole French nation to undertake "non-acting action": action without attachment that would make the country and its reassembled military forces — like Arjuna and his followers in the Gita — instruments not of private vengeance, but of divine justice.

Yet precisely the case of Arjuna and his army showed, Weil believed, that collective efforts required distinguished individual leaders to serve as their symbolic focal points. As Weil argued in one of her London essays, "the masses are not creative unless authentic elites infuse them with an inspiration" (*EL*, 105). The masses struggling to throw off Hitler's yoke needed an inspiration like that provided by Arjuna in the great Sanskrit poem: an example of power not only military but spiritual. For only the "upsurge of a true faith" (108) could dynamize the antifascist forces sufficiently for the struggles that lay ahead.

In this situation, the political responsibilities of the leaders of the Free French movement constituted at the same time — and even more crucially — a spiritual task. While they labored to restore the nation militarily and politically, they also had to take the lead in healing France's soul. Indeed, Weil warned, military liberation and political and economic reconstruction would prove futile if the spiritual challenge were not faced squarely. "The true mission of the French movement in London is a spiritual mission before being a political and military mission." The task could be defined as "spiritual guidance [*direction de conscience*] on the scale of an entire country" (*E*, 272–73).

Fortunately, the leaders of the Free French were well placed to carry out this function (*E*, 243–44, 250). It was to the movement based in London that the French people looked quasi-unanimously for guidance and hope: not only for military liberation, but for signs of the spiritual transformation French people sensed was indispensable. De Gaulle in particular, Weil stressed, had achieved the status of a living "symbol" whose significance went far beyond the dimensions of ordinary patriotism. To many French people, de Gaulle was not only "the symbol of France's fidelity to itself," but the incarnation of "everything in man that refuses the base worship of force" (244). What the people of France awaited from the Free French movement and its leaders was thus much more than a display of military prowess. Through words and above all actions (250–51), the movement had to "mold the soul of the country" (252).

Frontline Nurses

Weil hoped she, too, might have a role to play in "molding the soul" of her country as it struggled to free itself from Nazi domination. This sense of a calling fueled her desperate anxiety to reach London and the Free French headquarters. Yet when, by dint of extraordinary efforts, Weil actually arrived in England in December 1942, events did not unfold as she had anticipated.

André Philip, de Gaulle's commissioner of labor and the interior, had decided Weil should be employed in the civilian branch of the Free French organization, with the slightly vague job title of *rédactrice*. She was given a small private office and assigned the task of examining proposals for the postwar reorganization of France being sent to London by local Resistance committees (*SP* II, 451–52). Weil was bitterly disappointed to have been relegated to an office job. London, though closer to the scene of conflict than New York, was still very much "the rear," and therefore intolerable.[18] Weil remained determined to obtain a more active and dangerous mission as soon as possible and quickly began promoting this idea to the responsible officials with her customary intransigence.[19]

The plan in which Weil had placed her greatest hopes was her "project for a formation of frontline nurses" (*EL*, 187–95).[20] In an important sense, Weil's thinking on mystical faith and war culminates in the nurses project.

Weil's aim was the creation of a special corps of women medical workers prepared to serve on the very front line of battle, intervening with first aid to the wounded directly under enemy fire. The group of women would find itself "always in the most perilous locations" and would expect to "face as great or greater dangers" than the soldiers engaged in combat (*EL*, 188–89).[21] Weil emphasized the strategic advantages that the creation of the corps of nurses — at first on a small, "experimental" basis — could be expected to bring with it. Citing reports from the American College of Surgeons and the Red Cross, she argued that immediate medical aid on the front lines could sharply reduce the number of battlefield deaths due to shock, exposure, and hemorrhage (195). A positive effect on troop morale could also be expected. The difficulties and risks of the effort, on the other hand, would be minor from a military point of view. A group of just ten women would be sufficient for a "first try." Even if casualties among the nurses turned out to be heavy, the losses would be "minute in terms of numbers, on the scale of the war; one can say negligible" (189).

Of course, it was not only other women's lives that Weil was intending to put at risk, but in the first place her own. Though her description of the project does not say so explicitly, there is no doubt Weil saw herself as the group's natural leader.[22] Weil had taken Red Cross first aid courses in Paris and then again in New York (*SP* II, 430). She could hardly boast extensive medical experience, but in her proposal Weil was careful to stress that for women seeking to participate in this special unit, advanced medical knowledge was less important than "moral qualities" and the willingness to face danger (*EL*, 188).

Anticipating likely objections to the plan, Weil insisted: "In a general manner there is no reason to regard the life of a woman [...] as more precious than the life of a man; still less so if she accepts the risk of death. It would be very easy to exclude from such a group mothers, wives, and girls under a certain age limit" (*EL*, 189). This passage and the nurses proposal as a whole exhibit Weil's peculiar penchant for simultaneously endorsing cultural stereotypes regarding women and subversively bending those stereotypes to her own rebellious ends. Weil scorned the notion that her life was inherently "precious" because she was a woman. Weil was fully cognizant that such value was attributed to women's lives and bodies precisely in order to deprive women of autonomy. A body/life so precious to society could not simply be left to its owner to do with as she pleased. Accepting the implicit definition of her life as valuable (social) property, a woman forfeited the right to decide for herself when and how to protect her body and under what circumstances it could legitimately be placed at risk.

In the nurses group Weil sought to bring together a small contingent of women united in their refusal of this pattern. The nurses would defy conventional understandings of the limits of appropriate feminine roles when it came to dangerous political and military tasks. Traditional feminine norms and functions are indeed evoked in the nurses document. Yet when they first appear, it is to serve as a negative criterion, a ground for exclusion from the corps. The people most apt for participation in the nurses group would be single women possessing demonstrated qualities of courage and *"sang-froid"* (*EL,* 194) who had passed beyond their "first youth without becoming a wife or mother" (189). Thus, participants would be women who had matured without entering into the socially sanctioned arrangements — marriage and motherhood — by which women were conventionally expected to define themselves and their life goals. Not coincidentally, the ideal candidates would be women precisely matching Simone Weil's own social profile.

Yet while wives and mothers were barred from the special corps, the symbolic dimension of the nurses' function — for Weil its most crucial aspect — involved providing a living "tableau" expressive of "maternal tenderness" and of the Allied soldiers' "peaceful home" (*EL,* 193). It was neither possible nor desirable to turn French, British, and American soldiers into fanatical killing machines like those who filled the ranks of Hitler's armies, young men uprooted from their families from childhood onward and trained exclusively for war, permitted no sense of the "value of a home." But a passionate commitment to victory could be instilled in the Allied fighters precisely by "making the homes they defend as intensely present as possible in their minds," through potent symbols present on the battlefield itself. The nurses would be these symbols. "For this purpose," Weil wrote in the project document she sent to Schumann, "what could be better" than to have the Allied fighters "accompanied under enemy fire, amid scenes of the greatest brutality, by something that constitutes a living evocation of the homes they have had to leave behind: not a saddening evocation, but an exalting one? [. . .] This female corps would constitute precisely that concrete and exalting evocation" (193–94).

An ironic strategy determined Weil's rhetorical valorization of those "feminine" values and functions — marriage, home, "maternal tenderness" — that she herself had consistently and rebelliously rejected throughout her life. In the document submitted to the Free French authorities, Weil praised marriage and motherhood precisely in order to exclude wives and mothers from consideration for her corps of nurses. Conformity to the socially sacrosanct values of marriage and family precluded integration into the activity Weil herself regarded as genuinely sacred. Meanwhile, however, the assumed endpoint of Weil's sacred activity was voluntary death.

The "project for a formation of frontline nurses" provoked consternation among some of Weil's colleagues and superiors in the Free French organization, though the plan had its defenders.[23] More recent commentators have also been divided in their interpretations: some praising the heroism the nurses project exhibits, others reading it as a symptom of Weil's hubris or of an unbalanced mental state. Whatever one's assessment of Weil's mental condition in the last months of her life, I believe it is clear that the nurses scheme is no wild, aberrant impulse, but a project perfectly consistent with Weil's scrupulously reasoned religious and political teachings. Indeed, the project for a formation of frontline nurses crystallizes decisive aspects of Weil's thought, forging a synthesis of her most important (and, to some, most troubling) ideas. First, the nurses would translate belief into concrete action. Second, fulfilling their duty on the front lines of battle, the women would inevitably encounter extreme affliction, but would not cultivate affliction gratuitously. Third, the group of nurses would enact and be bonded by the spiritual consent to death. Finally, the nurses' gesture would fuse religious meaning and political efficacy in an act of poetic, performative power. We will consider these facets of Weil's project briefly, in turn.

From early in her career, Weil had maintained that ideas and beliefs are only meaningful to the extent that they inform concrete action. The principle was not, of course, original; to Weil it was one of those truths whose very obviousness makes them easy to ignore. Though often perceived as a "disembodied," dualistic thinker, Weil insisted tirelessly that the touchstone of philosophical and religious truth lay in the body and in the actions the body carries out (or fails to) under the impact of particular ideas. The more noble, elevated, and "spiritual" the principles involved, moreover, the more urgent the requirement to subject them to the test of bodily action. Nothing is easier than to hold idealistic religious views and generous ethical convictions as long as they remain merely a matter of private sentiment or abstract talk. When the stakes are raised to involve concrete consequences for the body of the believer, philosophical and religious thought shifts to an entirely new plane of seriousness.

When they are authentic, the love of God and the love of wisdom are practices in which the body is centrally engaged. In an entry near the end of her London notebook, Weil compared the cultivation of wisdom to physical activities such as sports, which have no meaning — indeed no existence — apart from the bodily habits and disciplines through which they are performed. "Philosophy (including problems of cognition, etc.), a thing *exclusively* in act and practice. That is why it is so difficult to write about it. Difficult in the manner of a treatise on tennis or running, but much more so" (*CS*, 335). Philosophy has no substance, no reality apart from the concrete patterns of behavior that it makes possible. Similarly, it is only through bodily action that religious ideas and values leave the shadowy realm of the imagination. A moral or religious motive is "only real in the soul when it has provoked an action executed by the body" (*E*, 256).

Discussing the "inspiration" the Free French movement must manifest to the people of France, Weil affirms: "Of course, it is not a matter of verbal inspiration. All real inspiration passes into the muscles and comes out in actions" (*E*, 251). The nurses project represented the means to realize — by translating them into embodied, "muscular" action — the mystical virtues Weil had cultivated and the ideas with which she had filled her notebooks: courage, compassion, charity, the "spirit of sacrifice" (*EL,* 192, 196), the "supernatural faculty" of being able to "step outside oneself [*sortir de soi*]" (*CS,* 335). That the nurses' task was to care for wounded bodies enhanced the project's spiritual value. Spiritual renunciation was fostered primarily not by edifying discourses, but by "serving others in their bodily needs." "To serve [others] freely in their needs as creatures is the best way" to purify one's own soul and to propagate the ideal of spiritual detachment (*CS,* 170; cf. *EL,* 77–79).

Weil was haunted by the simultaneous convictions that affliction was the key to the deepest levels of spiritual truth and that authentic affliction could not be chosen. The very definition of affliction postulated that it must be imposed on the subject against his/her will. Suffering must not be sought out with the express purpose of furthering one's own spiritual development. An action like that of the frontline nurses, however, by bringing into play notions of duty and obligation, offered a structure within which Weil believed it was legitimate to expose oneself to extreme forms of danger and pain. For in an important sense, according to Weil's analysis, she herself would not be personally *choosing* affliction by placing herself in the reach of enemy fire. Her actions under these circumstances would be determined by obedience to duty: that is, to obligations taken on with respect to the military authorities, to the suffering human beings she was called to serve, and to the ideal of the good.

In a letter to Schumann, Weil explained her views on affliction and its relationship to necessity and obligation: "If affliction were defined by pain and death, it would have been easy for me, when I was in France, to fall into the hands of the enemy. But [affliction] is defined first by necessity. One submits to it only by accident or by obligation." Obligation, however, required an "occasion to accomplish it" (*EL,* 214). Weil saw such an occasion in the frontline nurses plan: the opportunity to be placed "physically in affliction" (213), not by a personal whim but by the irrecusable demands of duty. On the battlefield, facing affliction's "extreme forms," Weil would at last reach the end of her long "wait for truth" (213).

The nurses program involved not merely action, but action implying the danger (if not certainty) of death. Far from detracting from its appeal, in Weil's view this sacrificial aspect constituted the project's decisive virtue. Weil saw in the proposed program an opportunity to enact in spectacular fashion the "consent to death" that was the heart of mystical wisdom and the precondition of authentic holiness.

As we have seen, Weil considered the attitude toward death the crucial test of philosophical insight and religious purity. "The saints are those who while still alive have really consented to death" (*CS*, 325). Weil's writings on the nurses corps do not employ the term "saint." But her description of the volunteers' psychological profile shows Weil believed successful recruits would be women consciously or unconsciously aspiring to holiness. Before placing themselves in the combat situation, Weil stressed, the nurses "would have to have made the sacrifice of their lives" (*EL*, 189). Inner "sacrifice" or spiritual consent to death was the primary prerequisite for potential volunteers. The women would then carry this contemplative renunciation into the realm of overt action, consummating their mystical detachment through the offering of their bodies. They would enact spiritual transformation as a physical and political event, showing how authentic religious inspiration expresses itself in bodily engagement. Where Bataille's mysticism turned away from the war in order to contest its utilitarian logic, Weil's mystical impulses drove her forward to use war itself as an instrument of spiritual purification and of ascetic self-fashioning. With her plan for the frontline nurses, Weil aimed to transform war into a sacrificial ceremony unleashing decreative mystical power at the same time that it furnished a politically and militarily dynamizing "inspiration" (191–92) that would galvanize the Allies' effective resistance to Nazi violence.

Performing Sacrifice

The number of lives saved through the efforts of the frontline nurses would be, Weil acknowledged, modest. Yet the project was not to be evaluated merely on the basis of its usefulness in medical terms. According to Weil, the principal benefit of the nurses' work would come in another area, one that would ultimately prove even more important for the Allied war effort. The frontline nurses' most crucial function was one of communication or "representation" (*EL*, 193).[24] The women's decisive contribution would be "symbolic" (193).

To characterize the nurses' effort as symbolic was not to minimize, but instead to underscore its importance. The creation and exchange of symbols determine human existence in its most vital aspects. And for Weil symbolic processes were never more crucial than in war. The outcome of the conflict with Nazi Germany hinged not just on battlefield tactics, arsenals, and industrial power, but on the capacity of the respective sides to generate potent symbols. As Weil had recognized in her essay on the *Iliad* and in her study of the concept of reading, war was a struggle for influence over minds just as much as an encounter of bodies and weapons. The nurses would play a role in shaping how the war was "read" by all parties involved; and to alter people's readings was palpably to influence the course of political and military events.

In this sense Weil spoke of the nurses' formation as fulfilling a "propaganda" function (*EL*, 192). In modern warfare, propaganda, the systematic molding of beliefs and motivations, is not a minor strategic device but an "essential factor" of victory (192). Thus the nurses, despite being noncombatants, could make a contribution of the "first importance" for the "general conduct of the war" (190).

In Hitler, the Allies faced an opponent whose genius lay in his grasp of the decisive role of propaganda in politics and warfare. Hitler had recognized the necessity not only of constructing a powerful military machine, but of using might in such a way as to "strike the imagination" of his own followers and his enemies (*EL*, 191). Much of Hitler's military success, Weil argued, stemmed in reality from his expert manipulation of images and ideas. Hitler had grasped instinctively the vital lesson that communication was not strictly a matter of words. Propaganda exerted its full force when it linked words to impressive images and spectacular actions. The Allies would have to learn and apply this lesson in their turn.

Already at the beginning of the war, Weil had noted that "Our propaganda cannot be made of words; to be effective it would have to be composed of dazzling realities [*réalités éclatantes*]" (*WOC* 2.3, 118).

The most potent means of communication and persuasion is not words but acts. Thus the form of German propaganda that "struck the imagination" most powerfully was not, according to Weil, Hitler's vehement speeches or the mass rallies at Nuremberg. The supreme form of Nazi symbolism came in the battlefield actions of special military formations "animated by a spirit of total sacrifice" (*EL*, 192). These elite formations included "the SS, the groups of parachutists who were the first to penetrate into Crete, and others" (191). Such groups are made up of "men chosen for special tasks, ready not merely to risk their lives, but to die" (191). The consent to death, fearlessly acted upon, was in Weil's eyes "the essential." The elite groups were "animated by an inspiration different from the mass of the army," an inspiration that resembled a "religious spirit" (191) and that lent the special formations an aura of sacred force. The elite troops did more than talk about readiness for sacrifice. They demonstrated that readiness in dazzling acts, consenting to death for the glory of the Reich. This consent transformed groups like the SS from mere soldiers into living symbols. Such troops become the precise (diabolical) equivalent of the religious "saints" Weil discussed, whose consenting obedience to the divine will is maintained even in death. The actions of Hitler's picked troops ascribed to the Führer more persuasively than any number of eloquent speeches the godlike capacity to command a loyalty stronger than death itself.

Victory for the Allies could depend, Weil argued, on "the presence among us of an analogous, but authentic and pure, inspiration" (*EL*, 192). The frontline nurses would call forth this "pure inspiration," constituting an equivalent on the Allied side of the SS and other Nazi elite formations. The nurses would signify (by embodying) the "spirit of sacrifice" (191–92) that the Allies must summon to achieve victory. Yet the nurses would represent an authentic religious emotion, in contrast to the Nazis' "ersatz of religious faith" (192). Where the SS draw their force from hatred, the frontline nurses would represent heroic action empowered by the opposite values: compassion, respect for human dignity, love of life. The frontline nurses on one side and the SS on the other "would make by their opposition a tableau preferable to any slogan. It would be the clearest possible representation of the two directions between which today humanity must choose" (193).

The almost certain death of the women involved was an acceptable price at which to purchase the creation of such a compelling symbol. Indeed, the communicative force of the "tableau" clearly depended on the nurses' genuine martyrdom. The spirit of absolute sacrifice that animated the women could only exert its influence over friends and foes if their sacrifice were carried through to the end. Weil envisaged this necessity with equanimity. The nurses' deaths would be consented to; therein lay their symbolic efficacy. But this consent was also the wellspring of a redemptive power that embraced but reached far beyond strictly military and political considerations. To be killed while maintaining an attitude of consent to the destruction one knew to be the will of God: this was the way of saintliness, the crowning of the mystical ascent.

The annihilation of the self, rehearsed in prayer and mystical experience, achieved completion on the battlefield, where suffering reached its pinnacle in death. "By dint of suffering, one wears out the *I*, and one abolishes it when the suffering goes all the way to death" (C2, 232). Weil's practice of mystical purification found its culmination here: in the image of the frontline nurses in which death became redemptive sacrifice, mystical truth became action, and action became "representation," communication, poetic creation.

The Art of Dying

The death Weil imagined for herself with the frontline nurses was crafted as an aesthetic work. The image of this death was not a momentary morbid fancy, but the fruit of years of sustained reflection. In it, Weil saw the culmination of the pattern of meaning she had discerned in (or imposed on) her life from early youth. Such a sacrificial climax presented itself to Weil as the divinely inspired, transfiguring conclusion of the composition that was her life.

Weil was deeply and passionately responsive to the beauty of art, affirming that works of beauty incarnate the real presence of God in the material world.[25] But she claimed that human life itself could be practiced as the highest form of art. Her aim was to "make of life itself the supreme poetry" (*WOC* 6.1, 424). Describing St. Francis of Assisi, Weil wrote: "Not only is his poem perfect poetry, but his whole life was perfect poetry in action. [. . .] Wandering and poverty were poetry for him" (*AD*, 119). The stuff of life itself, Weil believed, could and ought to be formed by an artistic labor like that practiced by a poet on the raw material of language or by a sculptor shaping a block of stone. The person should study, mold, and order the stuff of her or his own character and actions: selecting, refining, rigorously eliminating flaws, until the form of the human existence bodied forth an ideal of beauty (inseparable in Weil's mind from the moral good). Weil wrote of an "art whose medium [*matière*] is life" and that is "analogous" to art in the conventional sense, "but much more powerful" (*C2*, 173). From an early point, Weil regarded her own existence in this light, as a project or text. She sought to compose her life as a meaningful work with an orderly, coherent structure. In a letter to Albertine Thévenon probably written in 1935, Weil stated: "Maybe you don't know what it's like to imagine your whole life in front of you, and to make the firm and constant decision to make something out of it, to orient it from one end to the other by will and work, in a fixed direction. [. . .] Me, I'm like that" (*CO*, 18; cited in *SP* II, 485).

Weil's determination to author her life as a coherent work was complicated but simultaneously reinforced by the insights on the limitation of human agency that emerged out of her factory experience and her religious conversion. In the years after 1938, the idea became increasingly central for Weil that God, not the human individual, must be the author of any genuinely good human life, shaping its substance, "orient[ing] it from one end to the other [. . .] in a fixed direction," toward the love of the good. Weil's ideal now came to be described in terms not of individual human autonomy, but of complete obedience to the will of God. However, this shift increased, rather than lessening, the significance of the metaphor of poetic composition as an image for understanding how human existence should be conducted. For the truly great poet was, Weil maintained, not one whose creations sprang from his/her own imagination, but one who followed obediently an inspiration emanating from the divine, that is, from a source beyond and infinitely superior to the human personality and its resources. Great poetry, great art in general, was not a personal achievement, but — precisely — an exercise in pure receptivity and obedience to an impersonal inspiration. In literature as in the solving of mathematical equations, the personal was the source of error; pure beauty — like mathematical accuracy, like genuine, unselfish love — resulted from obedience to an impersonal principle (see *EL*, 17). Thus, poetic composition could continue after Weil's conversion to figure properly ordered human existence, once it was clearly grasped that God himself was the "supreme poet" (*CS*, 150) and human beings merely God's instruments, whose essential function was one of self-emptying, not assertive agency. This was the sense of Weil's repeated use of the metaphor of herself as a "pen" held by God (e.g., 81). The truly great human poet was the one who consented to be nothing: that is, to be nothing else than God's pen, a passive tool obediently tracing an inscription whose source was supernatural. The same principle applied to life.

This conception of God as the poet or artist shaping the material of a human life did not, however, lessen Weil's anxiety at the thought that she could fail in the execution of her vocation. Just as it was always possible for poets to write bad verses by failing to open themselves to the higher, impersonal inspiration, so it was entirely possible for human beings to fail in the composition of their lives through cowardice or disobedience. In life as in art, God offered inspiration but did not impose it. Human freedom was exercised in submission to or refusal of inspiration. One was as free to lead a flawed and mediocre life as to write flawed and mediocre poetry. One had to "earn" by dint of love the right to be subjected to a divinely ordained moral "constraint," in the same way one had to earn the highest forms of poetic inspiration through the exercise of humble attention (*C2*, 183).

Aesthetic and moral failure had a common source in the disobedient refusal to submit to the divine; Weil believed she herself was in such a state of disobedience as her stay in London prolonged itself in the early months of 1943. Weil's initial joy at reaching

Britain turned to deepening anxiety. It appeared more and more clear that the Free French authorities had no intention of letting her carry out her plan for the formation of frontline nurses or of allowing her to participate in any other dangerous mission. A letter Weil wrote to Schumann in early 1943 poignantly reveals the depth of her anguish in this situation.[26] Weil was convinced that her inability to persuade the French leadership of the value of the plan meant that she had failed in her spiritual vocation. Such a defeat imposed psychological torment and remorse Weil described to Schumann, in words not chosen lightly, as "worse than hell" (*EL,* 204). She predicted that the anguish and guilt that crushed her would soon lead to a state of total physical and psychological collapse, if she were not at last allowed to participate in a dangerous operation of the type represented by the nurses plan (212–13).

The stakes were so high for Weil precisely because of her belief that God wished to "write" her life in a particular way and charge it with a particular and potent meaning. The composition of her life was a divine work in which she was called to collaborate, a text dictated by God that it was her task to transcribe faithfully. Her existence was, or could be, an example of that "art" in which the substance of human destiny was endowed with a sacramental quality and became a means "to touch eternity" (*C2,* 173). Weil did not hesitate to affirm to Schumann that in pursuing the nurses project and her other plans for dangerous war missions, she was following a vocation imparted directly by God (*EL,* 203). She was persuaded that the type of death that awaited her with the frontline nurses corresponded to God's design for the final moments of her existence: a death that would be sacrifice and poetry, the enactment and communication of religious truth. Thus Rachel Feldhay Brenner is not mistaken in labeling the nurses project a proposal for a "human sacrifice."[27] Weil saw this sacrificial gesture as aesthetically necessary, politically liberatory, and divinely ordained.

Just as in a poem the final lines determine the value and impact of the whole text, so in a human life the concluding episode, death, is the most important. Death holds the key to the meaning of human life in its entirety. Realizing this is essential to making a "right use of death" and exploiting death's potential as our "greatest gift" (*CS,*

250). Death tests human values and commitments more rigorously than any other phenomenon and thus reveals truth with unexcelled clarity. "Reality appears only to him who accepts death" (250), while the "instant of death" demands to be regarded as "the norm and the goal of life" (*AD*, 33). This was why, Weil explained to Schumann, "Even when I was a child, and believed I was an atheist and materialist, I always had within myself the fear of failing, not in my life, but in my death. This fear has never ceased becoming more and more intense" (*EL*, 213).

God's purpose for her, Weil affirmed, involved precisely the culmination represented by the nurses project and by the death she could expect to encounter if the project were carried through. This sacrificial-symbolic death would complete and crown the composition of Weil's life. Her consented death with the frontline nurses would be a testament of love: a supreme poetic act, a potent inscription of religious desire, a revelation and affirmation of the saving power of sacrifice. In the final spasm of affliction, Weil would grasp truth, communicate truth, become truth. It was not only ironically Weil compared herself to Sophocles' Antigone (*SL*, 161). Weil's death would transmute and elevate a human existence into the substance of the tragic poetry she revered (the Sophoclean dramas, the *Iliad, Prometheus Bound,* the Passion narratives in the Gospels): poems of suffering undergone by lucid obedience to ineluctable necessity. Weil aimed to write such a death for herself, to transfigure the violence of war through spiritual consent, liberating redemptive power for the good of her country.

The "Real Metaphor"

Weil's late notebooks contain references to a concept that crystallizes what she may have hoped to achieve by offering her life with the nurses on the front lines of battle. This is the notion of the "real metaphor" [*la métaphore réelle*].

"The story of the Christ is a symbol," Weil wrote, "a metaphor. But in other times it was believed that metaphors occur as events in the world" (*CS*, 149). Religious people in other (for Weil, wiser) times considered that metaphor and thus meaning were not restricted to the domain of human discourse. Figures and events that "occur in the world" as parts of our real lives are also charged with meaning in complex ways, to which modern theories of knowledge have generally failed to do justice. In some cases it is possible to read these figures and events as metaphors inscribed in the substance of our material lives by God. Yet whether or not one acknowledges God as "supreme poet" (*CS*, 150), it is vital for epistemological and for practical political purposes to understand that we inhabit a world not of neutral objects but of living symbols, in which acts and appearances carry meanings we cannot do otherwise than "read" (*ENL*).

"We must rediscover the notion of the real metaphor," Weil asserts. "Otherwise the story of the Christ, for example, loses either its reality or its meaning" (*CS*, 163). As Max Weber showed, the disenchanted worldview of modernity is based on the idea that reality (the bare fact of something's existing) and meaning are categorially unrelated. Where the "primitive" mind discerned inherent significance in all types of objects and occurrences, modern understanding assumes that natural phenomena and nondiscursive human behavior possess no such intrinsic meaning. The only sense they have is the sense we give them, through patterns and practices that are contingent and in essence arbitrary. It is just this radical disjunction between "reality and meaning" that Simone Weil seeks to contest with her notion of the real metaphor. Weil's theory of perception as reading does recognize, of course, that our intelligence plays an active role in interpreting experience, that we project meanings (often wrong meanings) into appearances: for example, when on a dark path we "read" a tree as a lurking attacker (*ENL*, 17). Yet precisely the fact that it is possible to uncover certain readings as false shows that reading is not an arbitrary process. The relationship between our perceptual processes and patterns of meaning in the world is more complicated than the epistemological theories associated with modern physical and social science have acknowledged. The world speaks to us, bringing to light embedded meanings that challenge and transform our initial judgments (calling for corresponding changes in our practice).

This is patent in the area of our readings of human action. All action, according to Weil, is communication and in that sense "metaphor." Yet the richest and most important symbolic actions involve meanings that go beyond the conscious intentions and capacities of either actors or interpreters. Some human actions (those informed by the good) transcribe patterns of spiritual truth belonging to a higher realm. The episodes of a saintly life unite in themselves reality and meaning in this impersonal dimension. The events of Christ's Passion or of the lives of saints are real, factual. Yet they contain meaning not simply as an external, arbitrary quality assigned (read in) by interpreters, nor yet as a moral message the actors consciously sought to convey, but as an infused poetic structure invested in them by God. The events of these lives in fact constitute the primary mode of God's self-communication, the poetic medium (cf. *CS*, 150) through which the divine reveals and opens itself to human understanding and human love. To recover the capacity for discerning and interpreting such metaphors is necessary, Weil argues, if we are to grasp the full implications of our own moral and political acts: not only their immediate, pragmatic impact but their relation to patterns of spiritual value and cosmic law.

The "story of the Christ" (*CS*, 149) represented for Weil the key instance of such divine poetry. In the Incarnation, the Word became flesh, while human flesh was simultaneously transfigured as Logos, the Word of God. In Jesus' life and Passion, the events of a human destiny became the metaphors and symbols through which the divine communicated itself to the world. Yet if the story of Jesus was the decisive "example" (163) of the "real metaphor," it was not the only such example. This fact held deep significance for Weil's theology, moral thought, and politics. In Weil's view, Christians were to respond to the metaphor of Jesus' life not merely with passive admiration, but with active imitation. To learn to read spiritual metaphors, including the story of Christ, was just the beginning. Christians had to *become* real metaphors themselves. The point was not merely to grasp a discursive content, but to set forward a process of poetic communication, of writing, in and with the substance of one's own life.

The thrust of Weil's notion of the real metaphor is thus not only epistemological but political. Her thinking blurs the distinction between "real" political action and performance. For Weil, all action must be understood as symbolic, performative. This in no way denies the importance of concrete practical effects as a criterion for judging actions. Yet Weil believes conventional notions of the relevant "effects" of political action must be broadened. It is vital to distinguish between good and bad, effective and ineffectual actions. But evaluation must take into account the symbolic-performative dimension, that is, how actions are *read*. Thus Weil argues that the acts carried out by the Resistance (including her own proposed nurses project) are important not only for their immediate strategic impact, but as means of advancing the political "education of the country": nurturing the motives and collective feelings that will sustain further struggle (*E, 240*).

Christ's life as spiritual and political *"métaphore réelle"* sets in motion a multilayered sacrificial mimesis, in which the original model generates ever-renewed forms of imitation. A late passage of the London notebook delves further into the question of what it means to "take Christ as a model." Again, Weil appeals to artistic practice (in this case painting or drawing) to clarify the proper human attitude toward God's self-revelation in Christ:

> To take Christ as a model. Not by saying to oneself: he did such and such a thing, so...
>
> A bad painter looks at the young woman who is posing and says to himself: "She has a high forehead, arched eyebrows; I must put on the canvas a high forehead, arched eyebrows, etc...."
>
> A real painter, by dint of attention, is what he looks at. During this time his hand moves, with a brush at the end.
>
> Even more obvious for the drawings of Rembrandt. He thinks Tobias and the angel, and his hand moves.
>
> This is how Christ must be our model. [...]
>
> To think Christ with all one's soul. — And during this time, the intelligence, the will, etc., and the body act. (*CS, 334*; unbracketed ellipses in original)

To imitate Christ is to become Christ through pure attention. Not by reproducing mechanically gestures and words associated with the biblical Jesus, but by allowing one's soul to be filled with the thought of Christ and then taking the actions that this thought allows one to discern as necessary. Mind and heart saturated with the thought of Christ, the body moves; in this way one creates works (actions) that are "true" imitations of Christ, in which his spirit is authentically present. The essential factors are the inward attention that establishes contact with the divine and the outward action — movement of the body — that mediates and communicates this contact, allows it to impact and transform the world.[28] The virtue of the real metaphor lies in its ability to inspire such imitation, to continually engender further incarnations of itself. Such imitations will both preserve the metaphor's essential spirit and adapt that spirit to new historical tasks. This inscription of spiritual meaning in the material and political world was Weil's aim with the frontline nurses. Weil hoped her action would faithfully translate divine inspiration (though she acknowledged there could be no guarantees). As "wandering and poverty" had been "perfect poetry" in St. Francis, Weil's self-giving on the battlefield, the culmination of a life-long pursuit of "spiritual poverty" (*EL*, 104–5), would inscribe in poetic action a "sensible sign" (*C3*, 57) of divine love.

Death and Writing

Weil was denied the opportunity to transform her life (and death) into "poetry" in the way she had wished: sacrificing herself with the frontline nurses or on a suicidal sabotage mission in occupied territory. Arriving in London, Weil had been determined to break out of the limits imposed on her as an intellectual and as a woman and to participate actively, physically, in the dangers of the war effort. Not the smallest (nor for Weil the least bitter) irony of her career was the fact that, having vowed to give herself bodily to the struggle against Hitler, hoping to nurse the wounded under fire or parachute behind enemy lines, she spent her months with the Free French organization in a cozy office, reading and writing. As a *rédactrice,* her tasks were those not of a heroic shaper of "dazzling realities," but once again of a trafficker in mere words.

Of such words Weil produced in the months from January to April 1943 a quantity nothing short of prodigious. Writing was not the job she craved, but she gave herself to the task with a kind of fury. In London Weil authored not only the forceful essays collected posthumously in *Écrits de Londres,* including "La Personne et le sacré," but also the texts later published as *The Need for Roots,* a large number of papers addressing the reorganization of French political life and society after the war, a translation of selections from the Upanishads, a penetrating and provocative analysis of Marxism ("Y a-t-il une doctrine marxiste?"), and lengthy discussions of religious and theological questions.[29] In all, by David McLellan's reckoning, Weil produced in four months the equivalent of roughly eight hundred printed pages.[30] The manuscripts show that Weil's handwriting flowed with an almost supernatural steadiness, rapidity, and assurance in this period: page after page streaming out virtually without hesitations or corrections. She often worked around the clock, staying through the night at the office in Hill Street or walking home long after the last Underground train and continuing to work in her apartment for several more hours, all the while coughing steadily and violently. The force and substance of her life were poured in an almost literal way into the writing that filled her notebooks, in a procedure reminiscent of the transmutations and requalifications of matter and energy on which she speculated obsessively in her metaphysical texts. The physical collapse that occurred on April 15, 1943, was surprising only in having been so long in coming (see *SP* II, 492). Weil had written herself to the brink of death.

Weil was diagnosed with tuberculosis in both lungs, but the disease was at an early stage, and she was told her prognosis for recovery was good, given absolute rest and proper nourishment. However, she refused — or was to some degree physically unable — to take food in anything approaching the quantities her doctors insisted were required. Her condition remained initially static, then declined rapidly. To some friends and visitors, Weil said she could not allow herself to eat more than people in France, who were living under a regime of strict rationing. (Weil appears to have exaggerated to herself the severity of the rationing system in place in France at the time.) After roughly four months in the Middlesex Hospital, Weil was transferred to the Grosvenor Sanatorium in Ashford, Kent, in a condition that was clearly virtually hopeless. Weil had refused the pneumothorax operation in which her doctor at Middlesex had seen the best (and perhaps the last) chance for her recovery.

Whether Weil consciously sought to die is a question to which it is not possible to give an unequivocal response. In the later stages of her illness, she was at the very least indifferent to her chances of survival (*SP* II, 503–4). She was determined to share the suffering and hunger she believed to be those of ordinary people in France, though depriving herself of food put her life at risk, and she was aware of this fact. Weil understood the danger and accepted it from the moment it appeared this solitary sacrifice might rewrite the more spectacular self-oblation she had been unable to carry out on the battlefield.

It was not Weil's lot to be martyred like her heroine Joan of Arc, her body given to the flames at the hands of her country's enemies. Yet she could still allow (and will) her flesh to be consumed from within by the flame of hunger, fusing her body and spirit with those of the French men and women who were suffering, she believed, similar forms of deprivation. The inner fire of desire could still bring about a "transubstantiation" (*C2*, 210–11): action into communication; suffering flesh into moral exhortation; death into poetry.[31]

Mary Dietz has argued that by taking upon herself physically the hunger and pain of those in France, Weil may have felt she could focus compassionate spiritual attention on her wounded country and aid — symbolically but also literally — in France's spiritual rebirth.[32] This interpretation corresponds to Weil's notion of action as language and her teaching on economies of energy and the energy-collecting function of words, objects, and symbols. Attention was for Weil an objective, transforming force; she may have felt that energy focused on France through compassionate attention to and identification with the nation's anguish would concretely strengthen the nation's soul and aid in its healing. At the same time, the suffering of certain human beings possessed in Weil's eyes expiatory and in some cases redemptive qualities that could apply not only to the individual, but to the destiny of a wider community. The mimetic-expiatory economy of sacrifice was real for Weil. She had pronounced herself willing to act as a sacrificial "scapegoat" in the service of her country. In a letter referring to her scheme to be parachuted into France on a suicidal Resistance mission, Weil had written: "[T]he proposition [. . .] of the scapegoat [. . .] is an easy one for me. It implies nothing more than was incumbent on me in any case."[33]

As Weil's furious writing throughout her time in England had been a sacrifice of her vital substance, a willed transformation of her own flesh and energy into words, so her death, the final expenditure of energy and withdrawal into silence, remained a defiant *"écriture auto-sacrificielle"* (to adapt a phrase from Jean-Michel Heimonet).[34] In one of her final letters (to Closon), Weil herself commented on the degree to which the act of writing drained and absorbed her vital forces. Referring to her impassioned eight-page epistle, Weil observed: "Such a letter, in my condition, is madness. But it had to be written" (*SP* II, 508). The same appraisal could apply to all of Weil's literary output in London, to her oeuvre as a whole, and perhaps to her entire life. That life was relentless hunger for the impossible: a kind of madness, surely. But Weil's madness was (also) metaphor: a poetic figure, a sacred ceremony, an effort of communication. Her mad life, the "real metaphor," had to be written.

The final paragraphs of the same letter show that Weil had not entirely given up thinking about the future, despite her broken physical condition. But writing and death formed the horizon of that future. If she were to recover partially, Weil told Closon, she intended to "devote the small quantity of energy and life thus accorded" either to "writing [*rédiger*] what I've got in my belly" or else "to an activity in the cannon-fodder category" (cited in *SP* II, 509). Writing or sacrificial death were the two options Weil imagined for herself, if some usable portion of her health were restored. She expressed no preference for one possibility over the other. Perhaps because the two paths were in reality only one.

Ambiguities of Sacrifice

Some commentators have claimed that Weil's nurses plan — and perhaps her intellectual and political project as a whole — expressed a suicidal impulse commanded by crippling self-hate.

Weil's hatred of self is seen as linked to her Jewishness, on the one hand, and to her identity as a woman, on the other.[35] Rachel Brenner has argued this position in a forceful fashion. Brenner's discussion pays particular attention to Weil's plans for taking part in the war effort. Brenner proposes that Weil's "twofold self-denial communicates [her] uprootedness in a social system that estranged her as a woman and as a Jew" and argues that this self-denial culminates in Weil's "suicidal death."[36] For Brenner, Weil's demand for an active — if possible, fatal — assignment in the Resistance effort reflects a "two-pronged attempt to attain legitimacy" by erasing "femininity and Jewishness." Weil's "obsession to act in the Resistance coalesces with the compulsion to be baptized. Had these intentions been realized, Weil's transformation into a Christian martyr-soldier would have blotted out her 'otherness.' " This action, even as it ended her life, would at last have placed Weil "at the centre" of the Christian, male-dominated society "to which she wished to belong."[37]

Like Paul Giniewski's *Simone Weil, ou la haine de soi*, Brenner's reading focuses attention on aspects often left out of earlier, quasi-hagiographic accounts of Weil's thought and life. These themes, Weil's anti-Semitism and what has been termed her misogyny, are clearly relevant to an overall assessment of Weil's accomplishment as a thinker. Brenner argues persuasively that Weil internalized socially prevalent prejudices against Judaism and against women and that these factors combined with psychological conflicts of a more personal nature to create grave blind spots in Weil's liberative vision. Brenner juxtaposes Weil's attitude to that of Edith Stein, another intellectually gifted Jewish woman who underwent a conversion to Christianity in the same period. In contrast to Weil, Brenner argues, Stein was able to affirm Judaism and her own Jewishness even as she embraced Christianity, thus moving toward an "inner wholeness."[38] Weil, meanwhile, unable to resolve her psychological and social contradictions, was driven to a "rebellion of self-destruction." The "subtext" of Weil's provocative social and political activities "reveals an intensifying disposition toward dramatic self-sacrificial destruction." Moreover, "Weil did not want to die unnoticed. Her death, as she imagined it, was to be a spectacle of absolute fearlessness and selflessness."[39]

One must acknowledge the persuasive force of Brenner's argument that self-hatred was among the causal strands (conscious or unconscious) motivating Weil's determination to obtain a war mission that would expose her to the danger of death. Yet while Brenner's reading offers valuable insights, it also leaves important issues insufficiently addressed. It reveals some of the private demons and obsessions Weil grappled with in seeking to engage herself in the war effort. Yet, as Richard Bell contends, Brenner's account pointedly neglects what may be Weil's "central moral and political view," that is, the primacy of limitless obligation to the afflicted other.[40] And Brenner fails to acknowledge clearly enough that Weil was fighting not only her own mental phantoms, but a real and objective enemy, Nazism. It was Hitler's reign of sadistic terror Weil wanted primarily to help overthrow. By pathologizing Weil's actions, a heavily psychological reading may ironically lend support to regressive views of women as emotive beings whose behavior is generally shaped by their own *états d'âme*, rather than by the concrete demands of objective political reality.

Concentrating on the aspects of herself Weil fought against in joining the Free French movement, this interpretation fails to give sufficient attention to the causes Weil was fighting *for*. Weil was not simply seeking a random pretext for self-destruction and seizing on the Allied military struggle as the first plausible excuse. As Weil explained to Schumann, if the point had been merely to die, or even to die as a sort of martyr at the hands of the Nazis, there was no need to go as far as London. Such a fate could quite easily have been arranged in 1940, while Weil still found herself on French soil occupied by German troops. If Weil did not let herself fall into the hands of the enemy at that time, it was because she intended to make a meaningful contribution — meaningful both in terms of immediately practical military operations and of "propaganda," communication, "inspiration" (*EL,* 191) — to the war effort against Hitler.

Unhindered by the Bataillean scruple that the sacred must not be tied to utility, Weil wanted her death to have both beauty and a use. She intended for her self-expenditure to contribute to the struggle for justice, love, and human dignity. In a historical moment in which these values were under savage assault, Weil was determined to do what she could to defend them, though her mode of engagement defied conventional understandings of proper behavior for a woman. Can Weil be blamed for wanting to risk and if necessary lose her life in the struggle against Nazism? Can her reaction be diagnosed as unbalanced, the expression of a drive to "self-torture"?[41] Perhaps. But perhaps, too, the tyranny of Nazism would have claimed fewer victims in 1939–45 if more people throughout Europe and beyond had shown a similarly "tortured" compulsion to stake their lives without reserve in the fight against Hitler. Weil's "obsession to act with the Resistance"[42] may of course be judged pathological. Yet some may wish this particular obsessive pathology had been more widespread. As both Bataille and Weil grasped, there are moments when folly — the "folie d'amour" (EL, 56–57) — is more reasonable (or at least more desirable) than common sense.

Weil's hostility toward Jewish culture and womanhood must certainly be reckoned a significant and at times crippling factor in her thought and a destructive pattern in her personal existence. Yet it is possible — and just — to argue that Weil's "written" war (self-sacrifice as "supreme poetry") affirmed life-giving values of courage, compassion, and uncompromising resistance to oppression that feminists and others committed to struggles for social justice endorse. Weil's sacrificial performance must not be dismissed as simply pathological, unless one is willing to reject on the same grounds all causes and programs that claim the right to demand the sacrifice of individual lives in the service of collective liberation and the struggle against tyranny.

Few persons were less inclined than Weil to ignore the failures, abuses, and inadequacies of post-Enlightenment European civilization in general and France in particular. Yet Weil in 1942–43 was persuaded that for all their flaws, European culture and the French tradition contained spiritual treasures ("treasures of the past and anticipations of the future" [E, 61]) that, if lost, could never be recovered. Nazism was capable of eradicating these treasures and determined to do so. For Weil, this threat created a situation of moral obligation. If Weil's planned self-sacrifice was an attack against her Jewishness and her "female 'I,' "[43] it was also an attack for, a positive and committed defense of, the values she saw as menaced by Nazism: above all justice, compassion, liberty, and the duty of infinite respect toward every human being, inso- ● far as each is the bearer of an ineradicable aspiration toward the good (see *EL,* 74–79). Weil's self-sacrifice as a nurse tending the wounded on the front lines of battle was to be a text inscribing the fundamental moral principle of the primacy of the other being. The sense of Weil's text, of the poem into which she hoped to fashion her life and death, was not only destruction/decreation of her self, but radical commitment to the other.

Martyrs of Good, Saints of Evil

This chapter has emphasized the creative political significance of Simone Weil's wartime interventions, seeking to balance the disproportionately negative picture painted by some of Weil's critics. But if Weil the activist, *engagée* mystic was right (or at least more right than she is sometimes given credit for), does this mean that Bataille, adept of inner experience and rejecter of warlike action, was wrong? Should we conclude, rejoining critics like Sartre, that the commitment modeled by figures like Weil or philosopher and resistance fighter Jean Cavaillès was the proper course and Bataille's literary-mystical retreat a moral blunder?

To draw such a conclusion would be a mistake for several reasons. On one level, one might challenge the ostensible superiority of Weil's (or for that matter Sartre's) wartime attitude on purely pragmatic grounds. Weil's efforts to participate in active combat failed to produce meaningful military results; meanwhile Bataille's written performance challenged the logic of war in ways that continue to inspire substantive political debate decades after the fact. A case could surely be made for the superior political "use-value" of Bataille's provocative literary mysticism over Weil's abortive military projects. However, a different consideration is more important. To assume that a vindication of Weil's wartime attitude logically entails a condemnation of Bataille would be to reinscribe the dualistic schemas the last chapters have sought to render suspect. Weil and Bataille do not constitute two halves of an irreconcilable binary — hard-nosed *engagement* on the one hand, apolitical aestheticism on the other — between which the reader must *choisir son camp*. This book has striven to bring out the complex imbrication of politics and literary performance, aggressive commitment and religious self-stylization that both authors shared.

Of course, the temptation to read Weil and Bataille as incarnating two radically opposed political options is strong and sanctioned by Weil's own remarks in her draft letter to the Cercle communiste démocratique (see above, chapter 3). The differences between Weil's and Bataille's politics seem to have their roots at a deeper level, in the two authors' antithetical metaphysical commitments. At the center of Weil's metaphysics stands a Platonizing notion of the transcendent good, which Weil identifies with the Christian God. Bataille, meanwhile, urges an antipolitics based on what he terms evil: the transgressive force that drives the self beyond itself in ecstatic "communication."

Good and evil define an archetypal antithesis and ought by rights to correlate with irreconcilable political stances. Yet Weil's good and Bataille's evil are contraries that remain deeply intertwined. Their relation can be most fully understood by acknowledging that good and evil are two ways of naming the sacred, following the bipolar Durkheimian scheme. Hostile to each other, good and evil are bound together by an even more fundamental shared opposition to profane, homogeneous reality.

The hypothesis that good and evil are two ways of naming sacred force or a sacred attitude undergirds Bataille's argument in his 1949 review essay on Weil's *The Need for Roots*. A reading of Bataille's essay supports the view that Bataille's and Weil's positions are far from constituting a simple antithesis. Instead, a violent complementarity comes to the surface that furnishes the best account of the relationship between the two authors' politics. In analyzing *The Need for Roots*, Bataille argues, on the one hand, that a philosophy based on the good as an immutable cosmic principle is no longer tenable. On the other hand, however, Bataille affirms that "if a search for the good has been entire and burning," it leads its protagonist (Weil) directly into the territory of evil and communication, revealing unexpected convergences with Bataille's own theories (*BOC* XI, 539). The stakes involved in locating such points of rapprochement between ostensibly antithetical views are high. Indeed Bataille argues that, for contemporary thought, "no problem has more meaning" than the challenge of discerning areas of possible accord between a Christian metaphysics of the good and a post-Nietzschean philosophy of contestation and transgression. The moral and political destiny of European civilization after World War II hinges on this issue, as Western thinkers seek ways to renounce bankrupt absolutes without relinquishing all foundations for moral claims. In attempting to mobilize elements for a renewal of morality and community in the wake of the war's destruction, "the coincidence of utterly opposed minds" — Bataille's mind and Weil's — "can have a probative value" (539).

As a purely intellectual project, Bataille maintains, *The Need for Roots* is flawed, marked by flagrant logical inconsistencies that Weil's "vigor of expression" can mask only temporarily. "If one had to judge *The Need for Roots* from a practical angle, the book would not hold one's attention for long" (*BOC* XI, 536–37). Fortunately, however, there are more interesting things about Simone Weil than the practical content of her political theses. These more promising aspects of Weil's achievement are revealed in the "passion" that drove Weil to live and write as she did (536). "[T]here was in her a *marvelous* will to inanity: this is perhaps the source of an inspired bitterness that makes her books so absorbing — and the explanation of the death that she imposed on herself *outrageously* [*par outrance*]. (Her lungs were infected, yet she refused, in London, to eat more than a French ration)" (537). It is Weil's furious passion, her outrageous sacrificial excess, in short her sacred character, that guarantees her enduring importance.

According to Bataille, what Weil was unable to acknowledge is that, at their highest, evil and good fuse in the sovereign sphere of communication. She ignored "the 'evil' which is the way of good" (*BOC* XI, 545). The genuine highest good is communication, the compenetration of subject and object in violent ecstasy. But this highest good is inseparable from evil: the force that shatters the limits of the self. Weil was unable to face this reversibility of good and evil, since it would have "ruined her beliefs" (541). Yet her own writings and, even more, her own being bear witness to it. "In her writings as in her life," Bataille argues, Weil showed the scorn for calculations of utility, the "perfect irreducibility to interest," characteristic of the sacred (evil) realm (549). Weil "let herself fall prey to the seduction of useful works," yet she nevertheless "rendered to *evil* a testimony [*témoignage*] comparable to that of the mystics. Indubitably, there was in her, beyond useful works, a dominant attraction toward evil and the disturbance of the order of things that is affliction [*malheur*]" (546).

Beyond the difficulties of Bataille's somewhat tortuous effort to show that good and evil mean the same thing (or ought to), the key point is the coincidence of "writings" and "life" he discerns in Simone Weil and posits as the basis for a rapprochement between Weil's thought and his own. Bataille's essay presents Weil's life (her outrageous "passion," in all senses of the term) as integral to her work and indispensable for a correct evaluation of her political and philosophical contributions.

This accounts for the fact that Bataille spends a significant portion of the early part of his essay discussing in detail Weil's personality, eccentric habits, and physical appearance (*BOC* XI, 537). Bataille evokes Weil's personality and physicality not in order to dismiss her teachings, but to clarify what he views as the enduring power of her performance. Bataille focuses on Weil's person because for him Weil is the embodiment of what is most valuable in her own doctrines, the saint/symbol of her own most potent ideas. Bataille reads Simone Weil in terms of her "excessive zeal" (536) not just to write truth in the pages of her journals, but to embody a violent, shocking truth, to be that truth: that is, to make of herself and her life a "real metaphor." Bataille does not employ Weil's idiosyncratic technical term, but he has clearly grasped the performative strategy to which the term points. No doubt because the self-metaphorizing impulse was one Bataille knew, to adapt the language of the *Atheological Summa,* "from within." Neither Weil's philosophy nor his own, Bataille affirmed, could be judged in the abstract, apart from the question of how these doctrines found expression in the lives of flesh-and-blood beings. Weilian sacredness, like Bataille's own "heterology," was above all a "practice" that abandoned "speculation about abstract facts" to reach an engagement of the entire being (*BOC* II, 65). The best argument for taking Weil's thought seriously was not her spare, elegant prose or her system's conceptual rigor. The best Weilian argument was Weil herself: this complex, seductive, quixotic, excessive being whose courage "the impossible attracted" (*BOC* XI, 537).

As the "attraction to the impossible" threatens the simple polar opposition between good and evil, so it mutates the apparently clear distinction between bodily action in armed struggle and the performative self-sacrifice of the literary mystic. Bataille's essay condenses and confirms a key strand of this study's argument: the resistance of Bataille's and Weil's literary politics to simple labels and crude hierarchies. Our conclusion must break with the stereotyped view that praises Weil as a model of heroic political commitment while denouncing Bataille for political withdrawal and futile aestheticism. Yet at the same time, and just as forcefully, we must reject the opposite assessment, which would dismiss Weil's political acts as naive, ineffectual, and/or pathological while lauding Bataille's daring literary transgression. We have seen how, in both these figures, sacrifice and writing, political action and literary performance infiltrated and contaminated each other. In both, the boundaries between action and passivity, efficacy and inutility, *engagement* and retreat, life and literature were blurred. Yet if this blurring signifies a loss of comforting simplicity, it brings a corresponding gain in understanding of the inevitably complex, elusive procedures through which political meanings are produced, mutated, and overturned within a performative space determined by the "marvelous will" to a defiant freedom that hovers between ecstasy and "inanity."

This does not mean that dying on the battlefield and sacrificing oneself at the writing desk are the same thing or that these acts should be assigned the same value. In his postwar texts, Bataille would insist on a clear separation between "writing" and "action," giving primacy to the latter (see, e.g., *LRC*). Yet both Bataille's and Weil's careers demonstrate that the division is by no means tidy and that zones of confusion provide an arena for experimentation. What looks like battlefield action reveals itself as a literary exercise; meanwhile literary exercises channel alternative forms of force, revealing an unexpected capacity to shake ossified political habits and attitudes. Utilitarian commitment and sovereign (sacred) inutility exert mutual repulsion, but also a reciprocal seduction, between and within individuals. The two poles generate a field of tensions and reversible energies that is the theater of sacrifice, encompassing both the desk where Bataille spilled his ink in a tireless effort to communicate and the shell-torn battleground where Weil aimed to inscribe, as God's obedient *porte-plume*, her own death and her country's spiritual and political resurrection.

For all that separated them, Bataille and Weil shared a "converging moment" (*BOC* XI, 549) through a life/writing of sacred "outrageousness" [*outrance*]. Thus, Bataille could have the impression of having "responded," with his own pages and his own passion, "to the burning passion of each page of the work of Simone Weil" (549). In the incendiary excess of their sacred self-performance, both writers invoked "religion" as a way to advance political attitudes while overflowing a restrictive conception of politics. Beyond the limited objectives of military and political action, whose importance no one would deny, what mattered ultimately was outrageousness (sacredness, "burning") itself. Outrageousness that is not a project with a realizable objective, but an antiproject that assures its own "perfect irreducibility to interest" by following the attraction of the impossible whose shadow hovers beyond all limited, useful goals. Sacred *outrance* produces itself as a tension-riven state, an unappeasable hatred of satisfaction, spurred by the knowledge that good and evil are likewise "profoundly, inaccessible," approached but never captured by an "incessant wakefulness" (549). The pursuit of such impossible aims, Bataille and Weil believed, was salutary. Only the impossible goal stretches our faculties to their limits and beyond, opening the realm of radical loss where "being is given to us in an intolerable exceeding [*dépassement*] of being" (*BOC* III, 17). In the words of a Spanish poem Weil transcribed in her New York notebook: "Possible loves — are for fools — the wise have — impossible loves" (*CS*, 239; Weil's punctuation). Opposed in their ideological foundations, Bataille and Weil converged in the decision to perform on their own persons the experiment of a mystical politics broken open by "impossible love."

Conclusion

COMMUNICATION, SAINTHOOD, RESISTANCE

If someday I had the occasion to write with my blood my last words, I would write this: "All that I have *lived,* said, written, [. . .] I imagined it *communicated.* Without that, I could not have lived it.
— Bataille, *On Nietzsche*

Saintly being cannot close itself off from [. . .] the turbulent forces that strive for expression, because saintliness is always already situated within love and the risk of death.
— Edith Wyschogrod, *Saints and Postmodernism*

BATAILLE AND WEIL lived an epoch of convulsive social crisis, intellectual disillusionment, and war. Well before Derrida and Lyotard, Bataille, Weil, and other members of the generations that reached intellectual maturity in the France of the 1930s experienced their own version of the collapse of the *grands récits,* including those of Enlightenment liberalism, Marxism, the ideology of scientific progress, and traditional forms of religion. Over the course of the decades preceding World War II, the grounding philosophical and/or religious convictions that should have offered support for political and moral commitment fell away under the feet of many men and women. The opening pages of Weil's *Reflections on the Causes of Liberty and Social Oppression* bear witness to the intellectual and affective climate of the era:

The present period belongs to those in which everything which normally seems to constitute a reason to live vanishes. [. . .] That the triumph of authoritarian and nationalist movements is everywhere ruining the hopes honest people had placed in democracy and pacifism is only a part of our malady. The problems are much deeper and more extensive. (*RCL*, 9)

In a gloomy litany, Weil catalogs the real and threatened disasters of the epoch: material and moral misery of the working classes; bankruptcy of the "naive belief" in economic and technological progress; the loss of orientation among social leaders; the stagnation of art amid the "general disarray"; the disintegration of family structures under the impact of economic stress. "We are living an epoch deprived of a future," Weil writes. "The wait for what will come is no longer hope, but anguish" (9–11). It was in this climate that Weil and Bataille struggled to think, write, and act.

How, in the context of a country without a future, a society whose moral bases had collapsed, a civilization poised on the brink of suicide, was it possible to find meaning in life, to articulate ethical positions, to speak of beauty, loyalty, love? No area of individual or collective life appeared unaffected by the contagion of meaninglessness, violence, cynicism, and sham (*RCL*, 9). The language itself in which conventional philosophical and political discourse had been conducted appeared corrupted to the point of uselessness. For many, words like "democracy," "freedom," or "revolution" — to say nothing of the still more vacant abstractions of theology and old-fashioned moral philosophy — could elicit nothing but indifference, or a sneer. The old values were unquestionably defunct. But how (from what materials and according to what guidelines) were new values to be discovered or "created" (*BOC* II, 273)?

Even if new, legitimate values were somehow to emerge, moreover, it seemed doubtful they could be disseminated. Public debate on ethical and political questions — whether in the academy, the intellectual and artistic world, or the parliamentary institutions of bourgeois democracy — appeared to lead nowhere. Rational discussion degenerated into demagoguery or remained powerless in the face of immediate or threatened violence. An endless proliferation of mutually exclusive theories, claims, and programs filled a plethora of short-lived reviews, bulletins, journals, books, and manifestos, yet the outpouring of frantic intellectual energy generated few if any meaningful results. To argue political and moral positions honestly appeared impossible when the very language of discussion had been undermined by propagandistic misuse and when Hitler's example seemed to demonstrate conclusively that not ideas but brute force ultimately charted the course of history. How, even if good ideas could be devised, could they ever be convincingly expressed and allowed the chance to exert influence? The better political and social ideas were, Weil argued in the concluding pages of *Reflections,* the more likely they were to challenge fundamental societal assumptions, and the more certain it became that media enfiefed to the status quo would caricature or ignore these ideas, effectively preventing them from ever becoming matters of serious public debate.

These are the challenges with which Weil and Bataille found themselves confronted in the 1930s. They are issues that will perhaps strike us as not wholly unrelated to our own experience.

The difficulty Bataille, Weil, and their contemporaries confronted was the necessity both to create (or discover) values and to communicate them. The social context rendered these tasks urgent and inseparable. As Weil again noted in the later pages of *Reflections,* the structures of education, information, capital, and power in European society had created a situation in which those possessing the skills and tools for effective communication had nothing meaningful to say, while those with insights into the truth of the social mechanism were deprived of means of reflection and communication. How (if at all) could the two dimensions — truth and expressive power, content and form — be brought together? The problem may again strike us as not without relevance to our own historical moment.

Bataille and Weil, I have suggested, attempted to find a way out of the apparent impasse of political and philosophical meaning by putting into play — in their writing and in their lives — the notion of the sacred and closely related images and concepts: sovereignty; the good; radical evil; sacrifice; the impossible. Bataille and Weil were not alone in the 1930s in appealing to religious language as a means of stretching and revitalizing apparently moribund categories of political debate and ethical action. The originality of Bataille's and Weil's effort lay in their construction of themselves as sacred figures independent of all religious and political orthodoxies: figures whose sacrality contested hierarchical power, rather than legitimating it and seeking to appropriate its prestige. I have tried to show how Bataille and Weil responded to their era's crisis of meaning not (only) with conventional forms of philosophical analysis and literary production, but through practices of self-stylization, a construction or writing of the self as sacred. To the problem of how simultaneously to engender and transmit values not sanctioned by prevailing institutional powers, Bataille and Weil responded with a performative strategy of "incarnation," by becoming saints.

One might initially suppose (and be grateful for the fact) that the parapolitical tactics Weil and Bataille improvised amid an epoch of relentless crisis would have little practical relevance in our own day, whose aspect is less apocalyptic (at least for the affluent, educated citizens of wealthy countries). Yet the parallels between our own period and that of Weil and Bataille may indeed be closer than we assume. In *Saints and Postmodernism*, Edith Wyschogrod has analyzed the chaotic condition of contemporary moral theory, and the intellectual and social roots of that chaos, in accents at times curiously reminiscent of Weil's *Reflections*. To escape the impasse occasioned by our society's inability to think a coherent moral ideal, Wyschogrod recommends a turn to saintly figures as concrete exemplars of the moral lives we still know how to recognize, though we can no longer bring them under a unitary theory. While Wyschogrod can hardly be said to be expressing a majority view among contemporary moral philosophers (indeed, her point is that discerning a meaningful "majority view" in the field would be impossible), the emergence of a contemporary proposal that so effectively articulates intuitions implicit in Bataille's and Weil's self-production as sacred beings is, at least, suggestive. That accounting for Bataille's and Weil's practices was no part of Wyschogrod's agenda only renders the connection more intriguing.

Under the best of conditions, Wyschogrod argues, sophisticated philosophical doctrines cannot in themselves be counted upon to substantially alter human behavior. Moreover, in periods of cultural transition and conflict it becomes virtually impossible even to formulate, let alone effectively disseminate, a coherent moral or political philosophy capable of embracing the complexities of the historical situation, catalyzing broad consensus, and generating responsible action. Yet if the moral life an epoch demands cannot be exhaustively theorized, it can be (and is) lived, and this living itself can constitute a decisive form of communication, through the narrativization of moral truth Wyschogrod terms "hagiography."

Understanding hagiography, Wyschogrod writes, that is, understanding a life story given over to the sacred, "consists not in recounting its meaning, but in being swept up by its imperative force." Such participatory understanding "is a *practice* through which the addressee is gathered into the narrative so as to extend and elaborate it with her/his own life."[1] I have suggested that a similar intuition about the communicative "force" of sacred being guided Weil's and Bataille's self-scripting. Literary sainthood became Weil's and Bataille's preferred mode of communication insofar as sacred figures transmit, not philosophical or political theses, but an attitude, a style of existence, an orientation that perhaps cannot be precisely verbalized, but whose emotional atmosphere the "addressee" absorbs (by "contagion," as Bataille would have it [*BOC* V, 391]) through the hagiographic text. Writing as saints, consecrating themselves in writing, Bataille and Weil propagated through their texts/lives an emotional force inspiring readers to change: to affirm (discover or create) their own sacredness. "Gathered in" to the passionate narrative of saintly existence, readers would actively set forward the process (the living "practice") of communication, becoming (self-)writers in their turn, authoring their own lives as tales of love, sacrifice, and the contestation of oppressive power.

Work like Wyschogrod's reveals that Bataille's and Weil's self-stylizing strategies are perhaps not, in the end, so remote from our era's political and moral struggles. Yet the ultimate value and desirability of communication via the type of "imperative force" Bataille and Weil labeled sacred must for that very reason be even more rigorously questioned. Following Jean-Luc Nancy, one might see in Bataille's and Weil's politics of sainthood merely another, in the last analysis grimly predictable, permutation of the "fantasm" of sacred power and divinizing violence that has haunted — perhaps constituted — the West as a philosophical and political project.[2] Under the lens of Nancy's nuanced critique, the progressively sublimated violence of sacrifice reveals itself as interwoven with a certain construction of the Western subject and with the millennial dream of the subject's ecstatic dissolution in annihilating mystical "communion." For Nancy, the aporias of sacrificial thinking like that of Bataille and Weil combine with their era's record of genocidal violence to prove how urgently we should pursue "the end of real sacrifice and the closure of its fantasm," rejecting the apocalyptic threats and messianic promises of all would-be saints.[3]

From such a perspective, the study of Bataille's and Weil's mobilization of the sacred, beginning as a historical investigation, ends by placing us before a present responsibility: precisely, the responsibility to resist the saint's seduction. Truly to grasp the implications of the sacralization and aestheticization of politics enacted by Weil and Bataille would be to discern as an urgent political task for our own time the relentless banishing of the sacred, insofar as it marks and perpetuates the West's nostalgia for an "outside of finitude," for a beyond, a transcendence in the end always sought through violence.[4] On Nancy's reading, what we learn from Bataille, Weil, and other thinkers of their generations is above all a negative lesson, the lesson of an *échec* we can and must avoid repeating and that results when an "incandescent nihilism" haunted by notions of mystical fusion seeks a release from the artificial prison of modern Western subjectivity. Such release can only take the form of an *"oeuvre de mort"* that in various ways and degrees will transform human beings into things.[5] It is this sacrificial logic — equal to the logic of force as analyzed by Simone Weil — that at all costs, Nancy maintains, must be short-circuited. It is for the end of the dream (too often, nightmare) of the sacred as a whole that Nancy calls with his declaration that the farthest extreme of Bataille's thinking still remains bound to a deadly "fascination" with sacred violence. Nancy believes that "Nous ne pouvons qu'aller plus loin" (We have no choice but to go farther),[6] moving — with Bataille's help — beyond Bataille (and Weil), leaving behind at last the philosophical and political space determined by sacrifice and its simulacra.

The moral strength of Nancy's call is undeniable. We must measure the full toxicity of the *mise-en-question* transmitted in

Bataille's and Weil's performance of the sacred. For what is implied in the invocation of the absolute alterity of the sacred, if not a "sovereign" contempt for the profane world (the world of ordinary politics and everyday, impure people)? The saint is by definition a being who refuses the common lot. What are we to see, then, in the aspiration to sacredness, to heterogeneity, if not the proclamation of an attitude at once arrogant and nihilistic, a hunger to abolish (decreate) the basic structures of personal existence experienced as a humiliating constraint, and to do away, by the same gesture, with the exigencies and risks of moral choice and political agency as they confront the *commun des mortels,* in the name of devotion to a mysterious higher authority (God or "the experience")? It is difficult not to conclude that, beyond its challenge to specific forms of political oppression, Weil's and Bataille's cultivation of sainthood marks a virulent contestation of the human condition as such. That such a generalized feeling of outrage could surge up among people living an "epoch deprived of a future" is perhaps understandable. But we, who hope to have a future still before us, may judge the "attraction to the impossible" celebrated by Bataille and Weil as sheer romantic hubris. We may see here an effort to cloak with exalted words what is at bottom a puerile refusal to soil one's hands with the inevitably messy, frustrating business of merely "possible" politics and ordinary, "unsacrificeable" existence.[7] That neither Weil nor Bataille ever seriously regretted or sought to attenuate their intransigence is clear. Weil's death and her last writings are her inflexible testament in this regard. Whereas Bataille, speaking with Madeleine Chapsal only months before his death, rhapsodically praised Saint John of the Cross, not of course for his piety but for the rabid "rage" that inhabited him. "A rage against what?" Chapsal asked. Bataille responded: "Against the existing state of things. A rage against life as it is. . . . "[8]

Yet, while such pronouncements must give us pause, the negative assessment of Bataille's and Weil's stance I have just outlined is not the only one possible. The question will be whether we interpret the profound dissatisfaction with the human communicated in Bataille's and Weil's practices of literary/political sainthood as "nihilism," or rather as a call to the ongoing work of self-overcoming and self-creation (one can prefer a more or less Nietzschean version of this idea). The chapters of this study have attempted to provide a foundation on which the second, more affirmative, reading of Weilian and Bataillean sainthood can at least be entertained as a credible option. It is as models of the active, ongoing *écriture de soi*,[9] understood as a creative literary and political process, that I believe Bataille and Weil are most valuable and that their tactics, while bound up with the specific political crises of their era, also resonate beyond it.

The elusive, "sliding" quality of the sacred was one of the concept's most important advantages from Bataille's and Weil's perspective. In closing, I would like to focus on a particular aspect of this elusiveness. Connected to the Durkheimian polarity between "right" and "left" forms of sacrality is another fundamental ambiguity, one Bataille and Weil turned to advantage. In both Bataille's and Weil's work, passages can be found in which sacredness appears as what can best be termed a textual phenomenon: a particular way of writing or representing beings, relations, and practices: above all a mode of writing/performing one's self. Seen from this angle, sacredness or sainthood would be above all a style of self-production and specifically a literary-political attitude of mobile otherness adopted with respect to the normalizing, monopolar, monolithic power Bataille labeled "homogeneity" and Weil "the social." On this reading, sacredness appears not as a particular, fixed content or attribute, but as a shifting stance of perpetual self-giving in and as self-distancing: a stance that maintains the gap between the self and the social order, holding open that separation or wound as the free space for critique and spontaneous creative action.

If the sacred is seen in this way, sacredness or "sainthood" might be understood as a tactical self-positioning comparable to that described by David Halperin in his discussion (within the framework of an impressive piece of contemporary hagiography) of opportunities for a Foucauldian queer political praxis. Halperin analyzes queer "identity" not as a rigid essence but as a tactical posture of resistance. Queerness is not a stable feature, disposition, or set of predetermined behaviors. Instead, for Halperin, queer "identity" is or should be an "eccentric positionality" or "strategic possibility" defined by its oppositional character and subject at all times to shifts and revisions.[10] As another theorist has succinctly phrased it, "The great virtue of 'queer' [lies] precisely in its undefinability; [...] The point is precisely to refuse the accepted identities, the expected and predictable alignments or divisions."[11] Whatever its ultimate fate within the field of contemporary theory, the notion of queerness as "positionality" illuminates a significant aspect of the way in which notions of the sacred functioned for Bataille and Weil. Bataille and Weil frequently discussed sacredness, heterogeneity, or sainthood in terms that allow these qualities to appear as names or markers for a strategic stance or "potentially privileged site for the analysis of cultural discourses."[12] For these figures, sacrality names an intellectual style, a pattern of self-positioning in political spaces. Sainthood as practiced by Weil and Bataille is a systematically critical orientation to society and politics, always operating from a stance of heterogeneity and risk. Sacrality is the performative assertion of alterity and unmasterability. As Weilian good or as Bataillean evil, the sacred is a "sliding" positionality of resistance to the normalizing effects of dominant social value systems, the perpetual reassertion of a critical "nonidentity."[13] This sort of nonidentity, much more than a haughty rejection of communal bonds as such, was what Weil intended with her famous refusal to "live in a setting [*milieu*] where one says 'we' and to be a part of that 'we'" (*AD*, 26). To position/construct oneself as sacred is to model a movement confounding hegemonic forces' efforts to assign stable, manipulable social and political identities (e.g., "woman," "Jew," "philosopher," "leftist," or "homosexual") correlated with predictable patterns of thought and behavior. Weil's and Bataille's mobilization of religious language in political space functioned as a means to elude standard grids of ideological localization and control.

Yet numerous passages can also be cited in which both authors describe and invoke the sacred not as a "textual" phenomenon, but as a real and potent force capable of exerting a concrete influence on the world. This is patently true of Weil's absolute good (object of the saint's love and radical obedience), which she routinely characterizes as a binding and transforming energy, an "active force" (*E*, 336) whose powerful effects on individual human beings and communal milieus can be discerned, by the qualified observer, with a precision and assurance comparable to those attained in the prediction, verification, and measurement of physical forces by the natural sciences.[14] Meanwhile, Suzanne Guerlac has shown convincingly that Bataille, too, is concerned with the sacred not merely as a textual phenomenon or literary trope, but as a real affective force capable of generating real political effects. In contrast to his later admirers in the Tel Quel group, preoccupied above all with textual transgression and with "a question of philosophy, and of its end," Bataille himself pursued "the religious question of the sacred (which, since Durkheim, is related to the implicitly political issue of social cohesion)." As Guerlac indicates, this preoccupation has been a source of discomfiture for Bataille's antireligious admirers and exegetes, who have generally sought to "evacuate" the dimension of the sacred from their interpretations of his work.[15]

Which is it, then? Is the sacred a critical positionality, or is it an explosive emotional force unleashed through certain forms of individual and collective practice and capable of altering the shape of what it may no longer be appropriate to call "subjectivity"? Is sainthood a stance one adopts, a theatrical mask one borrows, or is it a heterogeneous force that borrows us (and that transforms, transmutes, perhaps "decreates" us in the process)? Bataille and Weil refused to decide this question in binary terms, and the protean (call it "formless" [BOC I, 217]) character of the sacred enabled this equivocation. Therein lay a part of its appeal. "The sacred" could point simultaneously and equally to an "eccentric positionality" and to an emotional energy, a *force agissante* unleashed through the communicative practices these writers sought to model. Precisely this double valence made the concept valuable for the revisionings of political and literary practice on which Bataille and Weil embarked.

Yet if sacredness is a force (the motor of the "sovereign operation"), it is never in these two writers the unilateral discharge of power. On the contrary, sacrality/sovereignty manifests itself as perpetual "revolt," never "the exercise of power" (BOC V, 221). Sacredness is the mobile, multifaceted contestation of all efforts to fix power in rigid hierarchies that place some human beings "at the disposal" of others (*RCL*, 52, 83–84). That this stratification and the resulting exploitation regenerate themselves perpetually within any complex social order as a consequence of its unavoidable division of labor only means that resistance to oppression must be just as tirelessly renewed. Sainthood became for Bataille and Weil a way to name (and, by naming, summon) the real energy of moral wakefulness necessary for this ongoing effort.

The sacred as Bataille and Weil embodied it was not the engine of a theocratic tyranny, nor an investment of certain structures of power with supernatural legitimation, but rather the endless contestation of *all* forms of authority that would confiscate autonomy or claim unconditional allegiance. The divine (the impossible) provided leverage for the relativization of all merely human, merely "possible" power claims. As the religious insurgents of all eras have known, men and women inhabited by the holy assume a "marvelous," though no doubt also dangerous, freedom vis-à-vis the established social order (*BOC* I, 270). For Bataille and Weil, such freedom — which may become an "obligation" (*EL*, 80–84) — is the liberty to venture perpetually into those "places" (social, political, religious, erotic) that are "most repugnant to decent society" (*BOC* I, 270). It is in the experience of this transgressive freedom that the emotive and political dimensions of sainthood (its dual aspects as active force and critical positionality) come together. It is to participation in this interminable performance, the never-completed "rites of liberation" (270), that Bataille and Weil incite.

In an optimistic moment, the restless, nonteleological movement of Bataillean and Weilian sainthood might be read as one of Foucault's "countless signs that our path is circular and that, with each day, we are becoming more Greek." Yet this nonlinear "motion" clearly does not herald the "return to a homeland or the recovery of an original soil which produced and which will naturally resolve every opposition." Bataille and Weil, situating — in the wake of Dionysos and the Crucified — "the experience of the Divine at the centre of thought," propose neither a definitive resolution through the conquest of a telos, nor the tranquil sleep of a return to origins. Instead, as "figures of tragedy" producing themselves in "extreme forms of language," they seek endlessly to "awaken us from the confused sleep of dialectics and of anthropology," not to mention conventional politics.[16]

Sacrality and sainthood as Bataille and Weil explored them do not in any sense signify a nostalgia for archaic orthodoxies, nor the desire to frame a new orthodoxy. On the contrary, the sainthood the two thinkers envisaged — which they (ironically) claimed for themselves or (less ironically) challenged others to attain — represented sovereign liberation from rigid orthodoxy, from all forms of intellectual and political domination. The impossible sainthood to which Bataille and Weil aspired was a call to creativity, to contestation as an affirmative stance.[17] In Weil's last letter to Perrin, she labeled it "a new type of sainthood, [...] an upsurge [*jaillissement*], an invention":

> We are living an epoch altogether without precedent. [...] Today, it is nothing merely to be a saint. What is needed is the sainthood the present moment demands, a new sainthood, it too without precedent.
>
> Maritain has said it, but he has only enumerated the aspects of the former sainthood that today, for a time at least, are outdated. He hasn't felt to what extent today's sainthood must contain miraculous novelty. [...] Keeping all proportions, and maintaining everything in its rank, it is almost analogous to a new revelation of the universe and of human destiny. It is the uncovering of a large portion of truth and beauty until now covered by a thick layer of dust. More genius is needed here than it took for Archimedes to invent mechanics and physics. A new sainthood is a more prodigious invention. (*AD*, 66–67)

In the present crisis, Weil pursued, the world needed "saints who have genius" as desperately "as a plague-stricken city needs doctors." Where there was such a need, there was ineluctable obligation (67): an obligation to sainthood, that is, to a self-"revelation" equivalent to tireless self-"invention."

Bataille, too, felt the call to communicate sacredness, though he found Weil's idea of "obligation" oppressive and preferred a spontaneous "loyalty" awakened by the *"sovereign presence"* of one's fellow human being (*BOC* XI, 541). The difference between divinely ordained "obligation" and ecstatic "loyalty" is hardly trivial. Yet just as significant may be the traits the two models and their authors share: their relentless discontent with the merely given; their determination to escape the "profane" realm of submission to established authority and to explore (if necessary, invent) the sacred region of tireless contestation and poetic self-creation. If, as Roger Caillois claimed, "the profane is the world of ease and security," then what counts most, perhaps, is leaving that world behind, whether one's departure take a left- or a right-hand turn. Once the boundary has been crossed, Caillois cautions, there can be no turning back. "One must walk without ceasing in the path of holiness or that of damnation, which abruptly join at unforeseen crossroads." For the pact with the devil is in truth "no less a consecration than divine grace."[18]

NOTES

Introduction

1. Bataille wrote the novel in 1935, but published it only in 1957. On possible reasons for the delay, see *ML*, 214–23; on patterns in Bataille's revision of the text in 1957, see Francis Marmande, *L'Indifférence des ruines*.

2. Emmanuel Mounier, describing the origins of the journal *Esprit* in a letter to Jéromine Martinaggi; cited in Jean Touchard, "L'Esprit des années 1930," 91.

3. Daniel Lindenberg, *Les Années Souterraines, 1937–1947*, 78.

4. See, for example, Simone Fraisse, "La représentation de Simone Weil dans *Le Bleu du ciel* de Georges Bataille."

5. André Breton, *Manifestes du surréalisme*, 147.

6. So far as my bibliographical researches have been able to determine, no extended comparison of Weil's and Bataille's thought has as yet been published. Weil scholarship in particular has pointedly ignored Bataille. Two short essays published in *CSW* constitute exceptions: Francis Chiappone, "Simone Weil, à mes yeux..."; and Fraisse, "La Représentation de Simone Weil." Bataille's readers in turn have paid scant attention to Weil, although a handful of studies touch on the relationship. Peter Tracey Connor deftly analyzes Bataille's review essay on Weil's *L'Enracinement* in exploring tensions between mysticism and philosophy in Bataille (Connor, *Georges Bataille and the Mysticism of Sin*, 72–79). An insightful essay by Sylvère Lotringer compares Weil's and Bataille's teachings on poverty, affliction, and sacrifice in the context of the challenge to meaning posed by the Holocaust (Lotringer, "Les Misérables"). In a brief but suggestive passage, Franco Rella points to similarities between Bataille's and Weil's doctrines of sacrifice (Rella, *The Myth of the Other*, 92–94). Bataille's biographer Michel Surya notes the ambiguous intensity of Bataille's feelings toward Weil (*ML*, 220–21).

7. Bernard Sichère, "Saint Bataille," in *Le Dieu des écrivains*, 25.

8. See Jean-Louis Loubet del Bayle, *Les Non-conformistes des années 30*, 53.

9. Arnaud Dandieu and Robert Aron, *Le Cancer américain*, 235; cited in Loubet del Bayle, *Les Non-conformistes*, 89.

10. Raymond de Becker, "Révolution spirituelle d'abord?"

11. See Michel Surya, "L'Arbitraire, après tout," 218–21. The most important of Chestov's texts in this connection is *La Nuit de Gethsemani*.

12. Before himself achieving martyrdom, Péguy had contributed through his writing to the fascination with saints that surfaced in French political rhetoric in the early decades of the twentieth century, predominantly but not exclusively on the conservative end of the ideological spectrum. See Connor, *Georges Bataille*,

227

19–21. Simone Weil was by no means insensible to the Jeanne d'Arc cult. Bataille found more inspiration in Jeanne's associate, the "sacred monster" Gilles de Rais (Bataille, *Le Procès de Gilles de Rais*, 11–17).

13. On the various stages of Sade's rehabilitation and ultimate canonization, see Carolyn Dean, *The Self and Its Pleasures*, 123–99.

14. See, for example, Breton, *Manifestes*, 38–39: "Swift est surréaliste dans la méchanceté. Sade est surréaliste dans le sadisme. [. . .]"

15. Louis Aragon, *Le Paysan de Paris*; Breton, *Nadja*; Breton, *L'Amour fou*.

16. Edith Wyschogrod, *Saints and Postmodernism*, xiii.

17. Wyschogrod views the "difficulties with moral theory" as highly complex, but related in the main to two problems: first, "the gap between theory and practice resulting from the confusion of moral and scientific discourse," and, second, "the incommensurate presuppositions of [various moral] theories," which render substantive dialogue among the proponents of competing theories impracticable in spite of the thinkers' best intentions (*Saints and Postmodernism*, 4).

18. Wyschogrod, *Saints*, 14–19.

19. Wyschogrod, *Saints*, 3.

20. See Philippe Lacoue-Labarthe and Jean-Luc Nancy, *Retreating the Political*, 140.

21. Lacoue-Labarthe and Nancy, *Retreating the Political*, 140.

22. Roger Caillois, *Man and the Sacred*, 13.

23. Certain aspects of the Durkheimians' oppositional definition of the sacred found support in Rudolf Otto's influential *Das Heilige* (1917), in which the experience of the sacred was characterized as the encounter with the "wholly other," an encounter initially situated outside of rational and moral categories. See Otto, *The Idea of the Holy*, 25–30.

24. Caillois, *Man and the Sacred*, 45.

25. Jean-Michel Besnier, "Georges Bataille in the 1930s," 169.

26. Besnier, "Georges Bataille in the 1930s," 169.

27. Lindenberg, *Les Années souterraines*, 23, 27, 198.

28. Philippe Lacoue-Labarthe, *La Fiction du politique*, 135.

29. Recent studies exploring politics and community in Weil include Diogenes Allen and Eric O. Springsted, *Spirit, Nature, and Community*; Richard Bell, *Simone Weil*; Lawrence Blum and Victor Seidler, *A Truer Liberty*; Charles Jacquier, ed., *Simone Weil*; Jean-Marie Muller, *Simone Weil*; Andrea Nye, *Philosophia*.

30. See in particular Rachel Feldhay Brenner, *Writing as Resistance*, esp. 75–95; Mary Dietz, *Between the Human and the Divine*, esp. 120–25, 189–93; Athanasios Moulakis, *Simone Weil and the Politics of Self-Denial*.

31. See, for example, Connor, *Georges Bataille*; Carolyn Bailey Gill, ed., *Bataille*; Amy M. Hollywood, *Sensible Ecstasy*.

32. Carolyn J. Dean, "Introduction."

33. Jean-Luc Nancy, "The Unsacrificeable."

1. Bataille's Sacrifice

1. See Jean-Michel Besnier, "Bataille, the Emotive Intellectual"; Besnier, *La Politique de l'impossible;* Peter Tracey Connor, *Georges Bataille and the Mysticism of Sin;* Jean-Michel Heimonet, *Le Mal à l'oeuvre;* Francis Marmande, *Georges Bataille Politique.*

2. Notably Mark C. Taylor, "The Politics of Theo-ry."

3. See Jean-Luc Nancy, "The Unsacrificeable," 34–38; Giorgio Agamben, *Homo Sacer,* esp. 112–15. And cf. Elisabeth Arnould, "The Impossible Sacrifice of Poetry." We should note that if, for Agamben, Bataille's effort to connect notions of sovereignty and "sacred life" must be considered "exemplary," the Bataillean conceptual apparatus remains inadequate for the intellectual tasks Bataille set himself. See Agamben, *Homo Sacer,* 112–13.

4. Allan Stoekl, *Agonies of the Intellectual,* 25.

5. Among the texts spanning virtually the whole of Bataille's authorship in which Durkheim's influence is palpable, see in particular "La Structure psychologique du fascisme" (*BOC* I, 339–71); Bataille's various contributions to *CdS; Théorie de la religion* (*BOC* VII, 281–361); "Le Sens moral de la sociologie" (*BOC* XI, 56–66); "La Guerre et la philosophie du sacré" (*BOC* XII, 47–57).

6. Stoekl, *Agonies,* 32.

7. Stoekl, *Agonies,* 33.

8. This is not to suggest that Durkheim lacks interest in the outer forms of aboriginal rites. On the contrary, as Taylor contends, Durkheim at certain moments seems to revel in "graphic" descriptions of the "genuinely wild and savage scene" of tribal festivals (Taylor, "Politics of Theo-ry," 9).

9. Nancy, "The Unsacrificeable," 25.

10. Nancy, "The Unsacrificeable," 23–24.

11. The English term "sacrifier" translates the French *sacrifiant:* the one at whose behest the ritual is performed. "Sacrificer" translates *sacrificateur,* designating the person — usually, a priest — who actually carries out the sacrificial operation.

12. See the review of Kraft-Ebing's *Psychopathia Sexualis* that was Bataille's first contribution to *La Critique sociale* (*BOC* I, 275–76).

13. Stoekl, *Agonies,* 51–52.

14. Taylor, "Politics of Theo-ry," 25.

15. Taylor, "Politics of Theo-ry," 27.

16. Taylor, "Politics of Theo-ry," 27.

17. Sylvère Lotringer, "Les misérables," 236; emphasis in original. The quotation from "La Notion de dépense" is from *BOC* I, 318.

18. See Lotringer, "Les misérables," 233.

19. Lotringer, "Les misérables," 237.

20. On the ambiguities of revolutionary political and aesthetic programs based on the glorification of "crime," see Carolyn J. Dean, *The Self and Its Pleasures,* esp. 123–220.

21. See Dean, *The Self and Its Pleasures,* 225–31; Nancy, "The Unsacrificeable," 28–30; Taylor, "Politics of Theo-ry," 29–33. And cf. Philippe Lacoue-Labarthe, *Heidegger, Art, and Politics.*

22. See Besnier, *Politique de l'impossible*, 184–86.

23. Besnier, *Politique de l'impossible*, 181–82.

24. Marmande, *Georges Bataille Politique*, 53, 52. It was by no means the smallest irony of Bataille's political odyssey that he committed himself to the revolutionary militancy of Contre-Attaque only months after completing the manuscript of *Le Bleu du ciel* (1935), one of the century's most searing indictments of literary-intellectual *engagement*. As Susan Suleiman notes, Bataille's "rousing public writings" for Contre-Attaque "could hardly be further from the vacillations and impotence of Troppmann," the politically indifferent antihero of his just-completed novel. "It was as if, in reaction to the anxieties and premonitions expressed in *Le Bleu du ciel*, Bataille sought to affirm, by means of his own 'surge of power,' the possibilities of virile political action" (Suleiman, "Bataille in the Street," 38).

25. See Suleiman, "Bataille in the Street," 37.

26. Maurice Blanchot, *La Communauté inavouable*, 27, 30.

27. See Surya's account of the sacrificial *péripéties*, ML 254–55. Cf. Blanchot, *La Communauté inavouable*, 28–32; Roger Caillois, *Approches de l'imaginaire*, 58–59.

28. Raymond de Becker, "Communautés chrétiennes," 781. The debut of the review *Acéphale* and the general orientation of the group were commented upon favorably in the pages of *Esprit*, and at least one member of *Esprit*'s inner circle, Denis de Rougemont, would become an active participant in Bataille's College of Sociology.

29. De Becker, "Communautés chrétiennes," 781.

30. Quoted in *ML*, 258.

31. Pierre Klossowski, *Le Peintre et son démon*, 182.

32. Jean-François Pradeau, "*Impossible* politique et antiphilosophie," 138. Cf. Bataille's review of Jaspers, *BOC* I, 474–76.

33. Pradeau, "*Impossible* politique et antiphilosophie," 133n.2.

34. Bataille had followed Alexandre Kojève's courses on Hegel at the Collège de France since 1934. As a seemingly irresistible momentum propelled the world toward war, Bataille found himself simultaneously seduced and horrified by Kojève's thesis that Hegel's "end of history" had arrived (with a hundred-year delay) in the person of Stalin. After Kojève spoke at the College of Sociology on December 4, 1937, Bataille drafted a letter to him, a shortened version of which was later published as an appendix to *Le Coupable*. Bataille was ready to admit as a "plausible supposition" that "as of now history is completed (except for the *dénouement*)." But he asks: "If action ('doing') is — as Hegel says — negativity, the question must then be asked if the negativity of those who have 'nothing more to do' disappears or subsists in the state of 'unemployed negativity' [*négativité sans emploi*]. Personally, I can only reach one decision, being myself exactly that 'unemployed negativity' (I could not define myself in a more precise fashion). [. . .] I imagine that my life — or its abortion, better yet, the open wound that is my life — by itself constitutes the refutation of Hegel's closed system" (*CdS*, 75–76).

35. J. G. Frazer, *The Golden Bough*, 1:4–6.

36. See Frazer, *Golden Bough* 1:7: "The union of a royal title with priestly

duties was common in ancient Italy and Greece. At Rome and in other Italian cities there was a priest called the Sacrificial King or King of the Sacred Rites (*Rex Sacrificulus* or *Rex Sacrorum*)."

37. Compare Bataille's unpublished essay "Sacrifice," *BOC* II, 238–43.

38. For an analysis situating Bataille in the broader context of modern French intellectuals' deployment of motifs of crime and madness, see Dean, *The Self and Its Pleasures.*

39. The most celebrated denunciation of Bataille's mysticism among his contemporaries came in Sartre's vitriolic review of *Inner Experience,* "Un Nouveau Mystique," originally published in *Cahiers du Sud* in 1943 and later included in *Situations I.* Sartre's attack will be discussed in chapter 4. The historian Daniel Lindenberg has evoked the apparent rupture in Bataille's intellectual trajectory in sarcastic terms characteristic of a number of Bataille's recent critics: "Le Bataille 'politique' d'avant-guerre mise sur la révolution prolétarienne violente [...]; ensuite il donne congé aux bruits et fureurs de Gog et Magog pour se replier sur son *Expérience Intérieure* et devenir ce 'nouveau mystique' qu'interpellera Jean-Paul Sartre" (Lindenberg, *Les Années souterraines,* 62). Recent analyses defending the political value of Bataille's mystical writing include Besnier, "Bataille"; Connor, *Georges Bataille;* and, from a quite different angle, Amy Hollywood, *Sensible Ecstasy.*

40. Nancy, "The Unsacrificeable," 21.

41. On the status of the "King of the Wood" as a divine figure "fallen on evil days," see Frazer, *Golden Bough* (1911 ed.), part 1: *The Magic Art and the Evolution of Kings,* 2:376–87.

42. Cf. Hollier's wry comment in his introduction to the *Le Collège de Sociologie:* "Ils se disaient sociologues. En fait, ils étaient fous — fous de la société, comme d'autres en ont été les suicidés, comme d'autres furent fous de Dieu" (*CdS,* 7).

43. Arnould, "Impossible Sacrifice," 95.

44. Frazer, *Golden Bough* (1911 ed.), part 1: *The Magic Art and the Evolution of Kings,* 2:381–83.

45. Philippe Pétain, "Appel du 20 juin 1940," 5.

46. See citations and discussion in Nancy, "The Unsacrificeable," 33.

47. Dean, *The Self and Its Pleasures,* 227.

48. Dean, *The Self and Its Pleasures,* 227.

49. Nancy, "The Unsacrificeable," 38, 27.

50. Nancy, "The Unsacrificeable," 29.

51. Nancy, "The Unsacrificeable," 21.

52. Nancy, "The Unsacrificeable," 37.

53. Agamben, *Homo Sacer,* 113–14.

54. See Thierry Paquot, "Utilité de l'inutile?"

55. Nancy, "The Unsacrificeable," 37–38.

56. Nancy, "The Unsacrificeable," 37.

57. Bataille, in an interview with Madeleine Chapsal, in Madeleine Chapsal, *Quinze Ecrivains,* 45.

2. Transforming the Warrior's Soul

1. See in particular Athanasios Moulakis, *Simone Weil and the Politics of Self-Denial*, esp. 147–68.

2. In *Les Indomptables*, Ginette Raimbault and Caroline Eliacheff have analyzed Weil's thought and life through the lens of a psychoanalytic and philosophical interpretation of anorexia nervosa (see esp. chapters 1, 3, 4).

3. Simone Weil, *Poèmes*, 13.

4. Raimbault and Eliacheff, *Les Indomptables*, 171.

5. David McLellan, *Utopian Pessimist*, 66.

6. See the discussion in Jean Bethke Elshtain, "The Vexation of Weil," 16–18.

7. Lawrence Blum and Victor Seidler, *A Truer Liberty*, 118.

8. Richard Bell, *Simone Weil*, 23.

9. See Blum and Seidler, *Truer Liberty*, 75.

10. Weil would return frequently to the idea of the "mark" burned into the bodies and souls of the oppressed by social violence. In the opening passage of her famous essay "The Love of God and Affliction," she again characterized the conjunction of extreme physical, psychological, and social suffering in terms of a "mark of slavery" with which affliction brands those of whom it takes possession (*PSO*, 85). The mark of slavery and abjection, once inflicted, is indelible and forces not only other people but the victims of affliction themselves to "read" in their own bodies and souls the distinctive sign of a creature that has sunk below the condition of full humanity. Affliction, Weil grasped, was a process of social writing, the inscription of "marks" separating the powerful and the powerless.

11. For recent assessments of Weil's experiences in Spain, see Domenico Canciani, "Débat et conflit autour d'une courte expérience," and Louis Mercier-Vega, "Simone Weil sur le front d'Aragon."

12. Cited in Blum and Seidler, *Truer Liberty*, 201. The phrase is from Weil's article "La Situation en Allemagne."

13. Blum and Seidler, *Truer Liberty*, 201.

14. Weil's account encompasses not only the slaves and captives of ancient epics, but the modern slavery of the proletariat, drawing on her own experiences in the factory. The Greek citation Weil placed as an epigraph to her factory journal is a verse from the *Iliad* in which Hector foresees the future enslavement of Andromache. Weil quotes the verse once again in the essay on force: "And perhaps one day, in Argos, you will weave cloth for another, / And the Messeian or Hyperian water you will fetch, / Much against your will, yielding to a harsh necessity" (*IPF*, 8; cf. *WOC* 2.2, 159, 170).

15. Blum and Seidler (*Truer Liberty*, 219) read Weil as pursuing Marx's important but insufficiently developed insight that both the powerless and the powerful are "constrained" in a situation of institutionalized economic and social oppression.

16. Mary Dietz has also compared Weilian changes in "reading" to the cognitive "paradigm shifts" discussed by Thomas Kuhn (Dietz, *Between the Human and the Divine*, 104n.10).

17. Moulakis, *Simone Weil*, 155.

18. Moulakis, *Simone Weil*, 163, 165.

19. My discussion in this and the following section draws substantially upon Richard Bell's recent treatment of the Weilian politics of compassion and attention in *Simone Weil*. The influence of Peter Winch's seminal analyses will also, no doubt, be perceptible (see Winch, *Simone Weil*). In addition, I seek to extend Mary Dietz's suggestive treatment of the politics of attention and beauty in Weil (see Dietz, *Between the Human and the Divine*). While regretting, along with Bell, Dietz's somewhat exaggerated emphasis on the individualistic strain in Weil's thought, I find considerable promise in Dietz's investigation of the political implications of Weilian "attention" and in Dietz's willingness to take seriously the connections Weil sought to uncover between politics and poetic practice.

20. Bell, *Simone Weil*, 159.

21. Dietz, *Between the Human and the Divine*, 96.

22. Bell, *Simone Weil*, 51; emphasis in original.

23. Dietz, *Between the Human and the Divine*, 96.

24. Bell, *Simone Weil*, 78.

25. Dietz, *Between the Human and the Divine*, 102.

26. Winch, *Simone Weil*, 182. See the analysis of this and related passages in Bell, *Simone Weil*, 47–51.

27. Blum and Seidler, *Truer Liberty*, 219.

28. Judith Van Herik, "Looking, Eating, and Waiting in Simone Weil," 70.

29. Gilbert Kahn, "Les Notions de pesanteur et d'énergie chez Simone Weil," 27.

30. Moulakis, *Simone Weil*, 201.

31. Among the incidents narrated in Weil's letters about her experience in Spain, one particularly striking story involves the humiliation and execution of a disarmed captive. The incident shows parallels with the tableau of the conquering warrior and kneeling captive (Achilles and Priam) that becomes for Weil an archetypal representation of human relationships molded by force (see *SL*, 107; and cf. Blum and Seidler, *Truer Liberty*, 235).

32. See Blum and Seidler, *Truer Liberty*, 224–26.

33. Blum and Seidler, *Truer Liberty*, 224.

34. See the essays in John M. Dunaway and Eric O. Springsted, eds., *The Beauty That Saves*.

35. See the discussion of this thesis in Kahn, "Les Notions," 27.

36. See Dietz, *Between the Human and the Divine*, 90–94.

37. My discussion here develops themes presented in Dietz's excellent chapter on Weil's political reading of the *Iliad* (see Dietz, *Between the Human and the Divine*).

38. Thus, though Weil's vision may at times seem to lack "any real sense of hope" (one could perhaps say the same of Homer's vision), by articulating clearly "the actuality and depth of human suffering," Weil nevertheless contributed to keeping alive amid the numbing brutality of war a compassionate moral sensitivity "that is fundamental to any radical thought" (Blum and Seidler, *Truer Liberty*, 195).

39. Dietz, *Between the Human and the Divine*, 94.

40. Gilbert Kahn has analyzed in detail Weil's speculative economies of energy transformation. Kahn shows how the experience of privation and the encounter with beauty function in Weil's theory as transformers of energy, shifting it from lower to higher registers through a complex dynamic of desire, denial, and the purification of attention. The basis of this spiritual mechanics is Weil's claim that "all desire is precious, for all desire encloses energy" (C2, 52). Kahn's discussion of Weil's views on the "uses" of sexual energy (the figuring of sexual desire as hunger) is particularly important. See Kahn, "Les Notions," esp. 27–28.

41. Distorted images of this process exist on the purely human level, among those enslaved to an obsessive passion. "Experience shows that supplementary energy when sufficiently concentrated pulls the vegetative energy after it." Examples of the total projection of the self's vital energies into an external object include "gamblers, misers, lovers, débauchés, collectors" (C2, 175).

42. Miklos Vetö, La Métaphysique religieuse de Simone Weil, 24.

43. See Judith Van Herik, "Simone Weil's Religious Imagery," 274. At the highest stages, desire purifies itself by ceasing to focus on objects. Because nothing we can desire is God, Weil writes, because desire reifies and ultimately destroys that to which it is attached, "One must desire nothing [il faut désirer rien]" (C3, 35–36). To possess God as an object is impossible. But through a hunger that refuses satisfaction, a desire actively focused on "nothing," one can open oneself to the supreme nourishment offered through and as grace. Weil's language strangely anticipates Lacan's insight regarding anorexia: "It is a matter of understanding in anorexia not that the child does not eat, but that he or she eats nothing [non pas que l'enfant ne mange pas, mais qu'il mange rien]" (Jacques Lacan, "La Relation d'objet," unpublished seminar [May 22, 1957]; cited in Raimbault and Eliacheff, Les Indomptables, 203).

44. See Diogenes Allen, "The Concept of Reading and the 'Book of Nature.'"

45. Allen, "Concept of Reading,'" 113.

46. See NB, 23; quoted in Dietz, Between the Human and the Divine, 102.

47. See, for example, Dietz, Between the Human and the Divine, 120–25.

48. Moulakis, Simone Weil, 154.

3. If Revolution Is a Sickness

1. Though the two organizations were distinct, La Critique sociale emerged out of the work of the Cercle, which had been formed after Souvarine's exclusion from the Communist Party in 1926. See Souvarine's account of the history of La Critique sociale in his preface to the reprint edition, La Critique sociale. On the origins and development of the Cercle communiste démocratique, see Anne Roche, "Introduction," and Jean-Louis Panné, "Aux origines." On Bataille's role, see esp. Jean-Michel Besnier, Politique de l'impossible, 163–90. Simone Weil, though never an official member of the Cercle, was conspicuously involved in its activities and contributed important texts to the later issues of La Critique sociale. Her personal influence on Souvarine and her impact on the Cercle's rise and eventual dissolution were decisive. See Jean-Michel Besnier, "Les Intermit-

tences de la mémoire," 81; Charles Jacquier, "Présentation," "Lettres de Simone Weil à Boris Souvarine"; Anne Roche, "Simone Weil et *La Critique sociale.*"

2. In a letter dated to July 1933, Souvarine wrote of Weil that she was the group's "only interesting recruit since Bataille." Cited in Surya, *ML* 178.

3. See Leo Bersani, "Literature and History," in *The Culture of Redemption;* Jean-Michel Heimonet, "Writing and Politics, Cryptology of a Novel"; Francis Marmande, *L'Indifférence des ruines;* Alan Stoekl, "Politics, Mutilation, Writing," in *Politics, Writing, Mutilation.*

4. See, for example, Bersani, "Literature and History," 116–17.

5. "In the midst of historical agitation," Bataille had written in "The Notion of Expenditure," "only the word Revolution dominates the habitual confusion and carries with it promises answering the unlimited demands of the masses" (*BOC* I, 318).

6. Both Simone Fraisse and Bataille's biographer Michel Surya have noted the particular intensity of Bataille's feelings toward Weil. See Fraisse, "La Représentation de Simone Weil dans *Le Bleu du ciel* de Georges Bataille," 91; Surya, *ML,* 220.

7. Cf. Bataille's lectures at the College of Sociology on simultaneous "attraction and repulsion" as the characteristic affective response called forth by the sacred (*CdS,* 120–68).

8. Susan R. Suleiman, "Bataille in the Street," 28.

9. Marmande, *L'Indifférence des ruines,* 25–26.

10. Stoekl, "Politics, Mutilation, Writing," 4.

11. Fraisse, "La Représentation de Simone Weil," 91.

12. See Denis Hollier, "La Tombe de Bataille," in *Les Dépossédés,* 74–87.

13. Simone Pétrement notes that Bataille was one of the first to discern a specifically Christian orientation in Weil's thought and character, at a time when Weil herself was still unwilling to acknowledge this affinity (*SP* I, 424).

14. Marmande, *L'Indifférence des ruines,* 31–42.

15. Bersani, "Literature and History," 111.

16. Bersani, "Literature and History," 111. "We find no attempt to provide a controlling perspective on Troppmann's perspective, to suggest that the material is being organized by anyone else."

17. On this episode, see Hollier, "La Tombe de Bataille," 85–87.

18. See Hollier, "La Tombe de Bataille," 90–94; for a somewhat different reading, cf. Stoekl, "Politics, Mutilation, Writing."

19. Bersani, "Literature and History," 111.

20. Stoekl, "Politics, Mutilation, Writing," 3–5.

21. Stoekl, "Politics, Mutilation, Writing," 3.

22. Bersani, "Literature and History," 110.

23. See above all Weil's celebrated essay "L'Amour de Dieu et le malheur," *PSO,* 85–131.

24. In part, Bataille can be seen as reading Weil against herself: using the emphasis on affliction characteristic of her later writings to call into question the theme of the revolutionary love of life that she had used as a rhetorical weapon to attack Bataille during the period of their association at *La Critique sociale.*

25. *SP* I, 353, quoted in Charles Jacquier, "Lettres de Simone Weil à Boris Souvarine," 2.

26. Bersani, "Literature and History," 115.

27. Stoekl, "Politics, Mutilation, Writing," 7–9.

28. Suleiman, "Bataille in the Street," 31.

29. See Maryline Lukacher, *Maternal Fictions*, 193–97.

30. Lukacher, *Maternal Fictions*, 190.

31. Lukacher, *Maternal Fictions*, 164.

32. Simone Fraisse notes this parallel, though without developing it (Fraisse, "La Représentation de Simone Weil," 82, 86).

33. Interestingly (and certainly not coincidentally), Simone Weil's longest contribution to *La Critique sociale* was a text titled "Reflections on War," in which she argued for a blanket refusal of war by the working classes throughout Europe. The article was published in *La Critique sociale* 10, along with Bataille's review of Malraux and Weil's notes on Rosa Luxemburg.

34. Bataille's remarks on Weil in his review of *The Need for Roots* also echo the theme of Weil not recognizing her own true nature (*BOC* XI, 537).

35. Suleiman, "Bataille in the Street," 31.

36. Hollier, "La Tombe de Bataille," 84.

37. Hollier, "La Tombe de Bataille," 84.

38. Lazare's attempt to associate herself with the separatists' revolt invites comparison with Weil's participation in the combat of the International Brigades during the Spanish Civil War. This episode came after the original composition of *Le Bleu du ciel* but would have been familiar to Bataille by the period of his later revisions.

39. Bataille appears to have received his information on these events from Aimé Patri, who accompanied Weil to Barcelona on a vacation trip in August 1933. See Fraisse, "La Représentation de Simone Weil," 87–88.

40. Hollier, "La Tombe de Bataille," 84.

41. Lukacher, *Maternal Fictions*, 166. Lukacher cites the English version of Hollier's article, "Bataille's Tomb: A Halloween Story," *October* 33 (1985).

42. Fraisse, "La Représentation de Simone Weil," 88.

43. Along with the drag queens of La Criolla, the scene involves another social category in which traditional notions of gender are destabilized: priests. Earlier, Lazare has listened with a priestly air to Troppmann's account of his necrophilia ("Elle était devenue aussi calme qu'un curé écoutant une confession" [*BOC* III, 407]); now he "call[s] her a priest" in the midst of his equivocal deathbed paroxysm. Priests, who have made themselves "eunuchs for the Kingdom of God," defy traditional gender patterns and are also in some sense self-mutilators, self-sacrificers, who draw spiritual power from an amputation of a part of their humanity. However, other incidents from Bataille's fiction (e.g., the climactic scene of *Histoire de l'oeil*) demonstrate that it is around these supposedly desexualized figures that the most powerful and perverse erotic energies often circulate. If Lazare/Weil is a priestly self-mutilator, it can also be recalled that Bataille himself, less than five years after completing his first draft of *Le Bleu du ciel*, will take the pseudonym of a sacrificial priest and criminal (Dianus) in writing *Le Coupable*.

44. Besnier, *La Politique de l'impossible*, 176–77; emphasis in original.

45. In the scene at La Criolla, after Michel has recounted Lazare's deadly game with the young worker Antonio, Troppmann is seized by a sudden and shattering realization: "The idea that, perhaps, I loved Lazare tore a cry from me that lost itself in the tumult" (*BOC* III, 445). A short time later, Troppmann will admit: "In the car, waiting for Michel, I was glued to the steering wheel — like an animal caught in a trap. The idea that I *belonged* to Lazare, that she possessed me, astonished me" (454).

46. It is possible to see in this remark a reference to any one of several small journals in which Simone Weil published political texts during the period in which Bataille knew her. The statement may also constitute an ironic nod to *La Critique sociale* itself.

47. While they were traveling together in Spain, Weil asked her friend Aimé Patri to help her train herself to resist torture by shoving pins under her fingernails. Patri, also a friend of Bataille's, apparently shared this story with him. He also recounted it to Simone Pétrement, who included it in her biography of Weil. See *SP* I, 351; cf. *ML*, 220.

48. While the novel may contain other *personnages à clef*, for example, Professor Melou, these characters are sufficiently "fictionalized" to make a positive identification difficult if not impossible. See Fraisse, "La Représentation de Simone Weil," 86. The identification of Dirty with Colette Peignot, though maintained by some earlier commentators, appears doubtful. See *ML*, 221.

49. Cf. Hollier, "La Tombe de Bataille," 90.

50. Boris Souvarine, "Prologue," 21.

51. Bersani, "Literature and History," 122.

52. Bersani, "Literature and History," 122, 120.

53. Stoekl, "Politics, Mutilation, Writing," 8, 18–20.

4. Exercises in Inutility

1. See, for example, Jean-Michel Besnier, *La Politique de l'impossible*, 211.

2. Between 1939 and 1945, Bataille wrote and published the major texts of his *Somme athéologique: L'Expérience intérieure* (published 1943); *Le Coupable* (1944); and *Sur Nietzsche* (1945). In addition, he completed "L'Alléluiah: Catéchisme de Dianus" and his *Méthode de méditation*. Yet the texts of the *Somme* represented only a portion of Bataille's production in this period. He also wrote and published the poems of *L'Archangélique* (1944) and part or all of some of his most important works of fiction, including the crucial short novel *Madame Edwarda* (1941, reedited 1945), *Le Mort* (probably written in 1942; *ML*, 502), *Le Petit* (published 1943), and *Julie* (written in 1944, unpublished at the time of Bataille's death), as well as sections of *L'Impossible*. The war years also saw the composition of Bataille's *Vie de Laure* and of at least a sizable portion of the manuscript of *La Limite de l'utile*, the abandoned project that would become *La Part maudite*.

3. For example, Peter Tracey Connor, *Georges Bataille and the Mysticism of Sin*, esp. 94–153; Amy Hollywood, *Sensible Ecstasy*, chapters 1–3.

4. See in particular Boris Souvarine's scathing assessment of Bataille's poli-

tics in his "Prologue." Souvarine, of course, had many reasons to feel resentment toward Bataille, and his position can hardly be regarded as unbiased. However, even sympathetic interpreters like Jean-Luc Nancy and Pierre Klossowski have discerned in Bataille's texts evidence of a fascination with Nazi ideals that may have dulled his desire to resist fascism intellectually, much less through more active forms of struggle.

5. Carolyn J. Dean, "Introduction," 4.

6. Dean, "Introduction," 4.

7. Søren Kierkegaard, *Training in Christianity and the Edifying Discourse Which "Accompanied" It.*

8. Martin Jay, *Downcast Eyes,* 216.

9. Dean, "Introduction," 4.

10. Hollywood, *Sensible Ecstasy,* chapter 1 (esp. ms. pages 55–63).

11. Jay, *Downcast Eyes,* 217n.18; cf. Rita Bischof, *Souveränität und Subversion,* 293.

12. Susan Suleiman, "Bataille in the Street."

13. Several commentators have shown how Bataille's "impossible" thought was shaped by the conflicting influences of Hegel (more properly Kojève) and Nietzsche. See, for example, Besnier, *Politique de l'impossible,* 23–128; Alan Stoekl, "Sur Nietzsche: Nietzsche in the Text of Bataille" and "Hegel's Return," in *Agonies of the Intellectual.*

14. Jay, *Downcast Eyes,* 216–17.

15. Dean, "Introduction," 4.

16. Dean, "Introduction," 4.

17. Dean, "Introduction," 4.

18. Michel Surya, for example, cites Bataille's initial thesis without exploring the mutations to which it is subjected in the later pages of the "War" chapter. *ML,* 293.

19. Souvarine, "Prologue," 19–20.

20. Pierre Klossowski, *Le Peintre et son démon,* 188.

21. Klossowski, *Le Peintre et son démon,* 188–89. Klossowski specifies that, in his view, Bataille did not share the "coquetry" of the particular brand of "satanism" symbolized by Jünger. Yet in submitting to the "fascination one discerns in the horizon of German *demi-culture,*" Bataille unconsciously tapped into deep-rooted impulses, an "ogrish side" [*côté ogre*], which linked him to fascism.

22. Both Rebecca Comay and Martin Jay dismiss the notion of a meaningful link between Bataille's and Jünger's notions of experience rather peremptorily. See Comay, "Gifts without Presents," 84; Jay, "Limites de l'expérience-limite," 52.

23. Leo Bersani, *The Culture of Redemption.*

24. Rebecca Comay is right to stress Bataille's rejection of the "heroic" dimension of Jünger's vision, which masks an ultimate "servility." Jünger's "*inneres Erlebnis* [. . .] announces itself, typically, as the heroic certitudes of pain and labor" (Comay, "Gifts without Presents," 84).

25. See Comay, "Gifts without Presents," 84.

26. In a 1951 review essay on Caillois's *L'Homme et le sacré,* Bataille would

return again to the relation between war and the sacred. The final lines of Bataille's essay are cited from Caillois's text and juxtapose the "festival" (with its theatrical, "imaginary" elements) and real bloodshed in war as two forms of sacred squandering between which a sort of moral (or perhaps "hypermoral") choice seems to impose itself (*BOC* XII, 57).

27. On the concepts of meaning and/as *glissement*, and the Bataillean impossible, see Catherine Cusset, "Technique de l'impossible," 171–89.

28. Cusset, "Technique de l'impossible," 178, 182.

29. Comay, "Gifts without Presents," 85.

30. Jay, "Limites de l'expérience-limite," 57. Jay shows that the participatory recognition of shared finitude does not involve a naive claim of complete "identification" with the other (57). But the death of a fellow being abruptly abolishes "the profound and solid reality that the person attributes to him or herself" (*BOC* II, 245–46). The anguished consciousness of death is the basis of the tragic bond, the union in separation, that establishes authentic community as a shared openness to death. "It is for this reason that it is necessary for communal life [*la vie commune*] to hold itself at the *height of death*" (*BOC* VII, 245).

31. On the relationship between the height of death and tragedy, see Bataille's sociological essays, above all "Le Sacrifice" and "La Joie devant la mort" (*BOC* II, 238–47).

32. Suzanne Guerlac, " 'Recognition' by a Woman!" 91; emphasis added.

33. Guerlac, " 'Recognition' by a Woman!" 91; emphasis in original.

34. As Bataille will claim in *Histoire de l'érotisme*, in connection with erotic desire, the simply given is not sufficient. "A dialectic is necessary" (*BOC* VIII, 549; cited in Guerlac, " 'Recognition' by a Woman!" 92) for the deepening in which the shattering truth of eroticism and of death becomes accessible. Like the "beautiful woman prostitute" who constitutes the erotic "object," the emblem or representation of death contemplated in mystical experience "guarantees this dialectic, and, in so doing, enables a certain consciousness" (Guerlac, " 'Recognition' by a Woman!" 92).

35. The vengeful Goddess of the ascetic's vision also recalls the scimitar-wielding female divinity of Troppmann's dream in *Le Bleu du ciel*. The "Angry Goddess" thus evokes the novel's constellation of "sacrificial" personages, including Troppmann and Dirty, but also Lazare. Following Susan Suleiman's reading, the dismemberment inflicted on the "Tibetan ascetic" could also be, like Troppmann's humiliation in the dream, a form of *political* (self-)punishment. See Suleiman, "Bataille in the Street," 31.

36. "Il est heureux de découvrir en soi-même, dans un mouvement d'une violence tout intérieure [...]" (*BOC* VII, 259).

37. See Bataille's *Method of Meditation:* "Ce que j'enseigne [...] est une ivresse, ce n'est pas une philosophie" (*BOC* V, 217n.).

38. *L'Expérience intérieure* appeared in 1943, receiving violently critical reviews from, among others, Sartre (in the *Cahiers du Sud*) and Patrick Waldberg (in the expatriate journal *VVV*, published in the United States). Bataille refused to mend his ways. He published *Le Coupable* in March 1944 — still under the Occupation — and *Sur Nietzsche* in 1945.

39. The "monstrous penis" episode in fact belongs to notes that Bataille edited out of *Le Coupable* when the book was prepared for publication. The text was included in Bataille's mixed-genre work *La Tombe de Louis XXX* (*BOC* IV, 165).

40. Forty years after the publication of *Inner Experience* (and twenty years after Bataille's death), insinuations would still be made that the appearance of the book under the Occupation amounted to an endorsement of the Occupation itself. See Souvarine, "Prologue," 20.

41. The weight of this choice emerges still more clearly when one recalls that Bataille had not previously been in a rush (to say the least) to set his work before the public under his own signature. The example of *Le Bleu du ciel* (completed in 1935, withheld from publication until 1957) suffices to indicate that Bataille was generally more inclined to defer the appearance of his work than to rush his writings into wide circulation. In fact, Bataille in 1943 had never published a book with a major publisher under his own name.

42. Besnier, *Politique de l'impossible*, 145.

43. Besnier, *Politique de l'impossible*, 145; the cited phrase from Bataille appears in *BOC* V, 479.

44. Hollywood, *Sensible Ecstasy*, chapter 1 (ms. page 51).

45. The pointedness of Sartre's choice of images suggests that he may have been aware of Bataille's peculiar concern with transgressive enactments of the *"vice solitaire."* It is possible that this could have come to Sartre's attention through a reading of — or rumors concerning — Bataille's fractured novel *Le Petit*, published in a small edition earlier in 1943. *Le Petit* includes the following: "Je me suis branlé nu, la nuit, devant le cadavre de ma mère" (*BOC* III, 60).

46. Sartre takes these terms and images directly from Bataille's text, though — as one suspects — without a great deal of regard for the settings in which they appear or the nuances of Bataille's subversive handling of religious language. "Car enfin M. Bataille écrit, il occupe un poste à la Bibliothèque Nationale, il lit, il fait l'amour, il mange. Comme il le dit dans une formule dont il ne saurait me reprocher de rire: 'Je me crucifie à mes heures.' Pourquoi pas?" (*NM*, 175) (the cited phrase from *L'Expérience intérieure* appears in *BOC* V, 70).

47. Bataille's self-stylization, his effort to model through writing a certain (sovereign or sacred) style of existence, invites comparison in particular with the life/work of Nietzsche, as suggestively analyzed by Alexander Nehamas in his *Nietzsche*.

48. *NM*, 152: "La prédication orgueilleuse et dramatique d'un homme plus qu'à demi engagé dans le silence [. . .]"

49. Hollywood, *Sensible Ecstasy*, chapter 2 (ms. page 120).

50. Jean-Michel Heimonet, *Négativité et communication*, 40–41.

51. For illuminating discussions of Bataille's use of these images in his meditative practice, see Connor, *Georges Bataille*, 1–7, and Hollywood, *Sensible Ecstasy*, chapters 2–3.

52. Connor, *Georges Bataille*, 104.

53. "Death is what is most terrible, and to maintain the work of death is what demands the greatest force." Bataille used Hegel's celebrated phrase as the epigraph to *Madame Edwarda* (*BOC* III, 9).

54. Hollywood, *Sensible Ecstasy*, chapter 2 (ms. page 121).
55. Heimonet, *Négativité et communication*, 25.
56. Besnier, *Politique de l'impossible*, 148.
57. Klossowski, *Le Peintre et son démon*, 189.
58. Fred Botting and Scott Wilson, "Literature as Heterological Practice," 195.
59. Connor, *Georges Bataille*, 118.
60. As a space of ambiguous excess, literature and art threaten established social structures: not because writers and artists deliberately *choose* to engage in subversion, but because, Bataille claims, they have no choice. *"Whether the writer wants it or not, the spirit of literature always sides with squandering, with the absence of definite goals, and with passion whose only purpose is to eat away at itself"* (LRC, 40). On the role of passion in Bataille's effort to redraw the boundaries of politics, see Jean-Michel Besnier, "Bataille, the Emotive Intellectual."
61. Cf. Botting's and Wilson's argument that it is not sufficient for the Bataillean poet to depict the sacred; he or she must " 'be' sacred." To this end, "[T]he poet is required to sacrifice him- or herself and take on a heterogeneous existence. The poet becomes a sort of Christ figure whose work is revered not least because of the suffering from which it has issued" (Botting and Wilson, "Literature as a Heterological Practice," 197).
62. Dean, 4–5.

5. The Spectacle of Sacrifice

1. Rachel Feldhay Brenner, *Writing as Resistance*, esp. 31–50, 75–95; Brenner, "Simone Weil."
2. Lawrence Blum and Victor Seidler, *A Truer Liberty*, 244.
3. Once the choice was made, Weil reproached herself bitterly with having come to this realization too late. In her London notebooks (1943), she would speak of her support of the pacifist cause in the years before 1939 as a "criminal error" (CS, 317).
4. See Jean-Marie Muller, *Simone Weil*, 105–6.
5. See Weil's letter to G. Thibon, cited in SP II, 434.
6. David McLellan, *Utopian Pessimist*, 229.
7. See, for example, Mary Dietz, *Between the Human and the Divine*, 112–25.
8. On the concept of decreation, see Miklos Vetö, *La Métaphysique religieuse de Simone Weil*, 19–44; cf. Rolf Kühn, "La Décréation."
9. Weil's effort to exploit physical suffering as a spiritual "opportunity" shows striking parallels with the mystical techniques of the late medieval women discussed by Caroline Walker Bynum in *Holy Feast and Holy Fast*.
10. For a nuanced discussion of Weilian psychology and metaphysics focused around the notion of the *"quart d'heure"* of decreative anguish, see Vetö, *La Métaphysique religieuse*.
11. Franco Rella, *The Myth of the Other*, 92–94.
12. See André Devaux, "Du bon usage de la mort selon Simone Weil."

13. Cited in Devaux, "Du bon usage de la mort," 260. The citation is from the second edition of Weil's *Cahiers* 1, 230. On the theme of death as "gift," cf. *C3*, 86: "La croyance à l'immortalité dissout la pure amertume et la réalité même de la mort, qui est pour nous le don le plus précieux de la Providence divine."

14. Devaux, "Du bon usage de la mort," 273.

15. Quoted in Vetö, *La Métaphysique religieuse*, 122.

16. Vetö, *La Métaphysique religieuse*, 122.

17. The phrase appears in another verse Weil translated and transcribed in the margins of her Sanskrit Gita. Quoted in Vetö, *La Métaphysique religieuse*, 122.

18. Michel Narcy, "Simone Weil dans la guerre," 413.

19. See the account of Weil's exchange with philosopher and Resistance leader Jean Cavaillès in André Comte-Sponville, *Une Education philosophique* (Paris: PUF, 1989), 290–91; quoted in Narcy, "Simone Weil dans la guerre," 414.

20. The idea of organizing a corps of specially qualified battlefield nurses had apparently come to Weil even before the German offensive of 1940. Several references in her correspondence hint that Weil's decision to accompany her parents to America was conditioned specifically by her impression that New York would be an advantageous place to enlist support for the nurses project among American, English, and Free French officials (*SP* II, 434).

21. The frontline nurses may have represented a compromise between Weil's desire to face the dangers of active combat and the principles of her earlier pacifism. The nurses would be in the thick of the fighting, their lives as much at risk as those of the soldiers. Yet the women would be present as a force of healing and compassion, rather than of death. The nurses' role corresponds quite precisely to the pacifism that Weil, in *The Need for Roots*, defined as the only legitimate type: one that would bear witness to an aspiration to spiritual perfection (*"cette perfection impossible"* [*E*, 204]) not by withdrawing from war, but by inventing for itself a "presence in the war, properly speaking," a presence "more painful and dangerous than that of the soldiers themselves," yet absolutely nonviolent (*E*, 204–5). On the other hand, Weil makes clear in several letters and notebook entries that she was also prepared to accept assignments with the Resistance that would have involved taking German lives.

22. Brenner, "Simone Weil," 269.

23. The author Joë Bousquet, a severely wounded veteran of World War I with whom Weil spoke before leaving France, approved of the plan and wrote a supporting letter. Certain English and American officials seem to have endorsed at least the sentiment behind the project, if not the details, though without committing themselves to aiding in its implementation. In contrast, Philip judged the project completely impracticable, and de Gaulle, on having been shown Weil's document, is reported to have exclaimed: "Mais elle est folle!" (*SP* II, 483).

24. See the brief but suggestive discussion of this theme in Narcy, "Simone Weil dans la guerre," 416–18.

25. "In everything that awakens in us the pure and authentic feeling of the

beautiful, there is real presence of God. There is a sort of incarnation of God in the world of which beauty is the mark" (*C3*, 43).

26. Though they were both in London at the time, Weil found it useful to formulate some of her ideas in writing. The long letter (*EL*, 201–15) begins: "Cher ami, Comme il est pratiquement difficile de causer vraiment à loisir, il n'y a peut-être pas d'inconvénient à employer la correspondence" (201).

27. Brenner, "Simone Weil," 269.

28. Compare Weil's "method for understanding images, symbols, etc.," *C2*, 291–92: "Non pas essayer de les interpréter, mais les regarder jusqu'à ce que la lumière jaillisse. C'est pourquoi il faut craindre de diminuer leur réalité illégitimement, comme si on dit qu'il n'y a pas de vrai bataille dans la Gîtâ. Il vaut mieux risquer de les prendre trop littéralement que trop peu. Il faut d'abord les prendre d'une manière entièrement littérale, et les contempler ainsi, longtemps. Puis les prendre d'une manière moins littérale et les contempler ainsi, et ainsi de suite. Et revenir à la manière entièrement littérale. Et boire la lumière, quelle qu'elle soit, qui jaillit de toutes ces contemplations. (La source qui jaillit du rocher). [...] D'une manière générale: méthode d'exercer l'intelligence, qui consiste à regarder."

29. For a relatively full and detailed inventory of Weil's astonishing literary output in this period, see *SP* II, 452.

30. McLellan, *Utopian Pessimist,* 245.

31. Maurice Schumann's description of Weil's last days underscores the poetic (and prophetic) dimensions of her withdrawal from life. For Schumann, Weil was already "a spirit almost freed from the flesh, and which was the Word [*le Verbe*]" (cited in *SP* II, 500).

32. Dietz, *Between the Human and the Divine,* 189–93.

33. Quoted in Brenner, "Simone Weil," 269. Brenner argues that "[Weil] wished to die" and that this letter "makes her intention clear."

34. Heimonet, *Négativité et communication.*

35. The classic in this category remains Paul Giniewski's *Simone Weil ou la haine de soi.*

36. Brenner, "Simone Weil," 263.

37. Brenner, "Simone Weil," 268.

38. Brenner, *Writing as Resistance,* 81.

39. Brenner, *Writing as Resistance,* 84–85.

40. Richard Bell, *Simone Weil,* 170.

41. Brenner, "Simone Weil," 264.

42. Brenner, "Simone Weil."

43. Brenner, "Simone Weil," 264.

Conclusion

1. Edith Wyschogrod, *Saints and Postmodernism,* xxiii; emphasis in original.

2. See Nancy's discussion of the relationship of sacrifice to the West's founding "double figure of ontotheology," Socrates and Christ (Jean-Luc Nancy, "The Unsacrificeable," 21–24).

3. Nancy, "The Unsacrificeable," 21.

4. Nancy, "The Unsacrificeable," 36–37.

5. Nancy, *La communauté désoeuvrée,* 80.

6. Nancy, *La communauté désoeuvrée,* 102.

7. Nancy, "The Unsacrificeable," 35–38.

8. Madeleine Chapsal, *Quinze écrivains,* 16–17; ellipsis in original.

9. See Michel Foucault, "Self Writing," 207–22.

10. David Halperin, *Saint Foucault,* 61, 74.

11. William B. Turner, *A Genealogy of Queer Theory,* 146.

12. Halperin, *Saint Foucault,* 60–61.

13. Turner, *A Genealogy of Queer Theory,* 146.

14. See *E,* 334: "On pourrait trouver dans les Evangiles, quoiqu'ils ne nous aient transmis qu'une faible partie des enseignements du Christ, ce qu'on pourrait nommer une physique surnaturelle de l'âme humaine. Comme toute doctrine scientifique, elle ne contient que des choses clairement intelligibles et expérimentalement vérifiables. Seulement la vérification est constituée par la marche vers la perfection."

15. Suzanne Guerlac, *Literary Polemics,* 22.

16. Michel Foucault, "Preface to Transgression," 29–30.

17. See Foucault, "Preface to Transgression," 29.

18. This characterization of the sacred and its adepts is drawn from the concluding paragraph of Roger Caillois's article "The Ambiguity of the Sacred," a 1938 text reprinted in *CdS,* 401–2. In rendering the passage in English, I have borrowed several turns of phrase from Meyer Barash's translation of the parallel passage in Caillois's *Man and the Sacred,* 59.

WORKS CITED

Agamben, Giorgio. *Homo Sacer: Sovereign Power and Bare Life.* Trans. Daniel Heller-Roazen. Stanford, Calif.: Stanford University Press, 1998.

Allen, Diogenes. "The Concept of Reading and the 'Book of Nature.'" In *Simone Weil's Philosophy of Culture: Readings toward a Divine Humanity,* ed. Richard Bell, 93–115. Cambridge: Cambridge University Press, 1993.

Allen, Diogenes, and Eric O. Springsted, eds. *Spirit, Nature, Community: Issues in the Thought of Simone Weil.* Albany: SUNY Press, 1994.

Andic, Martin. "Discernment and the Imagination." In *Simone Weil's Philosophy of Culture: Readings toward a Divine Humanity,* ed. Richard Bell, 116–49. Cambridge: Cambridge University Press, 1993.

Angèle de Foligno. *Le Livre des visions et instructions.* Trans. Ernest Hello. Paris: Tralin, 1921.

Aragon, Louis. *Le Paysan de Paris.* Paris: Gallimard, 1979.

Arnould, Elisabeth. "The Impossible Sacrifice of Poetry: Bataille and the Nancian Critique of Sacrifice." *Diacritics* 26, no. 2 (summer 1996): 86–96.

Atkinson, Clarissa, Constance Buchanan, and Margaret Miles, eds. *Immaculate and Powerful: The Female in Sacred Image and Social Reality.* Boston: Beacon, 1985.

Bataille, Georges. "Hegel, Death, and Sacrifice." Trans. Jonathan Strauss. *Yale French Studies* 78 (1990): 9–28.

———. "Letter to René Char on the Incompatibilities of the Writer." Trans. Christopher Carsten. *Yale French Studies* 78 (1990): 31–43.

———. *Oeuvres complètes.* Paris: Gallimard, 1970–88.

———. *Le Procès de Gilles de Rais.* Paris: Pauvert, 1965.

Becker, Raymond de. "Communautés chrétiennes." *Esprit* 29 (February 1935).

———. "Révolution spirituelle d'abord?" *Esprit* 16 (January 1934): 672–73.

Bell, Richard. *Simone Weil: The Way of Justice as Compassion.* Lanham, Md.: Rowman and Littlefield, 1998.

Bell, Richard, ed. *Simone Weil's Philosophy of Culture: Readings toward a Divine Humanity.* Cambridge: Cambridge University Press, 1993.

Bersani, Leo. *The Culture of Redemption.* Cambridge, Mass.: Harvard University Press, 1990.

Besnier, Jean-Michel. "Bataille, the Emotive Intellectual." In *Bataille: Writing the Sacred,* ed. Carolyn Bailey Gill, 12–25. London: Routledge, 1995.

———. "Georges Bataille in the 1930s: A Politics of the Impossible." *Yale French Studies* 78 (1990): 169–80.

————. "Les Intermittences de la mémoire." In *Boris Souvarine et La Critique sociale,* ed. Anne Roche. Paris: La Découverte, 1990.

————. *La Politique de l'impossible.* Paris: La Découverte, 1988.

Birou, Alain. "L'Articulation entre le surnaturel et le social chez Simone Weil." *Cahiers Simone Weil* 8, no. 1 (March 1985): 50–66.

Bischof, Rita. *Souveränität und Subversion: Georges Batailles Theorie der Moderne.* Munich: Matthes and Seitz, 1984.

Blanchot, Maurice. *La Communauté inavouable.* Paris: Minuit, 1983.

————. *L'Entretien infini.* Paris: Gallimard, 1969.

Blum, Lawrence, and Victor Seidler. *A Truer Liberty: Simone Weil and Marxism.* London: Routledge, 1989.

Boldt-Irons, Leslie Anne. "Sacrifice and Violence in Bataille's Erotic Fiction." In *Bataille: Writing the Sacred,* ed. Carolyn Bailey Gill, 91–104. London: Routledge, 1995.

Botting, Fred, and Scott Wilson. "Literature as Heterological Practice: Georges Bataille, Writing, and Inner Experience." *Textual Practice* 7, no. 2 (summer 1993): 195–207.

Botting, Fred, and Scott Wilson, eds. *Bataille: A Critical Reader.* Oxford: Blackwell, 1998.

Brenner, Rachel Feldhay. "Simone Weil: Philosopher, Socialist, and Christian Mystic — a Jew and a Woman Despite Herself." In *The Netherlands and Nazi Genocide: Papers of the 21st Annual Scholars' Conference,* ed. G. Jan Colijn and Marcia S. Littell, 259–75. Lewiston, N.Y.: Edward Mellen, 1992.

————. *Writing as Resistance: Four Women Confronting the Holocaust.* University Park: State University of Pennsylvania Press, 1997.

Breton, André. *L'Amour fou.* Paris: Gallimard, 1987.

————. *Manifestes du surréalisme.* Paris: Gallimard, 1970.

————. *Nadja.* Paris: Gallimard, 1986.

Bynum, Caroline Walker. *Holy Feast and Holy Fast: The Religious Significance of Food to Medieval Women.* Berkeley: University of California Press, 1987.

Caillois, Roger. *Approches de l'imaginaire.* Paris: Gallimard, 1974.

————. *Man and the Sacred.* Trans. Meyer Barash. Glencoe, Ill.: Free Press, 1959.

Canciani, Domenico. "Débat et conflit autour d'une courte expérience, ou les guerres d'Espagne de Simone Weil." In *Simone Weil: L'expérience de la vie et le travail de la pensée,* ed. Charles Jacquier. Arles: Sulliver, 1998.

Certeau, Michel de. *La Fable mystique.* Paris: Gallimard, 1982.

Chapsal, Madeleine. *Quinze écrivains.* Paris: René Julliard, 1963.

Chestov, Léon. *La Nuit de Gethsemani, essai sur la philosophie de Pascal.* Paris: Grasset, 1923.

Chiaponne, Francis. "Simone Weil, à mes yeux..." *Cahiers Simone Weil* 13, no. 4 (December 1990): 405–12.

Comay, Rebecca. "Gifts without Presents: Economies of 'Experience' in Bataille and Heidegger." *Yale French Studies* 78 (1990): 66–89.

Connor, Peter Tracey. *Georges Bataille and the Mysticism of Sin*. Baltimore: Johns Hopkins University Press, 2000.

Cusset, Catherine. "Technique de l'impossible." In *Georges Bataille après tout*, ed. Denis Hollier, 171–90. Paris: Belin, 1995.

Dandieu, Arnaud, and Robert Aron. *Le Cancer américain*. Paris: Éditions Riéder, 1931.

Dean, Carolyn J. "Introduction." *Georges Bataille: An Occasion for Misunderstanding* (special issue). *Diacritics* 26, no. 2 (summer 1996): 3–5.

———. *The Self and Its Pleasures: Bataille, Lacan, and the History of the Decentered Subject*. Ithaca, N.Y.: Cornell University Press, 1992.

Devaux, André. "Du bon usage de la mort selon Simone Weil." *Cahiers Simone Weil* 16, no. 4 (December 1993): 259–73.

Dietz, Mary. *Between the Human and the Divine: The Political Thought of Simone Weil*. Totowa, N.J.: Rowman and Littlefield, 1988.

Dunaway, John M., and Eric O. Springsted, eds. *The Beauty That Saves: Essays on Aesthetics and Language in Simone Weil*. Macon, Ga.: Mercer University Press, 1996.

Durkheim, Émile. *The Elementary Forms of the Religious Life*. Trans. Joseph Ward Swain. London: George Allen and Unwin, 1915.

Elshtain, Jean Bethke. "The Vexation of Weil." In *Power Trips and Other Journeys: Essays in Feminism as Civic Discourse*. Madison: University of Wisconsin Press, 1990.

Ernst, Gilles. "La Mort comme sujet du récit: Dianus de Georges Bataille." In *La Mort dans le texte*, ed. Gilles Ernst, 179–192. Lyon: Presses Universitaires de Lyon, 1988.

Farron-Landry, Béatrice. "Détachement, renoncement et origine du mal selon Simone Weil." *Cahiers Simone Weil* 2, no. 2 (June 1978): 71–83.

Foucault, Michel. "Preface to Transgression." In *Bataille: A Critical Reader*, ed. Fred Botting and Scott Wilson, 24–40. Oxford and Malden, Mass.: Blackwell, 1998.

———. "Self Writing." In Foucault, *Ethics: Subjectivity and Truth*, ed. Paul Rabinow, 207–22. New York: New Press, 1997.

Fraisse, Simone. "La Représentation de Simone Weil dans *Le Bleu du ciel* de Georges Bataille." *Cahiers Simone Weil* 5, no. 2 (June 1982): 81–91.

Frazer, J. G. *The Golden Bough: A Study in Comparative Religion*, Vol. 1. London: Macmillan, 1890; later edition, London: Macmillan, 1911.

Gill, Carolyn Bailey, ed. *Bataille: Writing the Sacred*. London: Routledge, 1995.

Giniewski, Paul. *Simone Weil ou la haine de soi*. Paris: Berg, 1978.

Guerlac, Suzanne. *Literary Polemics: Bataille, Sartre, Valéry, Breton*. Stanford, Calif.: Stanford University Press, 1997.

———. " 'Recognition' by a Woman! A Reading of Bataille's *L'Erotisme*." *Yale French Studies* 78 (1990): 90–105.

Halperin, David. *Saint Foucault: Toward a Gay Hagiography*. New York: Oxford University Press, 1995.

Heimonet, Jean-Michel. *Le Mal à l'oeuvre: Georges Bataille et l'écriture du sacrifice*. Marseilles: Parenthèses, 1986.

———. "The Modernity of Mysticism: Bataille and Sartre." *Diacritics* 26, no. 2 (summer 1996): 59–73.

———. *Négativité et communication*. Paris: Jean-Michel Place, 1990.

———. "Writing and Politics, Cryptology of a Novel: *Le Bleu du ciel* of Georges Bataille." In *German and International Perspectives on the Spanish Civil War: The Aesthetics of Partisanship*, ed. Luis Costa et al. Columbia, S.C.: Camden House, 1992.

Hillenaar, Henk, and Jan Versteeg, eds. *Georges Bataille et la fiction*. Amsterdam: Rodopi, 1992.

Hollier, Denis. *Les Dépossédés: Bataille, Caillois, Leiris, Malraux, Sartre*. Paris: Minuit, 1993.

———. "The Dualist Materialism of Georges Bataille." In *Bataille: A Critical Reader*, ed. Fred Botting and Scott Wilson, 59–73. Oxford: Blackwell, 1998.

———. *La Prise de la Concorde: Essais sur Georges Bataille*. Paris: Gallimard, 1974.

Hollier, Denis, ed. *Le Collège de Sociologie, 1937–1939*. Paris: Gallimard, 1995.

———, ed. *Georges Bataille, après tout*. Paris: Belin, 1995.

Hollywood, Amy. "Bataille and Mysticism: A 'Dazzling Dissolution.'" *Diacritics* 26, no. 2 (summer 1996): 74–85.

———. *Sensible Ecstasy: Mysticism, Sexual Difference, and the Demands of History*. Chicago: University of Chicago Press, forthcoming.

Hubert, Henri, and Marcel Mauss. *Sacrifice: Its Nature and Function*. Trans. W. D. Halls. Chicago: University of Chicago Press, 1964.

Idinopulos, Thomas A., and Josephine Z. Knopp, eds. *Mysticism, Nihilism, Feminism: New Critical Essays in the Theology of Simone Weil*. Johnson City, Tenn.: Institute of Social Sciences and Arts, 1984.

Jacquier, Charles. "Présentation." "Lettres de Simone Weil à Boris Souvarine." *Cahiers Simone Weil* 15, no. 1 (March 1992): 1–5.

Jacquier, Charles, ed. *Simone Weil: L'Expérience de la vie et le travail de la pensée*. Arles: Sulliver, 1998.

Jay, Martin. *Downcast Eyes: The Denigration of Vision in Twentieth-Century French Thought*. Berkeley: University of California Press, 1993.

———. "Limites de l'expérience-limite: Bataille et Foucault." In *Georges Bataille après tout*, ed. Denis Hollier, 35–60. Paris: Belin, 1995.

Kahn, Gilbert. "Les Notions de pesanteur et d'énergie chez Simone Weil." *Cahiers Simone Weil* 9, no. 1 (March 1986): 22–31.

Kierkegaard, Søren. *Training in Christianity and the Edifying Discourse Which "Accompanied" It*. Trans. Walter Lowrie. Princeton, N.J.: Princeton University Press, 1967.

Klossowski, Pierre. *Le Peintre et son démon*. Paris: Flammarion, 1985.

Kühn, Rolf. "La Décréation: Annotations sur un néologisme philosophique, religieux et littéraire." *Revue d'histoire et de philosophie religieuses* 65, no. 1 (1985).

———. *Deuten als Entwerden: Eine Synthese des Werkes Simone Weils in hermeneutisch-religionsphilosophischer Sicht.* Freiburg: Herder, 1989.

Lacoue-Labarthe, Philippe. *La Fiction du politique.* Paris: Christian Bourgois, 1987.

Lacoue-Labarthe, Philippe, and Jean-Luc Nancy. *Le Mythe nazi.* La Tour d'Aigues: Éditions de l'Aube, 1990.

Lacoue-Labarthe, Philippe, and Jean-Luc Nancy. *Retreating the Political.* Ed. Simon Sparks. London: Routledge, 1997.

Levinas, Emmanuel. *Difficile liberté: Essais sur le judaïsme.* Paris: Albin Michel, 1976.

Libertson, Joseph. *Proximity: Levinas, Blanchot, Bataille, and Communication.* The Hague and Boston: Martinus Nijhoff, 1982.

Lindenberg, Daniel. *Les Années souterraines, 1937–1947.* Paris: La Découverte, 1990.

Little, J. P. "Simone Weil's Concept of Decreation." In *Simone Weil's Philosophy of Culture: Readings toward a Divine Humanity,* ed. Richard Bell, 25–52. Cambridge: Cambridge University Press, 1993.

Lotringer, Sylvère. "Les Misérables." In *Georges Bataille, après tout,* ed. Denis Hollier, 233–44. Paris: Belin, 1995.

Loubet del Bayle, Jean-Louis. *Les Non-conformistes des années 30.* Paris: Seuil, 1969.

Lukacher, Maryline. *Maternal Fictions.* Durham, N.C.: Duke University Press, 1994.

Marmande, Francis. *Georges Bataille Politique.* Lyon: Presses Universitaires de Lyon, 1985.

———. *L'Indifférence des ruines: Variations sur l'écriture du Bleu du ciel.* Marseilles: Parenthèses, 1985.

McLellan, David. *Utopian Pessimist: The Life and Thought of Simone Weil.* New York: Poseidon, 1990.

Mercier-Vega, Louis. "Simone Weil sur le front d'Aragon." In *Simone Weil: L'expérience de la vie et le travail de la pensée,* ed. Charles Jacquier. Arles: Sulliver, 1998.

Moulakis, Athanasios. *Simone Weil and the Politics of Self-Denial.* Trans. Ruth Hein. Columbia: University of Missouri Press, 1998.

Muller, Jean-Marie. *Simone Weil: L'Exigence de non-violence.* Paris: Desclée de Brouwer, 1995.

Nancy, Jean-Luc. *The Birth to Presence.* Stanford, Calif.: Stanford University Press, 1993.

———. *La Communauté désoeuvrée.* Paris: Christian Bourgois, 1990.

———. *Des Lieux divins.* Mauvezin: Trans-Europ Repress, 1987.

———. "The Unsacrificeable." Trans. Richard Livingston. *Yale French Studies* 79 (1991): 20–38.

Narcy, Michel. "Simone Weil dans la guerre, ou la guerre pensée." *Cahiers Simone Weil* 13, no. 4 (December 1990): 413–23.

Nehamas, Alexander. *Nietzsche: Life as Literature.* Cambridge, Mass.: Harvard University Press, 1985.

Nye, Andrea. *Philosophia: The Thought of Rosa Luxemburg, Simone Weil, and Hannah Arendt.* New York and London: Routledge, 1994.

Otto, Rudolf. *The Idea of the Holy.* Trans. John Harvey. New York: Oxford University Press, 1958.

Panné, Jean-Louis. "Aux origines: Le Cercle communiste démocratique." In *Boris Souvarine et La Critique sociale,* ed. Anne Roche. Paris: La Découverte, 1990.

Paquot, Thierry. "Utilité de l'inutile?" *Les Temps Modernes* 602 (December 1998/January–February 1999): 109–20.

Pétain, Philippe. "Appel du 20 juin 1940." In *Les Messages du Maréchal,* 4–5. St-Étienne: Éditions du Secrétariat Général de l'Information, 1942.

Pétrement, Simone. *La Vie de Simone Weil.* Paris: Fayard, 1973.

Pradeau, Jean-François. "*Impossible* politique et antiphilosophie." *Les Temps Modernes* 602 (December 1998/January–February 1999): 132–46.

Raimbault, Ginette, and Caroline Eliacheff. *Les Indomptables: Figures de l'anorexie.* Paris: Odile Jacob, 1989.

Rella, Franco. *The Myth of the Other: Lacan, Deleuze, Foucault, Bataille.* Trans. Nelson Moe. Washington, D.C.: Maisonneuve Press, 1994.

Roche, Anne. "Simone Weil et La Critique sociale." *Cahiers Simone Weil* 7, no. 3 (September 1984): 233–42.

Roche, Anne, ed. *Boris Souvarine et La Critique sociale.* Paris: La Découverte, 1990.

Rolland, Patrice. "Approche politique de *L'Enracinement.*" *Cahiers Simone Weil* 6, no. 4 (December 1983): 297–318.

Sartre, Jean-Paul. "Un Nouveau Mystique." In *Situations I,* 143–88. Paris: Gallimard, 1947.

Sichère, Bernard. *Le Dieu des écrivains.* Paris: Gallimard, 1999.

Souvarine, Boris. *A contre-courant: Écrits 1925–1939.* Paris: Denoël, 1985.

———. "Prologue." *La Critique sociale,* reprint edition. Paris: La Différence, 1983.

Stoekl, Allan. *Agonies of the Intellectual: Commitment, Subjectivity, and the Performative in the Twentieth-Century French Tradition.* Lincoln: University of Nebraska Press, 1992.

———. *Politics, Writing, Mutilation.* Minneapolis: University of Minnesota Press, 1985.

———. "Recognition in *Madame Edwarda.*" In *Bataille: Writing the Sacred,* ed. Carolyn Bailey Gill, 77–90. London: Routledge, 1995.

Suleiman, Susan Rubin. "Bataille in the Street: The Search for Virility in the 1930s." In *Bataille: Writing the Sacred,* ed. Carolyn Bailey Gill, 26–45. London: Routledge, 1995.

————. "Simone de Beauvoir and the Writing Self." *Esprit Créateur* 29, no. 4 (winter 1989): 42–51.

Surya, Michel. "L'Arbitraire, après tout." In *Georges Bataille, après tout,* ed. Denis Hollier, 213–32. Paris: Belin, 1995.

————. *Georges Bataille: La Mort à l'oeuvre.* Paris: Séguier, 1987.

Taylor, Mark C. "The Politics of Theo-ry." *Journal of the American Academy of Religion* 59, no. 1 (spring 1991): 1–37.

Touchard, Jean. "L'Esprit des années 1930." In *Tendances politiques dans la vie francaise depuis 1789.* Paris: Hachette, 1960.

Turner, William B. *A Genealogy of Queer Theory.* Philadelphia: Temple University Press, 2000.

Van Herik, Judith. "Looking, Eating, and Waiting in Simone Weil." In *Mysticism, Nihilism, Feminism: New Critical Essays in the Theology of Simone Weil,* ed. Thomas A. Idinopulos and Josephine Z. Knopp. Johnson City, Tenn.: Institute of Social Sciences and Arts, 1984.

————. "Simone Weil's Religious Imagery." In *Immaculate and Powerful: The Female in Sacred Image and Social Reality,* ed. Clarissa Atkinson, Constance Buchanan, and Margaret Miles. Boston: Beacon, 1985.

Vetö, Miklos. *La Métaphysique religieuse de Simone Weil.* Paris: Harmattan, 1997.

Versteeg, Jan, ed. *Georges Bataille: Actes du colloque international d'Amsterdam.* Amsterdam: Rodopi, 1987.

Weil, Simone. *Attente de Dieu.* Paris: La Colombe, 1950.

————. *Cahiers.* 3 vols. Paris: Plon, 1953–56.

————. *La Condition ouvrière.* Paris: Gallimard, 1951.

————. *La Connaissance surnaturelle.* Paris: Gallimard, 1950.

————. *Écrits de Londres.* Paris: Gallimard, 1957.

————. *Écrits historiques et politiques.* Paris: Gallimard, 1960.

————. *L'Enracinement.* Paris: Gallimard, 1990.

————. "Essai sur la notion de lecture." *Etudes Philosophiques,* n.s., no. 1 (January–March 1946): 13–19.

————. *First and Last Notebooks.* Trans. Richard Rees. London: Oxford University Press, 1970.

————. *Formative Writings.* Ed. and trans. Dorothy Tuck McFarland and Wilhelmina Van Ness. Amherst: University of Massachusetts Press, 1987.

————. *Gravity and Grace.* Trans. Arthur Wills. New York: G. P. Putnam's Sons, 1952.

————. "The *Iliad,* or the Poem of Force." Trans. Mary McCarthy. Wallingford, Pa.: Pendle Hill, 1957.

————. *Intimations of Christianity among the Ancient Greeks.* Trans. Elisabeth Chase Geissbuhler. London: Routledge and Kegan Paul, 1957.

————. *Lettre à un religieux.* Paris: Gallimard, 1951.

————. *The Need for Roots.* Trans. Arthur Wills. New York: G. P. Putnam's Sons, 1952.

————. *Notebooks.* Trans. Arthur Wills. New York: Putnam, 1956.

————. *Oeuvres complètes.* Paris: Gallimard, 1988–.

————. *Oppression and Liberty.* Trans. Arthur Wills and John Petrie. London: Routledge and Kegan Paul, 1958.

————. *Pensées sans ordre concernant l'amour de Dieu.* Paris: Gallimard, 1962.

————. *La Pesanteur et la grâce.* Paris: Agora/Pocket, 1991.

————. *Réflexions sur les causes de la liberté et de l'oppression sociale.* Paris: Gallimard, 1985.

————. *Selected Essays, 1934–1943.* Trans. Richard Rees. London: Oxford University, 1962.

————. *Seventy Letters.* Ed. and trans. Richard Rees. London: Oxford University Press, 1965.

————. *La Source grecque.* Paris: Gallimard, 1953.

————. *Waiting for God.* Trans. Emma Craufurd. New York: G. P. Putnam's Sons, 1951.

Winch, Peter. *Simone Weil: The Just Balance.* New York: Cambridge University Press, 1989.

Wyschogrod, Edith. *Saints and Postmodernism.* Chicago: University of Chicago Press, 1990.

INDEX

Acéphale, 18–24, 40, 129, 147, 149,
  159
Achilles, 63–64
Aeschylus, 46
Affliction [*malheur*], xviii, xxiii,
  61, 95–96, 176–77, 179, 186,
  188–89, 196, 199
Agamben, Giorgio, 1, 39
Alain (Émile Chartier), xiii, 57, 78,
  169, 170
Amor fati, 76, 131
Angela of Foligno, 124, 134, 136,
  162
Aragon, Louis, xx
Attention, 74, 194, 199, 202
  as antidote to force, 59–63, 80
"attraction and repulsion" (Bataille),
  xv, 88, 90, 96

Bataille, Georges
  accusations of fascist sympathies,
    29–30, 125, 150–51
  mysticism, 2, 29–37, 124–26,
    129–33, 133–42, 149–58
  political involvement during 1930s,
    17–29
  political "withdrawal" during
    World War II, 29–37, 124–26,
    133–68
  relation to father, 128
  relation to Simone Weil, xi–xvi,
    82–88, 92–99, 102–20, 207–12,
    223–25
  self-construction as transgressive
    "saint," xxvii, 32–35, 130,
    160–67, 215–25
  theories of sacrifice, 1–41
  views on writing, 127, 141–42,
    154–55, 162, 164–66

Baudelaire, Charles, xx
Beauty, 64, 76, 77, 80, 85, 88, 173,
  192, 214
  and political culture, 65–67
Bell, Richard, 49, 59, 60, 61, 205
Bersani, Leo, 91, 103, 122, 140
Besnier, Jean-Michel, 111
Bhagavad Gita, 68, 179–80, 182
Blanchot, Maurice, 18
Body, 59, 79, 100–101, 106, 109,
  131, 147–49, 167, 185, 188, 199
  mother's, 101–2, 109
  Weil's attitude toward, 43–44,
    68–72, 172–73, 187
Brasillach, Robert, 124
Brenner, Rachel Feldhay, 195, 203–7
Breton, André, xiii, xx, 17, 157

Caillois, Roger, xxii, 22, 24, 225
Castration, 99, 106, 109
Cercle communiste démocratique, 84,
  86, 87, 102, 104, 208
Cervantes, 82
Chapsal, Madeleine, 219
Chestov, Léon, xix
Christianity, xii, xiii, xxii, 21, 26–27,
  29, 87, 117, 129, 177
  Bataille's interpretation of, xv,
    26–27
  Weil's embrace of, xiv, 171, 204
College of Sociology, xv, 24–29, 37
Communication, xvii, xix, xxviii,
  31–32, 34, 37, 127, 145, 190,
  195, 197–200, 208, 213, 215,
  217
Community, 4, 9, 19, 22–24, 28, 37,
  116, 145, 202, 209
Contre-Attaque, 17
Crime, 6, 15, 19, 25, 28, 89, 123, 154

La Critique sociale, xii, xiv, xv, xxvii, 10–11, 16, 80–85, 87–88, 92, 94, 99, 111, 117, 170

Dean, Carolyn, xxv, 125, 127, 134, 150, 167–68
Death, xi, 4, 82–83, 87, 99–101, 106, 110–11, 115, 117, 120, 159–60
  anticipated in mystical experience, 72, 146–49, 172–78
  attraction to as basis of political commitment, 116–23
  as communication, xviii, 200, 204
  consent to, xviii, 170, 178, 186, 191, 200
  as "greatest gift" (Weil), 195–96
  "height of" [*hauteur de mort*] (Bataille), 142–46, 164
  "joy before" (Bataille), 129–33
  as key to meaning in human existence, 126, 143, 170, 195–96
  Lazare/Weil's attraction to, 104–5, 108–10, 117
Decreation, xxvii, 74, 170, 173, 207
Desire, 68, 73, 97, 121, 144, 173, 176, 196
Dietz, Mary, 60, 61, 66, 202
Don Juan legend, 89–90, 92–93, 95, 99, 106
Drag, 109–10, 149
Durkheim, Émile, xxii, 2–9, 12, 24, 32, 38, 222
  Bataille's debt to, xxiii, 2, 34
  theory of sacrifice, 2–7
  theory of the sacred, xxii–xxiii

Energy: Weil's theories of, 63, 65, 68–73, 79, 173–76, 201
Engagement, xii, xxviii, 17, 79, 86, 87, 89, 93–94, 102, 105, 107, 122, 207, 211
Eroticism, 1, 37, 94, 101, 110, 132, 146, 155, 162
Esprit, xvi, 21
Evil, xxvii, 159, 161, 207–12, 215
Excess, xii, 89, 94, 96, 102, 108, 112, 132, 158, 167, 176

Expenditure, 10–17, 87, 91, 93–94, 98, 100, 104, 106–8, 112, 119, 129, 162, 176

Fascism, xii, xiii, xxiv, 1, 12, 16, 25, 36, 85, 94, 111, 116, 120, 171
Force, 3, 23, 221–22
  in Homer's *Iliad,* 53–56, 63–67
  hunger as form of, 43–47
  internalized in mysticism, 70–73
  relation to cosmic law, 75
  relation to social oppression, 47–49
  Weil's concept of, xxvi–xxvii, 40, 41–81
Foucault, Michel, 169, 223
Fraisse, Simone, 108, 109
Francis of Assisi, 193, 200
Frazer, J. G., 25, 30, 151
Freedom, 44, 46–52, 59, 61, 152, 167, 211, 214, 223
  and spiritual "obedience," 194
  Weil's early concept of, 50–51
Front populaire, xiii, 17

Galileo, 41
Giniewski, Paul, 204
God, xvii, xviii, 6–8, 21, 31, 62, 69, 71, 72, 75, 77, 131, 136, 146, 152, 155, 163, 172, 175, 177, 178, 187, 193–99, 212
  death of, 21
  identification with Platonic good, 208
  as "supreme poet" (Weil), 193–94, 197
The good, xxiii, 207–12, 215
Grace, 69, 71, 79, 225
Gravity, 41, 74
Guerlac, Suzanne, 146, 222

Halperin, David, 220
Headlessness, 89, 97–99, 101, 110
Hegel/Hegelianism, 25, 96, 131, 146, 154
Heidegger, Martin, 163
Heimonet, Jean-Michel, 157, 203

Heterogeneity/heterogeneous, xxii, xxiii, xxvi, 8, 11, 12, 16–17, 35, 37, 111, 116, 164
Hitler, Adolf, xii, xxiv, xxviii, 16, 29, 36, 53, 67, 78, 80, 169, 182, 185, 190–91, 205, 215
Hollier, Denis, 106, 108
Hollywood, Amy, 128
Horror
  "lyricism" of, 140–41
  and mystical contemplation, 139–44, 158
Hubert, Henri, 1, 3, 6–8, 31
Hunger, xxvii, 42–44, 59, 175, 202
  as path to knowledge (Weil), 46, 52, 72–73

Ignatius Loyola, 157–58
Iliad, 41, 53–56, 58, 63, 68, 70, 177, 196
  as political statement, 65–67
The impossible, 1, 23, 73, 113, 116, 153, 211–12, 215, 219
Incest, 101–2
Inner experience (Bataille), xxvii, 32, 125, 151–58
  as literary self-stylization, 154–56
  relation to Jünger's *inneres Erlebnis*, 133–43, 144
  See also mysticism; sacrifice; writing
Irony, 89, 91, 120–23, 163, 224

Jaspers, Karl, 23
Jay, Martin, 127, 132
Jesus, 26–27, 33–34, 196–200
Joan of Arc, xix, 181, 202
John of the Cross, 219
Jünger, Ernst, 136–42, 143, 148, 159
Justice, xiv, xxi, 44, 60, 66–67, 205–7

Kant/Kantian, 37, 47, 163
Kenosis (self-emptying), 30
Klossowski, Pierre, 22, 138
Kojève, Alexandre, 24–25, 131

Labyrinth, 22
Lacoue-Labarthe, Philippe, xxi, xxii

Laure (Colette Peignot), 85, 87, 92–93, 117
Leiris, Michel, 24
Looking/eating (Weil), 62–63
Loss, 10, 15, 97–99, 106–7, 112–13, 147, 212
Love, 32, 77, 80, 88, 104, 106, 108, 111, 158, 177, 194, 205–6, 212, 214, 217
  as cosmic governing principle, 76
  of life as basis of revolutionary commitment (Weil), 84–86, 102, 118–19
Luxemburg, Rosa, 85, 86, 94, 95, 104, 170

Madness, xiv, 7, 23, 32, 104
Malraux, André, 82–84, 86–87, 170
Marcel, Gabriel, 125
Marxism, xii, 11, 13, 16, 47–48, 61, 87, 90, 92, 94, 99, 118
Masson, André, 19, 22
Mauss, Marcel, 1, 3, 6–8, 10, 31
Mother, 101–2, 108–9
Moulakis, Athanasios, 57, 63, 78, 79
Mounier, Emmanuel, 21
Mysticism, xiv, xxv–xxvi, xxvii, xxviii, 2, 43, 68, 78, 124
  in Bataille, xxvi–xxvii, 2, 29–30, 124–25, 129–33, 133–42, 149–58
  and political contestation, 78, 152–53, 158–65
  in Weil, xxviii, 68, 70–73, 80, 172–78
  See also inner experience; sacrifice
Myth, xxiv

Nancy, Jean-Luc, xxi, xxii, xxvi, 1, 38–40, 217–18
Nazism, xxiv, 16, 80, 91, 120–21, 125, 137, 167, 170, 189–91, 205–6
Necessity, xxiii, 75–76, 188

Necrophilia, 86, 89, 100, 101–2, 103–4, 108, 110, 116
as basis of revolutionary politics, 116–23
Nietzsche, Friedrich, xiii, 22–23, 28, 129, 131, 152, 220
Non-acting action (Weil), 63, 74, 179, 182

Oppression, xii, 41–51, 53, 90, 96, 107, 206

Pacifism, xiv, 52, 87, 169, 170–71, 213
Pascal, Blaise, xix, 83
Patri, Aimé, 109
Péguy, Charles, xix
Performance/performativity, xv, xvii, xviii, 1, 2, 67, 147–49, 154–55, 162, 189–92, 197–99, 210, 212, 220–21
Pétain, Philippe, 35–36, 124
Plato/Platonic, 74, 208
Poe, Edgar Allan, xx
Poetry, 12–13, 33, 38, 43, 65–66, 76, 192–96, 200, 202
Potlatch, xxvi, 11, 19, 38
Power, 14, 49–50, 129, 132, 166, 222
Bataille's College of Sociology lecture on, 25–29
determining people's "readings" of one another (Weil), 64
relation to sacred, 25–26
writing as contestation of, 166
Priam, 63–64
Priests, 100
Project/projective thinking, 153–54, 212
"Project for a Formation of Frontline Nurses" (Weil), 67, 183–89

Reading [*lecture*], xxvii, 42, 56, 60, 62, 64, 76, 197–98
"Real metaphor" (Weil), xxviii, 196–200, 203, 210

Religion, xxiv, xxv, 2, 24, 40, 80, 83, 104, 187
as basis of alternative politics, xvi, xxv, 17–18, 23–24, 33, 212
Durkheim's theory of, 3–4
and Nazism, xxiv, 191–92
polar opposition to military force (Bataille), 25–26, 146–49, 164
Representation, 2–3, 5, 9, 11, 32–33, 147–50, 164, 189–92, 196–200
Revolution, xvi, 20–21, 82–86, 88–89, 107, 112, 118, 123, 214
as emotive state, 82–83, 112
and impossibility, 114–15
linked to perversion (Bataille), 111
in Malraux's *La Condition humaine,* 82–86
rooted in love of life (Weil), 84–85, 102
as sacrifice, 10–17, 118
subject of dispute between Bataille and Weil, 82–88, 111–20
Rimbaud, Arthur, xx
Ritual, 3, 5, 9, 28, 107, 143–44, 146

The sacred, xv–xvii, xxii–xxv, 4–5, 17, 22–24, 81, 88, 96, 111, 154, 164, 205, 208, 210, 219
ambiguity of, xxii–xxiv, 4–5, 111–12
Bataille's concept of, xv, 26–27
Durkheim's theory of, xxii–xxiii, 4–5, 220
"left" and "right," xxiii, 26–27, 33–34, 208, 220
as mode of self-production, 219–20
as political stance/force, xvi, xxi–xxii, 17, 215, 220–25
Weil's understanding of, xxiii
Sacrifice, xxii, xxvi, xxviii, 1–40, 69, 100, 125, 176, 188, 195, 202, 215
in *Acéphale,* 20
Bataille's theories of, 1–40, 42, 136–42, 142–46, 147–49, 151–52

centrality to Western intellectual tradition, xxvi, 1, 38, 217–19
cosmic creation as, 173
of the god, 6–7
Lazare/Weil's avidity for, 102, 105–7, 117
of the mother, 101–2
Nancian critique of, 1, 38–40, 217–18
relation to war and mysticism, 129, 133–42, 151–52, 159–60, 189, 192
revolution as, 10–17, 82, 87, 112
as spiritual "comedy," 147–49
and writing, 32–34, 142–46
Sade, xiii, xix, xx
Saint/Sainthood, 1, 36, 107, 189, 207, 210, 213, 216
Bataille's and Weil's self-stylization, xvii–xix, xxvii, 32–35, 130, 160–67, 189, 207, 210, 215–25
Bataille's understanding of, xxvii, 32–35, 130, 160–67, 215–25
and contemporary ethics, xx–xxi, 216–17
as critical positionality, 220–21
as political stance, xvi, 219–25
role of concept in French political thought, xvi, xix
Weil's understanding of, xxi–xxii, 178, 224–25
Wyschogrod's definition, xx, 216
Sartre, Jean-Paul, xviii, xix, 125, 134, 147, 154–56, 159, 162, 207
Self, xvii, 8, 35, 42, 71, 129, 131, 154–56, 172–78
as literary project, xvii, xix–xx, 154–56
mystical loss of, 71–72, 131–32, 145, 175
and Weilian decreation, xxvii, 74, 172–78
writing of, 219–22
Self-mutilation, 7–9, 30–33, 106, 113, 115, 116
as political subversion, 9

Sexual perversion, xiii, 86, 108, 111
as gesture of revolt, 9
Shamanism, 22
Sichère, Bernard, xvi
Sin, xviii, 31
Smith, William Robertson, 4
Sophocles, 196
Soul, xii, 56, 60, 61, 65, 70–71, 79, 174–75, 187–88, 199
"of a country" (Weil), 183
Souvarine, Boris, 80, 84, 85, 92, 120, 134, 137
Sovereignty, 16, 24, 112, 141, 150, 161, 163, 167–68, 215, 222, 224
Spinoza, Baruch, 103
Stalin, Joseph, xiii, 92
Stein, Edith, 204
Stoekl, Allan, 5, 99
Suffering
as key to knowledge, 46, 96
redemptive, 72, 192, 196
and Weil's *malheur,* 96
Suleiman, Susan, 89, 106
Sun, 8, 69, 97–98, 100, 108, 121
The supernatural (Weil), xvii, xviii, 60, 64, 65
Surya, Michel, 128

Taylor, Mark C., 11
Tel Quel, 222
Thibon, Gustave, xvii
Tragedy, 5, 20, 23–24, 28, 31, 33, 196, 223
Transgression, xxv, xxvii, 6, 97, 101–2, 105–6, 137, 147, 154, 208, 211

Values, xx, 82–84, 89, 95, 104, 111, 116, 120, 206, 214–16
Van Gogh, Vincent, xxvi, 7, 34–35
Violence, xxvii, 2, 5, 9, 26, 29, 31, 40, 42, 49–50, 61, 62, 65, 68, 103, 105, 137, 159, 214
internalization of in mysticism, 29–37, 70–73, 129–33, 149–58, 173, 176–78
and the sacred, 40, 217–18

Violence (continued)
   united with consciousness, 127,
      146
   and writing, 32–34, 115–16
Virility, xxvii, 86, 95, 109, 129–30,
      132

Waiting [*attente*], 60, 78, 174
War, xxvii, xxviii, 29, 41, 53–56,
      58–59, 62, 64, 71, 75, 79, 103,
      159–60, 195–96
   in Bataille's "Heraclitean
      Meditation," 129–33
   and French national renewal,
      180–83
   as opportunity for spiritual trans-
      formation, 53–56, 129–33,
      178–83
   relation to sacrifice and mystical
      ecstasy, 129–33, 133–43, 178–
      83
   setting for deployment of force
      (Weil), 53–56, 63–64
   as "stimulant of the imagination"
      (Bataille), 127–29
Weil, Simone
   attitude toward body, 43–47,
      68–72, 172–73, 187
   attitudes toward femininity,
      women, 184–92, 203–7
   death, 201–3
   early view of revolution, 83–85
   effort to shape life as poetic project,
      xvii, 192–96, 200–203, 207, 210
   factory experience, 51–52, 54
   involvement with Free French
      movement, 68, 171–72, 183–84,
      194–95, 200
   mystical theology and experiences,
      68, 70–73, 80, 172–78
   participation in Spanish Civil War,
      52–53, 54
   rejection of Jewish identity, 203–7
   as sacred figure for Bataille, xiv–xv,
      88, 111, 116–20, 209–12
   view of war as spiritual opportunity,
      178–89
Winch, Peter, 60, 61
Wittgenstein, Ludwig, 56
Writing, xix, 10, 30, 32, 34, 38, 102,
      113–16, 217
   Bataille's views of, 127, 154–55,
      162, 164–66
   and "black irony," 122
   and death, in Weil, 192–96,
      200–203
   and inner experience, 154–55
   and sacrifice of mother, 102
   of the self, xvii–xviii, 220
   and violence, 115–16, 127, 140,
      142–46
Wyschogrod, Edith, xx, 213, 216–17

ALEXANDER IRWIN is assistant professor of religion at Amherst College. He is the author of *Eros toward the World: Paul Tillich and the Theology of the Erotic* and the coeditor of *Dying for Growth: Global Inequality and the Health of the Poor.*